Feasting Free on Wild Edibles

for david
love,
nancy

BRADFORD ANGIER

Feasting Free on Wild Edibles

... a one-volume edition of *Free for the Eating* & *More Free-for-the-Eating Wild Foods*

Stackpole Books

Feasting Free on Wild Edibles

*First published in 1972
as a one-volume edition of
Free for the Eating and More Free-
for-the-Eating Wild Foods*

Copyright © 1966 and 1969 by
Bradford Angier

Published by
STACKPOLE BOOKS
Cameron and Kelker Streets
Harrisburg, Pa. 17105

*Published simultaneously
in hardbound and soft-
covered Rubicon editions*

Printed in U.S.A.

Library of Congress Cataloging in Publication Data

Angier, Bradford.
    Feasting free on wild edibles.

    1. Cookery (Wild foods) 2. Plants, Edible.
I. Angier, Bradford. More free-for-the-eating wild
foods. 1972. II. Title.
TX823.A48 1972   641.6   72-6088
ISBN 0-8117-0609-5
ISBN 0-8117-2006-3 (pbk.)

*For our intimates Dr. and Mrs. Thomas James Gray—
Tom, a medical doctor long engrossed in company with
Vena and myself in all the problems of living off the
country—and Rita, his helping and sharing laboratory
technician, who has made our numerous field trips
pleasanter and more rewarding.*

Contents

Part I
FREE FOR THE EATING

    • members of the rose family • berries • cherries • delicious ready-to-eat fruits • tasty recipes for pies, muffins, flapjacks, syrups, jams and jellies, sherbet, fruit with dumplings, wines and cordials • methods of drying, canning, and storing

    • wild varieties of spinach and celery • plants good from the ground up • using frequently overlooked parts of plants • tips for solving the problem of leftovers • flavor enhancers for soups and stews • recipes for homemade pickles, table mustard, and mayonnaise • medicinal preparations

Part II
MORE FREE-FOR-THE-EATING WILD FOODS

> Consult the Directory of Wild Edibles to locate instantly all wild plants treated in this book.

Directory of Wild Edibles

Acknowledgments

The author is indebted for some of the illustrations in Part I to the New York State College of Agriculture at Cornell University and their bulletin *Wild Foods* by Eva L. Gordon, the U.S. Department of Agriculture, and Vena Angier. All the illustrations in Part II are by Arthur J. Anderson.

Introduction

SOME OF THE best foods in the world are free. Long before we thought of raising them in our gardens and on our farms and ranches, all our commonest fruits and vegetables were growing wild.

Wild foods have always been important in this young country. The Pilgrims derived considerable nourishment during their first desperate winter from groundnuts, which are similar to small potatoes. California's Forty-Niners, plagued by scurvy because of the scarcity of food in some of the gold camps, were introduced to miner's lettuce by the Indians and Spanish. Farther north, scurvy grass performed a similar function, both preventing and curing the vitamin-deficiency disease among early frontiersmen. When regular rations on the Lewis and Clark expedition had to be reduced to one biscuit a day, it was the sweet yellow fruit of the papaw that kept the men going.

Even today, in this age of space flight and split atoms, sustenance tasty enough to satisfy us in times of plenty and nourishing enough to keep us healthy if survival ever becomes a problem, grows free for the taking in yards, vacant lots, fields, along roadsides and seashores, on mesas, streambanks, lake edges, and within marshes and sequestered woodlands—ready and waiting for those who recognize the bounties they hold.

Each year thousands among North America's millions of campers, fishermen, and hunters become lost or stranded in the wilderness, many fatally. Yet almost invariably, where such individuals suffer and all too needlessly die, a choice of wild foods is free for the eating.

It's easy to avoid picking any of the limited number of poisonous wild plants in North America by just surely identifying everything before you pick it—and this book, a complete one-volume edition of the author's *Free for the Eating* and *More Free-for-the-Eating Wild Foods,* with its detailed descriptions and drawings, not only affords ample means for doing so, but also eliminates borderline plants that might reasonably cause confusion. Start with only a few wild edibles, if you want, perhaps with those you've already known for years, although perhaps not as foods. Each year add a few more.

What hobby can yield the same amount of pure and vigorous pleasure with so little outlay, and such delicious returns, as the gathering of wild foods? When you become interested in them, each excursion outdoors is transformed from a purposeless stroll to an eager, rewarding quest. Each trip becomes an opportunity for making new wild edible acquaintances and enjoying hours of stimulating exhilaration.

One thing to keep in mind when preparing many of the recipes in this book is the advisability of using freshly ground black pepper when pepper is called for. It will make a considerable difference in the flavor of many wild foods; so you should have at the very least a small, inexpensive pepper mill.

The reader who has prepared and sampled even a few of the wild delicacies discussed in this book will be well on his way not only to exciting new adventures in gourmet dining but also to accumulating knowledge that can make the difference between life and death in an unforeseen emergency.

Part I

Free for the Eating

Wild Fruits

IT'S DIFFICULT TO travel across a corner of North America, from the very deserts to the glittering ice cakes of the Arctic Ocean, that doesn't regularly yield wholesome and often delectable wild fruit.

Besides the numerous common grapes, cherries, and plums, the uniquely flavored little wintergreens, and the crab apples, that thrive wild from the southern states to Alaska, there are the startlingly red but less familiar berries of the staghorn sumac that, crushed in water and sweetened, give a drink like lemonade. Also not to be overlooked are the sustaining red berries of the kinnikinic, whose leaves are still a familiar backwoods tobacco substitute.

It's not hard to find the common blueberries, gooseberries, cranberries, and their ilk that every year fill out by the thousands of tons. And there are such abounding members of the rose family as strawberries, blackberries, and raspberries, whose young stems and stalks are also tasty, and whose leaves can be profitably steeped for tea.

PRICKLY PEAR

(Opuntia)

There is also the unlikely prickly pear—the little thorny knobs, ranging from the size of apricots to the size of large lemons, that bulge from the padlike joints of cactus. Actually, the spine-bristling skin of this fruit of the cactus is so unmistakable that any difficulties lie not in identifying but in picking. It's best to go about this with leather gloves and a knife.

Depending on the kind of cactus, the ripened colors of prickly pears vary from tawny green and purplish black to the choicest of them all— the big red fruits of the large *Opuntia megacantha* of the continental Southwest. To eat any of these Indian figs, as they're also known, slice off the ends, slit the hide lengthways, and scoop out the pulp.

ROSE

(Rosa)

Delicious wild foods grow everywhere. For example, there is a familiar berry that, although you've maybe never sampled it, has the flavor of fresh apples. More important, its juice is from six to twenty-four times richer in Vitamin C than even orange juice. Throughout much of the continent you can pick all you want the greater part of the year, even when temperatures fall a booming 60° below zero. As for recognizing the fruit, no one with a respect for brambles and a modicum of outdoor knowledge is going to get the wrong thing by mistake. It is the rose hip, the ordinary seed pod of roses everywhere.

Some thirty-five or more varieties of wild roses thrive throughout the United States, especially along streams, roadsides, fences, open woods, and in meadows, often forming briary thickets. The hips or haws, somewhat roundly smooth and contracted to a neck on top, grow from characteristically fragrant flowers, usually pink, white, or red. Remaining on the shrubs throughout the winter and into the following spring, they are available for food in the North when other sources of nourishment are covered with snow.

These rose hips have a delicate flavor that's delectable. They're free. They're strong medicine, to boot. Studies in Idaho found the scurvy-preventing vitamin in the raw pulp running from 4,000 to nearly 7,000

ROSE
Hips, Leaves, and Stems

milligrams a pound. Daily human requirements, estimated to be 60 to 75 milligrams, provide a yardstick for this astonishing abundance.

Three rose hips, the food experts say, have as much Vitamin C as an orange. We don't pay much attention to these gratuitous vitamins in the United States and Canada. But in England during World War II, some five million pounds of rose hips were gathered from the roadsides and put up to take the place of then scarce citrus fruits. Dried and powdered, rose hips are sold in Scandinavian countries for use in soups, for mixing with milk or water to make hot and cold drinks, for sprinkling over cereals, etc., all of which they do admirably.

This cousin of the apple, one of the many members of the rose family, is nutritious whether eaten off the bushes, cut up in salad, baked in cake or bread, or boiled into jam or jelly. As a matter of fact, plain dried rose hips are well worth carrying in a pocket for lunching on like raisins. To prepare them for this latter use, just cut each in half.

Remove the central core of seeds. Dry the remaining shell-like skin and pulp quickly in a cool oven or in a kettle suspended above the fringes of a small campfire.

One good way to use rose hips is turn them into syrup. Snip the bud ends from a freshly gathered batch. Then cover the fruit with water and boil rapidly until soft. Strain off the juice. Return the pulp to the kettle, add enough water to cover, and make a second extraction. For every 2 cups juice, add 1 cup sugar. Boil until thick. Pour into sterilized bottles. That's all. Poured over steaming sourdough pancakes on blue-black mornings when the Northern Lights are still ablaze, this syrup never lasts long.

Here's an extra hint. Don't throw away the pulp. Press it through a sieve to remove seeds and skins. Add one half as much sugar as pulp. Put in clove, cinnamon, and any other spices or flavoring agents to taste. Heat covered until the sugar is dissolved. Then uncover and cook slowly until thick, stirring to prevent sticking. Pack in sterilized jars and seal. Voila! Fruit butter.

With rose hips up to sixty times richer in Vitamin C than lemon juice—and richer in iron, calcium, and phosphorus than oranges—you might as well get the most good out of them while insuring maximum flavor. The best way to do this is to use the rose hips the day they are picked and to gather them while they are red but slightly underripe on a dry, sunny day.

But even after frost or later in the winter when they are shriveled and dry, rose hips are still worth picking. Earlier in the season, the petals themselves, varying in flavor like different species of apples, are delicious if you discard the bitterish green or white bases. Dark red roses are strong-tasting, the flavors becoming more delicate as colors become subdued through the light pinks.

Even the seeds are valuable, being rich in Vitamin E. Some backwoods wives grind them, boil in a small amount of water, and then strain through a cloth. The resulting vitamin-rich fluid is used in place of the water called for in recipes for syrups, jams, and jellies.

The flowers make a rather tasty tea, if each heaping teaspoon of dried petals, twice that amount of fresh petals, is covered with a cup of boiling water, then steeped for five minutes. A little honey or sugar helps bring out the fragrance. Leaves, roots, and the rose hips themselves are also occasionally used for tea.

BLUEBERRY
(Vaccinium)
(Gaylussacia)

Like numerous other members of the heath family, the blueberry genus thrives in acid soil, and I've seen thousands of acres of new bushes, heavy with berries, spreading over fire-blackened lands in Maine. Although botanists differ, some thirty-five different members of this species, from low shrubs to high bushes, grow throughout the United States and Canada, mostly in open woods and clearings. None is poisonous. Other names include whortleberries and bilberries.

One major difference among the many varieties is between so-called blueberries and huckleberries which, if you care, is easily resolved. Blueberries proper have many fine, easily chewable seeds. Huckleberries, which also have distinguishing waxy spots on their foliage and fresh shoots, contain ten larger seeds. Blueberries and huckleberries are good eating throughout the continent. A few species, though, it should be added, take on their true goodness only after being cooked, as you can readily find out for yourself.

A lot of game is the tastier for these mostly sweet, juicy, generally

BLUEBERRY
Left: in flower. *Right:* with fruit.

reddish to blue and blackish-purple berries, which, too, sometimes ripen to a greenish or yellowish color. Black bear roasts and stews are especially choice when these animals have been putting on fat by stuffing themselves with blueberries. Several species of grouse feed mainly on blueberries summers and early falls. Deer, moose, and rabbits browse on the foliage, fruit, and pretty little bell-shaped flowers.

Blueberries commonly grow so thick that you can often gather them by the bushel, stripping them indiscriminately in large handfuls or shaking them onto spread sheets. One way to clean them later is to drop them, a few at a time, from the pails onto a slanted blanket, tightly stretched a few feet below. Let the ripe blueberries roll into a large wide basin set just below the lower edge of the blanket. Most of the harder green berries will bounce free. The leaves and twigs will remain on the blanket, which can occasionally be brushed clean. Finally, rolled around in water to remove a little more debris, the plunder will be ready to eat.

This fruit excels in pies. Here's the best way we know of going about a blueberry pie. This pie isn't so solid with thickeners such as arrowroot, tapioca, or cornstarch that it will hold solidly together while you punctuate the occasional forkful with conversation. As a matter of fact, most diners who sit down to this particular dessert find they are glad to hold up on the repartee awhile and to finish off with a spoon.

All you need besides the pastry is 4 cups fresh blueberries, 1 cup sugar, and ¼ cup melted butter or margarine. As for the cooking, it takes place in a single operation. Line a greased pie pan with pastry. Mix the berries, sugar, and shortening. Pour them into the uncooked shell. Top with the upper crust, being sure to cut vents. Bake in a preheated oven, moderately hot, about 50 minutes, or until the crust is golden tan.

Or maybe on occasion you'd prefer blueberry slump. For this, bring 4 cups blueberries, 1½ cups sugar, 4 tablespoons cornstarch, and 1 teaspoon nutmeg slowly to a boil in a heavy saucepan.

While the mixture is heating, make a batter by first creaming 4 tablespoons of sugar with 3 tablespoons of shortening. Add ½ cup milk and blend thoroughly. Mix 1½ cups sifted flour, 1½ teaspoons baking powder, and ¼ teaspoon salt. Stir rapidly into the other ingredients.

Then begin dropping the batter, spoonful by spoonful, over the bubbling berries. Cover and cook at the same speed for 10 minutes. Serve hot with cream, milk, or vanilla ice cream.

Hot blueberry frying-pan bread, good anywhere, is especially easy to cook when you're away on vacation. The following basic mix, given here in man-and-wife proportions, will stay fresh for 6 weeks or more in camp if kept sealed, dry, and reasonably cool. For it you'll need: 2 cups all-purpose flour, 3 teaspoons double action baking powder, ½ teaspoon salt, and 6 tablespoons oleomargarine.

If this mix is being readied at home, sift the flour before measuring it. Then sift together the flour, baking powder, and salt. Cut in the margarine with 2 knives, with an electric mixer at low speed, or with a pastry blender until the mixture resembles coarse meal. For somewhat better flavored and more nourishing bread, add 4 tablespoons of powdered skim milk.

Place in plastic bags. Seal with a hot iron or with one of the plastic tapes. A large quantity can be made at once, of course, and divided into the smaller portions. Before using, it is a good idea to stir the mixture lightly.

When everything is ready to go, mix in 1 cup freshly washed and still damp blueberries, carefully stirring until each is coated with flour. Then quickly mix in ⅓ cup cold water to make an easily handled dough. Shape this, with as little handling as possible, into a cake about an inch thick. Dust the loaf lightly with flour, if you have any extra, so it will handle more easily.

Lay the bannock in an already warm frying pan. Hold it over the heat until a bottom crust forms, rotating the pan a little so the loaf will shift and not stick. Once the dough has hardened enough to hold together, turn the blueberry bannock, perhaps using a spatula or a plate and supporting the loaf long enough to invert the frying pan over it, then turning everything together. When it seems ideally browned, test by shoving in a straw or sliver. If any dough adheres, the loaf needs more heat.

Maybe you'd prefer muffins. Then just add 2 tablespoons sugar, 2 well-beaten eggs, and 1 cup milk to the mix and berries. Stir just enough to dampen all the dry ingredients. Fill greased muffin rings, improvised if you want from aluminum foil, about ⅔ full. Bake in a hot oven about 20 minutes. Eat at once.

Blueberry flapjacks are something special. Make the regular batter and drop it, ⅓ cup at a time, on a hot, lightly greased griddle. Sprinkle 2 tablespoons of blueberries over each flipper. When the hot cake starts showing small bubbles and its underside is golden, turn and brown the other side. Have the butter dish loaded and enough syrup ready to match the appetites.

CRANBERRY

(Vaccinium)

Wild cranberries, regarded by many as the most important berry of the north country, grow along the northern borders of the contiguous forty-eight states and from Alaska to Newfoundland, south to Arkansas and Virginia. Commercial varieties, 60 per cent of which are raised in Massachusetts, are delicious, but the wild varieties have more flavor and color.

Three species of this prime bear food liven bogs, marshes, rocky or dry, peaty, acid soil, and open coniferous woods across this continent, where they are also known as lingenberries, lowbush cranberries, American cranberries, cow berries, rock cranberries, lengon, swamp cranberries, *pommes de terre,* and partridgeberries.

Although they cling to the vines all winter and when kept fresh by snow are available many months as an emergency food, cranberries are at their best after the mellowing frost. Many people in the know then pick them by the bushel, often using homemade tooth-edged scoops and then cleaning the loot by bouncing the berries on slanted blankets, as described under blueberries.

Wild cranberries vary some, but they are essentially low evergreen shrubs or vines, rising some six inches above the wilderness floor and often growing so thickly that they form lush verdant mats. The leathery green leaves are small, generally rather glossy above, paler and bristled or spotted beneath. The small whitish or reddish flowers, which have four deep petal-like divisions, are attached to the ends of slender stems in such a way that colonists early called the plant craneberry, because the blossoms, which nod when ground winds are blowing, are shaped like the heads and necks of those birds. The name was later shortened to cranberry.

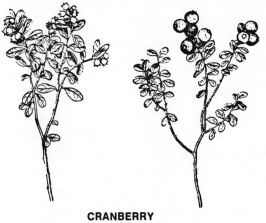

CRANBERRY
Left: in flower. *Right:* with fruit.

The berries, which are green before they ripen, are edible but unappetizing raw, although, thinly sliced, a few will lend a holiday touch to a green salad. Cooked with enough sugar to mellow their tart acidity, they're an entirely different story. The preserving acidness of the firm fruit, incidentally, has long been one of its most valuable characteristics on this continent, dating from the days when early Massachusetts settlers successfully shipped ten barrels of them across the Atlantic to King Charles II.

They can be stored without preserving, if the fully ripe berries are gathered on dry days and kept in cloth sacks in a cold place. Do not use tight containers, as the cranberries then tend to mold unless kept frozen.

If you're temporarily without handier facilities, it may be valuable, too, to know that wild cranberries can be easily and successfully dried. The best method, although you can improvise, is to strew the fruit on shallow trays that have been lined with cheesecloth and to leave them in a warm place like an attic, or an oven with the door partly open, until they become shell-like and easily mash to a powder. We find this characteristic especially handy in log cabin living. To use these dry berries, just soak them in water and then boil them a few minutes. Add sugar to taste.

There are lots of ways to use cranberries, but our favorite year in and year out, both as a dessert and as a pleasantly pungent supplement to meat, is cranberry sauce. You may have your own method of making this, but with wild berries try stirring 1½ cups of water and 1 cup of sugar together in a saucepan. Bring to a boil and simmer for 10 minutes. Then drop 2 cups of cranberries into the syrup and let bubble until the fruit pops. If someone in the house is trying to lose weight, try cutting the sugar in half and adding instead a level teaspoon of salt.

To serve with your meat for a change, how about a raw cranberry relish that will keep in the refrigerator for weeks? Start by putting 4 cups of cranberries through the meat grinder. Add the pulp and juice of 2 oranges, the chopped rind of 1 orange, the juice of 1 lemon, and 1½ cups sugar. Mix well and allow to stand a day before using for the first time.

Colorful cranberry jelly is always good, and it is very easy to make without failures. Pour ¾ cup boiling water over 2 cups of cranberries in a saucepan and bring quickly to a simmer. After 5 minutes, add ¾ cup sugar and cook another 5 minutes. Then strain, pour into hot sterilized glasses, and seal.

HIGHBUSH CRANBERRY

(Viburnum)

Despite the name, this shrub of the *Viburnum* family, some twenty species of which occur in the United States, is not a cranberry. A lot of people, too, object to its distinctively sweetish-sour odor and flavor. They do at first, that is. It has become one of my favorite berries, especially when I let a few frozen fruit melt on my tongue like sherbet in late fall and winter. I wouldn't swap the provocatively different jelly it makes for any other in the world.

The juicy red highbush cranberries, which often have an attractive orange hue, are also sometimes called squash berries and mooseberries. They are at their best for cooking just before the first softening frost, although they continue to cling to their stems throughout the winter and are thus one of the more useful emergency foods in Alaska, Canada, and the northern states, where they are to be found usually the year around. Even when soft and shriveled in the spring, they are particularly thirst-quenching, and once you get to recognize the clean but somewhat musty odor, you're never going to get the wrong berry by mistake.

Highbush cranberries grow as straggly or erect shrubs whose slender

HIGHBUSH CRANBERRY
Top: leaves and fruit. *Bottom:* blossoms.

grey branches are generally all within reach of the average adult. The usually three-lobed leaves, whose edges are toothed, resemble those of the maple. Like those of that familiar tree, they become brilliant in the fall. The berries which are actually drupes, each enclosing a large flattened seed, appear in easily picked groups whose flavor becomes milder as they age.

Now for that beautifully sparkling, salmonish-red jelly of perfect texture and unique flavor! This latter will be improved if the still firm berries are picked before the first freeze, while about half ripe. Bring each 2 cups of these to a boil in 3 cups of water. Mashing them as they cook, simmer for 5 minutes. Then strain. Add ⅔ cup sugar to every cup of resulting juice and bring to a bubble. Then pour into hot, sterilized glasses and seal immediately. A lot of people don't care for this at first, but with repeated samplings, many of them come to agree that there's no other jelly quite as good.

PAPAW

(Asimina)

This fruit so relished by raccoons and possums, sometimes called "false banana" because of its appearance, is also widely known as "custard apple" in deference both to its deliciousness and its family. Like the highbush cranberry, papaws usually call for an acquired taste. But once you come to like their creamy sweetness, they can become one of your favorite fruits. They are sometimes found in city markets, but they are at their best harvested when ripe, which in the North may mean after the first frost.

This hardy cousin of similar tropical fruits is native from New York southward to Florida and west to Nebraska and Texas. Preferring ground that is moist and fertile, it is most often seen in stream valleys and on the lower adjoining hills. It grows, too, in small clearings and along shaded roadsides. Papaws planted during landscaping often turn out to be doubly valued for their decorativeness as well as for their fruit.

A big shrub or a small tree, the papaw occasionally grows some forty feet high in the South, with a trunk perhaps as much as a foot in diameter. Northward, however, even the taller trees are often fifteen to twenty feet high, with trunks only a few inches thick. The papaw's large and often drooping leaves, which give it a tropical appearance, are from six to twelve inches long and, growing on short stems, are dark green above and paler beneath.

In early spring, just as these first leaves are starting to open, it blossoms with greenish flowers that later turn to a brownish or reddish purple. Growing from where the branches are met by the stems of the previous year's leaves, these are unusual in that they have six petals in

PAPAW
Left: bud and leaf scar. *Center:* branch with flowers and leaves. *Right:* fruit.

two sets of three. The inner trio bunch together in a little chalice around which the outer three are outstretched like a saucer. About one and one-half inches wide, these produce slender fruits that look like short bananas, from several to about five inches long, with smooth, greenish-yellow hides that become brown a day or two after the papaws are plucked.

Despite the nuisance of several large dark seeds, the papaw has a wealth of bright yellow pulp whose mellow sweetness makes it really something to feast on outdoors, as the hungry members of the Lewis and Clark expedition discovered on their homeward journey. They are quickly gathered, often from the ground. You can also pull them slightly green and put them out of the way in a dark and dry place to ripen.

The custardlike consistency of the ripe fruit, whose odor is also fragrant, blends well with a number of desserts. For 2 people, make a sauce by beating the yolks of 3 eggs briefly, then stirring in 2 cups of milk and ½ cup sugar. Cook in the top of a double boiler until it thickens slightly. Then mix with a cup of papaw pulp that has been strained through a colander. Allow to cool, and then put in the refrigerator. Serve chilled, snowily topped with the beaten whites of 3 eggs into which, after they have become stiff, 6 tablespoons of sugar have been whipped.

Frozen papaw will also make you hope that no unexpected company drops in at the last moment. It's easy to make, although you have to go at it in stages, with everything at the same temperature to begin with. Start by separating 3 eggs. Beat the yolks until thick, add ½ cup sugar, and whip until creamy. Beat the whites until they form peaks, pour in ½ cup sugar, and continue beating until stiff. Then beat 1 cup of heavy cream until it, too, is stiff. Gently combine all these ingredients and fold in a cup of strained papaw pulp. Then just freeze.

RASPBERRIES and BLACKBERRIES

(Rubus)

Even expert botanists have trouble trying to tell the numerous members of the raspberry and blackberry family apart. In fact, they can't even agree how many varieties there are in the United States, the estimates varying from about 50 to 390, including the raspberries, the hordes of true blackberries, the cloudberries, baked-apple berries, salmonberries, dewberries, thimbleberries, and a lot more. Me, I don't try to identify them all. I just eat them.

All members of the rose family, these produce closely and deliciously related fruits in commonly varying shades of red, yellowish, and black. Size and softness differ, too, but they are all berries that are made up of many small, generally juicy, pulp-filled ovals, each of which contains a hard seed. They grow over most of the continent, even in the Arctic where their high Vitamin C content is of particular importance. Despite their usually minute differences, they generally resemble market varieties of raspberries and blackberries and are easily recognized by all.

RASPBERRY
Left: with buds and flowers. *Right:* with fruit.

More than one opening day in Maine I've jumped a deer by coming upon a raspberry patch when it was just getting light enough to see. We have to watch the bushes in our yard in British Columbia to see that our horses don't nip them to nothingness. All in all, the *Rubus* family rates at the very top as a summer food for stock and wildlife. Too, the leaves and stems are eaten extensively in the spring, and later on few of the shriveled remains of the berries go to waste.

The tender young peeled sprouts and twigs of raspberries and blackberries are also edible by humans, being something pleasant to chew on when you're in the woods and fields. The leaves provide another of the wilderness teas. You can make a refreshing drink from the ripe berries, too, pressing jars full of them, filling in the spaces with vinegar, and letting stand for a month. Then strain off the juice and seal what you don't use right away in sterilized containers. To serve, sweeten to taste and dilute with iced water.

Besides devouring countless of these raw from the often thorny vines and bushes, we annually enjoy luscious quarts of them with just milk and sugar. But there are other things you can do with these berries which, in dollars and cents, constitute the most valuable wild fruit crop in North America.

Here is a variation of blueberry slump adjusted to raspberries. This recipe can also be used for blackberries and the other varieties by changing the proportions of the sugar and spices according to the natural flavor of the wild fruit.

Mix 1 cup of sugar, 1 tablespoon shortening, ½ teaspoon cloves, ½ teaspoon cinnamon, and 1 tablespoon of cornstarch in a pan. Slowly add 1 cup of boiling water and, continually stirring, bring to a simmer for a minute. Add 3 cups of raspberries to the syrup. While the mixture is bubbling, proceed as in the blueberry slump recipe.

How about an outstanding and easily made pie? Not bothering with a bottom crust, just fill a deep pan with berries that have been mixed with a little flour to absorb the excess juice and thus help to prevent overflowing, as well as to give the syrup more body. Sweeten to taste. Then roll out a pie crust that is thicker than usual, cut this into strips, and crisscross over the fruit. Bake in a moderate oven from forty to sixty minutes or until the crust is golden brown.

These wild berries will speedily cook up into a custardlike dessert that will always be enjoyed whenever it is served. Just stir 4 cups of fruit, ½ cup of hot water, and 1 cup of sugar together in a pan, slowly bringing them to a boil and then briefly simmering until juicy. Moisten 2 tablespoons of cornstarch with twice that much cold water and then about an equal amount of the hot juice. Turn this into the berries and, stirring, let bubble and thicken for 2 minutes. Cool before eating.

BLACKBERRY

Blackberry cordial, which, incidentally, has long been a favorite home remedy for diarrhea, is easy to make when these berries are plentiful. You'll need 8 quarts for this particular recipe, although this latter can be easily halved or quartered. In any event, pick over and wash the black-berries, place in a kettle with 2 quarts of cold water, boil until mushy, and then strain.

For every quart of resulting juice, stir in 2 cups of sugar. Then tie 1 tablespoon each of cloves, nutmeg, cinnamon, and allspice in a cotton cloth. Drop in the juice and boil for 20 minutes. After this has cooled, add 1 pint of brandy or whiskey to every quart of syrup. Pour into sterilized bottles and cork securely. This will mellow with age.

Blackberry wine appeals to some, especially where the bushes are thick with this fruit. After carefully picking over and cleaning a mess of berries, drop them into a crock and crush them thoroughly. Let the mashed berries remain there for a week stirring them daily. Then strain out all the juice.

For every 3 quarts of juice, use 1 pound of sugar. Boil this with the least amount of water required to dissolve it. Then pour the hot syrup into the juice. Leave in the crock for another full day. Then pour into sterilized bottles or jugs, covering these only with a cloth, as gases will be escaping during the fermentation. When this bubbling process has stopped, taste the wine. If it does not seem sweet enough, add to taste cold sugar syrup, made by slowly simmering 1 cup of sugar in ½ cup of water until syrupy. Bottle.

To avoid possible fines, confiscation, and other difficulties, anyone planning to make blackberry or any other wine from wild edibles or anything else should first inform himself about the rather complicated federal restrictions and regulations. You may do this by writing the Alcohol and Tobacco Tax Division, Internal Revenue Service, U.S. Treasury Department, Washington, D.C. Incidentally, there is a provision whereby, subject to certain limitations, "the duly registered head of any family may, without payment of tax, produce for family use and not for sale an amount of wine not exceeding 200 gallons per annum." There are many local laws, too.

SERVICEBERRY

(Amelanchier)

Also known as juneberries, the numerous members of this family are used like the blueberries they resemble. Millions were once gathered to flavor pemmican.

Four or five species of serviceberries, which are primarily North American shrubs and trees, are native in the East and up to about twenty in the West. Bearing delicious fruit from Alaska to Newfoundland and south to California and the Gulf of Mexico, they thrive in such habitats as open woods, rocky slopes and banks, and in swamps. Various other common names include saskatoon, shadbush, shadblow, shadberry, sugar pear, and Indian pear. Incidentally, some frontiersmen still make an eyewash from the boiled green inner bark.

One very steep Peace River bank I know, several hundred feet high and a short walk from our British Columbia cabin, was covered with serviceberries. Falls I've counted as many as six black bears eating the fruit on it at once. Then a forest fire burned it off, and the bears don't go there any more. Grouse and pheasant like the fruit and buds, while hoofed browsers, especially mule deer, feed on the twigs and foliage.

The daintily conspicuous, white, longish, five-petaled blossoms appear while the leaves are just expanding and are among the first spring flowers of our native woody plants. They cover the tough, flexible shrubs and small trees which have small alternate leaves, varying from elliptical to almost round, and at least partially toothed. These change from green to a beautiful rusty red in autumn. The loose bunches of berries, whose five-toothed summits cause them to resemble large blueberries, are red when young, becoming purplish or almost black.

The sweet juicy pulp surrounds ten large seeds, which add to the flavor when the fruit is cooked. As a matter of fact, although for years I have lived within a few feet of enough serviceberries to supply a good-sized restaurant, I have never much cared for the fruit raw. Cooked, though, especially when the then mild sweetness is enlivened with acid, that's another story. Too, the cooked seeds become even softer and impart an almondlike piquancy to the fruit.

SERVICEBERRY
Left: with fruit. *Right:* with flowers.

Drying also considerably alters the otherwise somewhat insipid taste for the better. The serviceberries thus treated can be substituted in recipes for currants and raisins. The Indians used to preserve them this way by the thousands of bushels, spreading them in the sun and later beating some of them into a mash which was molded into cakes and dried. The dried berries were also used in puddings and in the famous pemmican which, if you want, you can duplicate today. Essentially, this most nourishing and notable of concentrated outdoor foods is, by weight, ½ well-dried lean meat and ½ rendered fat, both pounded together. Dried serviceberries are mixed in for flavoring.

Today most serviceberries are preserved by canning, and their dark nutty juiciness is invigorating when they're opened in the winter, when maybe snow is whispering on the windows. Bring to a bubble 2 cups of water and 4 cups of sugar. Carefully pour in 6 cups of serviceberries and simmer a minute or 2. Stir in 3 tablespoons of lemon juice. Then pack the hot berries in sterilized pint jars, cover with the hot juicy syrup, and seal. Process the jars 20 minutes covered by boiling water or, if you have a pressure cooker, 10 minutes at 1 pound pressure.

Canned serviceberries make superior pies, although they can also be used fresh for this purpose. For the latter, mix 4 cups of ripe serviceberries with 1¼ cups sugar, 4 tablespoons melted butter or margarine, and 2 tablespoons lemon juice. Bake in a double crust in a moderate oven for 50 minutes or until the crust is a rich brown. The slabs will be runny, and you'll probably have to finish up with a spoon, so serve in deep dishes.

Serviceberry jam is another improvement on the raw berries. Start by putting the washed fruit through a medium-fine food chopper. Then measure 4 cups, add only enough water to cover, and simmer until the berries are tender and pulpy. Add 3 cups sugar, the juice of 2 lemons, the shredded pulp of 2 oranges with all the juice, and the grated rind of those oranges. Let bubble gently half an hour, pour into sterilized jars, and seal.

MAY APPLE

(Podophyllum)

Springtimes these attractive plants poke up like miniature forests of little opening umbrellas. Preferring moist rich woods and banks, their creamy-white flowers are later familiar from southeastern Canada to Florida and west to Minnesota and Texas. These produce sweetly scented, lemon-yellow fruits which, when delectably ripe, are relished by many.

This native perennial, a member of the barberry family, is also known as mandrake, wild lemon, and raccoon berry. Only the fruit is edible. The

MAY APPLE
Left: stem with flower and leaves. *Right:* fruit.

root, which Indians collected soon after the fruit had ripened and used in small quantities as a cathartic, is poisonous. So are the leaves and stems.

Each spring the long horizontal roots, which stay alive year after year, shoot up single-stemmed plants twelve to eighteen inches high. These roots, incidentally, are dark brown, jointed, and very fibrous. Internally yellow, they are mostly about half the size of a finger.

The solitary stems bear either one or two large leaves which open like tiny parasols. It is the latter plants that produce the single flowers which nod on short stems that rise from the fork of the leaves. About two inches wide, these oddly scented blossoms have from six to nine waxy white petals and twice that number of golden stamens.

The sweet yellow fruit, the size and shape of small eggs, ripens from July to September, depending on the climate, generally when the dying plants have dropped to the ground. Despite numerous seeds and a tough skin, it is very enjoyable in moderation raw, although there are those who, as in the case of serviceberries, prefer the May apple cooked.

The raw juice, however, really touches up sweet lemonade and other fruit drinks, while in some parts of the country there are those who add it and sugar to wine.

You can make a luscious, thick, pulpy jam from May apples. Clean about 2 quarts of fully ripe fruit, being sure to remove all stems. Place a layer in the bottom of a kettle. Crush them with a potato masher, repeating this process until all the fruit has been mashed. Add ½ cup water and heat short of simmering for 20 minutes, stirring now and then.

Then press the fruit through a colander. To 4 cups of the resulting juicy pulp, add a package of powdered pectin and a pinch of salt. Put back on the heat. When it starts to bubble, stir in 4 cups of sugar. Bring to a full boil, remove from the heat, skim, and seal in hot sterilized jars.

The heat does alter the delicate flavor of the fruit, although many think this is for the better, there are those who prefer the natural taste of May apples. For these, here is an uncooked jam that will keep for several months in the refrigerator. Clean and crush 2 quarts of ripe May apples as before, add ½ cup water, and heat to lukewarm only—100° F. on your thermometer. Press through a colander. Stir a package of powdered pectin into the still warm juice and pulp and let stand 20 minutes. Add 1 cup light corn syrup to prevent the sugar from crystalizing in the cold. Then thoroughly mix in 4 cups of sugar and a pinch of salt. Pour immediately into sterilized containers and store in the refrigerator.

WINTERGREEN

(Gaultheria)

These spicy little red berries, which, when very young, I used to pick and eat on a New Hampshire slope slick with pine needles, are the first wild fruit I remember gathering. I still enjoy both them and the wintergreenish leaves of this small evergreen plant, which is one of the most widely known of all the wild North American edibles. The some twenty-five names accorded it, including teaberry and checkerberry, support this conclusion.

The familiar wintergreen flavor, though, so common to drugstores and markets, is no longer made from this plant, but, when not obtained synthetically, from the distilled twigs and sometimes shreds of bark of the black birch. In older times, quantities of wintergreen were gathered around October, dried, and then packed for shipping. Before the volatile oil was distilled off, they were soaked in water for about twenty-four hours, which will give you an idea if you ever want to make any of your own.

Wintergreens are diminutive members of the heath family, often thriving in the shade of evergreens. A pleasant part of the woods of the

Northeast, this midget relative of the salal of the Pacific Coast grows in forests and clearings from eastern Canada to the Gulf states and as fa. west as the Great Lakes. Western wintergreen, *Gaultheria shallon,* grows on the other side of the continent from California to British Columbia. Although less spicy than the eastern species, the larger and still esteemed berries were highly regarded by the Indians.

The wintergreen is a trail plant whose thin, shrubby stems weave through woodland moss and evergreen needles, sending up from two to six erect branches that are usually less than six inches tall. These bear tiny, frosty, bell-like flowers from June to September. These hang below the small, shiny evergreen leaves which, for the most part,

WINTERGREEN
Left: **with flowers.** *Right:* **with berries.**

cluster at the tops of the branches. The leaves, whose wintergreen fragrance when crushed makes them unmistakable, are tough when mature, one or two inches long, and oval with little bristling teeth.

The firm berrylike fruit, which is inconspicuous though bright red, can be an important emergency food when found in great enough quantities, as it clings to the stems all winter. It is sometimes seen in the eastern markets and is often turned into pies. The only use I have ever made of these sweetly dry berries, though, has been to enjoy them while hunting, fishing, hiking, or just plain relaxing in the wilderness.

The evergreen leaves are well worth chewing, especially when young, because of their characteristic flavor and are a food of the ruffed grouse and white-tailed deer. These leaves, when freshly gathered, make a very palatable tea, a teaspoon to a cup of boiling water. Tearing them first into small pieces provides even more flavor, which can be helped along by cream and sugar.

ELDERBERRY

(Sambucus)

You can use the flowers of the common elderberry in your cooking, feast on the berries, and make flutes from the limbs. As a matter of fact, some Indians knew this member of the honeysuckle family as "the tree of music" because of the way they made wind instruments from the straight stems. These were cut in the spring, dried with the leaves on, and then the soft pith of their interiors was poked out with hot sticks. In fact, this is a way to make spouts for gathering sap from maples, birches, and other trees.

The common or American elderberry, sometimes known as the sweet elder, is a shrub growing from four to twelve feet high and occasionally in the South reaching the proportions of a small tree. The stems often spring in erect groups from tangled roots in moist, fertile soil along fences, walls, roadsides, ditches, banks, streams, and in fields from the Maritime Provinces to Manitoba and south to Florida and the Gulf of Mexico.

The green-barked stems, the larger of which were sometimes used for arrows, are mostly filled with porous white pith when young, this core becoming smaller with maturity. The bark, too, changes with age, becoming a grayish brown. The opposite leaves are compounded of from five to eleven leaflets, the lower of which are often lobed.

Creamy flat clusters of blossoms, which decorate and pleasantly scent the *Sambucus canadensis* in June and July, are made up of dozens of tiny star-shaped flowers. In late summer and early fall these become juicy, round berries, each with three or four rough seeds.

Quantities of these purplish black berries can be picked in a hurry. But even when at their ripest, they are none too palatable when fresh, although some of the game birds feast on them eagerly. However,

ELDERBERRY

there's an easy way to improve the flavor. Just pick and clean the mature berries as usual. Then dry them on trays in the sun or oven or on outspread newspapers in a hot, dry attic. The difference will be astonishing, and this way they will keep well, too.

When you get tired of dried elderberries simmered with a little sugar and lemon to taste, if that ever happens, why not enjoy some of the elderberry pies you may have heard about from your grandmother? A good crust for these can be made by sifting 2 cups flour and ⅛ teaspoon salt together. Cut in 6 level tablespoons butter or margarine. Add 6 tablespoons cold water and mix gently. Roll into a thin sheet and line a heavily greased pie pan. Reroll the remaining pastry for cutting into strips to crisscross over the top.

As for the berries, stew enough of them with a minimum amount of water to fill 4 cups. Then thicken with a little flour to absorb the excess juice and to furnish a thicker syrup. Mix with 1½ cups of sugar, or more, if that doesn't taste sweet enough, and 4 tablespoons of melted butter or margarine. Pour into the shell, cover with the pastry strips, and bake in a preheated moderate oven ¾ hour or until the crust is golden brown.

Or if you'd rather, have a cobbler instead. Mix 2½ cups of dried elderberries, again stewed with a minimum amount of water, 1 cup of sugar, and the juice of 1 lemon. Pour into a greased casserole or deep pan and dot liberally with butter or margarine. Crisscross with pie pastry, made in half amounts from the recipe above, rolled out and cut into strips. Bake in a hot oven, preheated as always, until the crust is brown.

Once you can identify the small white flowers of the common or American elderberry, *Sambucus canadensis,* these showy flat-topped clusters can be washed, shaken dry, stripped from the stems, and beaten in batters that are slightly thinner than usual for pancakes, waffles, and muffins.

You can make elderberry pancakes by sifting together 2 cups flour, 2 teaspoons double-action baking powder, 2 tablespoons sugar, and ½ teaspoon salt. Beat 2 eggs and mix with 2 tablespoons melted butter or margarine and 1½ cups milk. Rapidly combine everything and quickly stir in 1 cup of elderberry flowers. Bake on a hot griddle that has been sparingly greased with bacon rind. Turn each pancake only once, when it starts to make small bubbles, and cook only half as long on the second side. These have a delicate flavor, and even when we have maple syrup, we prefer just butter and sugar on them.

Or if you like fritters, you can dip the entire flower cluster with the tough stem removed into a batter, then fry in deep hot fat until brown. Start the batter by beating 2 eggs, into which stir ½ cup sugar, 1 tablespoon cooking oil, 1 teaspoon vanilla, and 2 cups milk. Sift together 3 cups flour and 5 teaspoons double action baking powder; then beat everything quickly together until smooth. These hot fritters, carefully removed so as not to break the crust and drained on a folded length of paper toweling, are good either plain with the main meal or afterwards with whipped cream.

Elderberries will provide outstanding jelly with the cooperation of an equal bulk of apples, which may be wild, too. Wash these latter and cut them into sections without peeling or coring. Then cover everything with water and simmer until soft, after which mash and strain.

Measure the juice, bring it to a bubble, skim, and add an equal bulk of sugar. Continue boiling until a spoonful falls off the spoon in a sheet. Fill hot, sterilized jelly glasses to within ½ inch of the top. Immediately fill to the rim with paraffin, broken into small pieces and melted over very low heat. Cover with a cloth, cool, label, and then store in dry, cool darkness.

Elderberry wines and cordials have come down through the centuries. They can be readily made by substituting this fruit in the recipes given for blackberries.

STRAWBERRY

(Fragaria)

Everyone knows the wild strawberry, similar to domestic varieties but usually far smaller and always infinitely sweeter. Some four species sweeten the air from the Arctic Circle to Florida and California, growing wild nearly everywhere except in arid country. Deer like to browse on these juicy members of the rose family, which are found in open woods, fields, clearings, and along dry hillsides and shaded banks, often so abundantly that a few square feet provide a meal.

I personally know of no more delicious berry, wild or otherwise. And those who finally feel the need for something to offset the delicate sweetness can brew strawberry tea, dropping 2 full handfuls of the saw-toothed leaves into 4 cups of boiling water and allowing them to steep for 5 minutes. Too, a refreshing drink can be made from the strawberries themselves by first partially crushing them and then stirring them in cool water.

The stems and stalks of this popular perennial are also tasty. Incidentally, fresh wild strawberries have additional value by being a rich source of Vitamin C, about one-half to two-thirds of a cup equalling the Vitamin C content of an orange.

Recipes for strawberries are legion, but over the hungry years we have found the following 4 to be particularly efficacious with the wild varieties. They are simple. For instance, there's strawberry shortcake. All you need for this tiptop treat is wild strawberries and hot bannock.

To match about 2 quarts of berries, freshly picked and left standing drenched with a cup of sugar, you'll need for the bannock: 2 cups sifted flour, 2 tablespoons sugar, 2 teaspoons baking powder, 1 teaspoon salt, 4 tablespoons shortening, and ¼ cup cold milk or slightly more.

Sift all the dry ingredients together into a bowl. Work in the shortening; then quickly stir in enough cold milk to make a soft dough.

Knead this dough very briefly on a floured board. Roll it out about ½ inch thick. Lay half of the dough in a greased pan and dot it with chunks of canned butter. Spread the other half on top. If you prefer individual biscuits, just cut the dough into ovals with a floured can top or glass. Baking in a very hot oven takes 12 to 15 minutes.

Afterwards carefully separate the steaming layers, ladle the sweetened berries between and above, and fall to it. Raspberries, blueberries, serviceberries, blackberries, and similar wild fruits are also good with this hot bannock.

The shortcake tastes even better with whipped cream made from evaporated milk. In case you want to try it in the woods sometime,

STRAWBERRY

there's a simple gimmick to this. Milk and utensils have to be icy cold. This can be arranged easily enough by submerging bowl, beater, and can of milk in a mountain stream.

So chilled, most evaporated milk quickly whips to about triple volume. A couple of teaspoons of lemon juice, canned or fresh, can be used to increase the stiffness after the milk is partially whipped. Some bush cooks also use an envelope of unflavored gelatin, dissolved in a minimum of water, for this purpose.

How about some wild strawberries fried? Clean 4 cups of fresh strawberries, except for their stems. Chill the berries as much as possible; if you're vacationing, perhaps by partly immersing them in a brook or spring. Keep the berries dry.

For the batter, beat 1 egg with 1 cup milk. Then add 1 tablespoon melted butter or margarine, ⅛ teaspoon salt, ¼ cup sugar, and 1 teaspoon vanilla. Blend thoroughly. Mix 1½ cups flour with 3 teaspoons baking powder. Combine with the egg mixture and beat until smooth.

Hold each chilled berry by its stem and dip carefully into the batter. Then drop into hot deep fat and fry until well browned. This will take about a minute. Save what you don't eat on the spot to mete out, with whipped cream if you have it, for dessert.

Here's an open strawberry pie that will really command attention. To make the 9-inch pie shell, sift together 1 cup sifted flour and ½ teaspoon salt. Cut in ½ cup of shortening. Handling this quickly and lightly, add only enough water, about 3 tablespoons, to make a dough that will hold together when rolled. Roll out and spread on a greased pie pan. Bake in a hot oven for 12 to 15 minutes or until done.

Simmer together 1 cup of crushed wild strawberries, ½ cup sugar, and 2 tablespoons of cornstarch until thick and syrupy. Meanwhile, pack the cooked pie shell with the ripest and juiciest wild strawberries available. Drench them with the hot syrup. Chill and serve.

This pie is delicious, too, when similarly prepared with raspberries, blackberries, and such. Sweetening may be varied to taste.

The cheeriness of homemade wild strawberry jam is especially suited to stormy winter days. For 2 pints, which will go a long way, you'll need 4 cups apiece of sugar and crushed berries. Stir the strawberries, measured after mashing, with the sugar in a large pan. Bring to a boil, continuing to stir until the sugar is melted. Keep at a rolling boil for 14 minutes. Then skim off the white foam and seal in hot sterilized glasses.

CURRANTS and GOOSEBERRIES

(Ribes)

Some eighty species of currants and gooseberries grow across the United States and Canada, from Alaska to Labrador southward to North Carolina, Texas, and California. Although differing considerably, they closely resemble cultivated varieties. All produce fruit that is edible raw and particularly when cooked, although the bristliness and odor of some of the berries call for an acquired taste, especially when devoured directly from the bushes.

Although thriving under varied conditions, especially in the West, they are typical of open, moist places, and they often grow by streams, springs, and bogs. Important Indian foods, they were among those soon adopted by the settlers and frontiersmen.

Double-crust gooseberry pie was famous back in colonial days. Just cream ¼ cup butter or margarine, add 1 cup brown sugar, and blend well. Beat 2 eggs slightly and stir in. Add 3 tablespoons evaporated milk, 2 cups ripe gooseberries, and ¼ teaspoon vanilla. The crust ingredients are the same as with strawberry pie, although in double amounts because of the addition of a top crust. Bake in a hot oven for 15 minutes to seal the crust and deter any running over. Then lower the heat to moderate and bake for 15 minutes more or until the pastry is brown on top. You can make this with ripe currants, too.

Gooseberry tarts have long been favorites, and are especially good in cold lunches when you're in the woods. We also make these with cur-

CURRANT
Left: **with flowers.** *Right:* **with fruit.**

rants. In fact, with tarts in particular, we enjoy the varying flavors of the different varieties of gooseberries and currants that grow near our cabin in British Columbia and which are all easily recognizable because of their maple-shaped foliage and their likeness to domestic species.

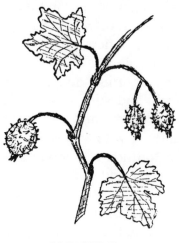

GOOSEBERRY

Just simmer the cleaned berries, with barely enough water to prevent scorching, until they come apart. Then remove them from the heat, sweeten liberally to taste, and put aside to cool. When they are cool, spoon them into pastry shells made by fitting the aforementioned pie pastry into greased muffin tins. Cover with a top crust brushed with melted butter, and bake in a moderate oven until the crust is nearly done. Remove long enough to brush with beaten egg and then put back in the oven to glaze for 4 minutes. We find these best cold.

Currant wine is simple to make, if the impulse ever seizes you. Wash and clean 10 pounds of currants and pour, along with 5 pounds of sugar, into a 2-gallon crock. Fill the crock to within an inch of the brim with cold water. Then spread cheesecloth across the top and leave in a warm place. For the next 6 weeks, carefully stir the mixture twice weekly. Then strain and allow to stand for an additional 2 weeks to settle. Finally, strain the resulting currant wine and store in sterilized bottles.

We'd rather use any excess currants for jelly which, especially when mixed with a bit of dry mustard, really does things for lamb and venison sandwiches. Mashing 12 cups of ripe clean currants, simmering for 10 minutes in 1½ cups water, and then straining through a jelly bag makes 6 cups of juice. Mix a 3-ounce package of pectin with this while it is still hot and, stirring constantly, add 6 cups of sugar and bring to a full hard boil for a minute. Then take from the heat, skim, and quickly pour into hot sterilized glasses. Immediately fill to the brims with melted paraffin, cover to protect from drafts which might break the glass, and leave to cool. Label and store as usual.

Gooseberry jam is more than worth the trouble. Just clean your berries, cut off the blossom ends, mix with an equal weight of sugar, and let stand overnight. Then bring to a rolling boil, and stirring, let boil for 20 minutes. Skim, pour into hot sterilized jars, and seal immediately.

PARTRIDGEBERRY

(Mitchella)

Partridgeberries are so easily recognizable that they make a good emergency food. Too, they are available from autumn to spring, clinging

PARTRIDGEBERRY

conspicuously to the trailing evergreen shrubs throughout the winter. You will find them in moist woodlands and clearings from Nova Scotia and New Brunswick to Florida, west to Minnesota, Arkansas, and Texas. Other names include twin berries and checkerberries.

We have a single species of partridgeberry on this continent. Another grows in Japan. Ours is a slender, creeping vine, six to twelve inches long, putting down new roots along its prostrate stem. The small, shiny, smooth-edged leaves grow on short stems in opposite pairs. Dark green and sometimes white-veined, they are oval or heart-shaped and usually no more than one-half inch long on average, although they run closer to three-fourths of an inch in some sections.

The June flowers burst out in pairs, often with the past year's coral red berries. These fragrant pairs of half-inch blossoms, each with four pinkish or white petals, grow together at their bases in such a way that it takes two blooms to make one berry. The fruit, too, has a distinctive Siamese-twin aspect.

It ripens during the usual fall hunting seasons, and I often enjoy its aromatic pleasantness while wandering through the woods. Although seedy and on the dry side, it will take the edge off hunger. Ruffed grouse, bobwhite, wild turkey, and small animals including the red fox like it, too.

MULBERRY

(Morus)

Mulberries ripen in early summer and at this time of the year are one of the favorite foods of songbirds and small game. They are also widely popular in jellies and pies, especially when their sweetness is modified by a touch of lemon. We have gathered them by the gallon for these purposes just by shaking a heavily laden branch over an outspread tarpaulin.

Although up to some dozen species of mulberries are distributed over our north temperate regions, the best of the fruit comes from the native red mulberry. This is a small tree, generally twenty to thirty feet high with a trunk diameter of one to one and a half feet, which prefers the rich moistness of bottomlands and foothill forests but which has been introduced to many yards and streets. A standby of Indians and of early European explorers and settlers, it grows from New England to the Dakotas and south to Florida and Texas, being especially prolific in the Ohio and Mississippi valleys. The soft but tough wood has been used for everything from furniture and fence posts to ships.

The often crooked branches of the red mulberry commonly spread into dense, broad, round domes. These become dark green with sharply toothed leaves, from three to five inches long and almost as wide, which are irregular in shape from their generally heart-shaped bases to their pointed tips. The undersurfaces are paler than the rough tops and often slightly downy. The stems have a milky sap. Incidentally, the

MULBERRY
Left: winter twig. *Center:* branch with leaves and fruit. *Right:* bud and leaf scar.

twigs are sweetish and, especially when tender in the spring, edible either raw or boiled. The flowers grow in greenish spikes in the joints between leaves and branches.

Despite the name, the ripe fruit of the red mulberry somewhat resembles that of the blackberry in color as well as shape, becoming dark purple when ready to eat. Even though you'll no doubt eat as you pick, you may collect what seems to be an excess. If so, don't overlook the excellence of the juice as a warm-weather drink, either pressing this through cheesecloth or extracting it with an electric juicer. A little lemon juice and sugar, stirred in to taste, will improve the flavor. We like to dilute this juice about half and half with crushed ice.

Mulberry jelly is bright, quivery, and worth the trouble if you live where the berries are plentiful. Mash 4 cups of cleaned fruit in a kettle. Add ¼ cup water. Bring slowly to a simmer, then boil rapidly for 10 minutes. Pour into a jelly bag to drip without squeezing. Add 1 teaspoon of lemon juice to each cup of juice.

Return to the kettle. Stir in 2 cups sugar and a package of pectin, and boil until the juice will fall in a sheet from the side of a spoon. Skim, pour immediately to within ½ inch of the tops of hot sterilized glasses, fill the remaining space with melted paraffin, cover to protect against drafts, and when cool, put away on a dark, dry shelf.

Mulberries and steaming hot dumplings make a happy match. If you're just cooking for 2, ready 3 cups of the ripe fruit. Mix these with 1 cup sugar or, better, sweeten to taste. Add the juice of a lemon. Bring to a simmer in a large pot. When you're ready to sit down to the main meal, drop on a white dome of dumplings and cover tightly.

Enough dumplings for 2 diners are a cinch to make. About 12 minutes before mealtime, mix 2 cups flour, 2 teaspoons baking powder, and 1 teaspoon salt. Work in 2 tablespoons butter, margarine, or other solid shortening. Make a bowl-like hollow in the center. Have everything ready to go, for these dumplings should be cooked and served immediately.

Now pour 1 cup milk into the well in the center of the dry ingredients. Mix quickly and gently with a folding, rather than a stirring or whipping, motion.

Moisten a large spoon in the mulberry juice. Use it to place large spoonfuls of dough, apart from one another, atop the boiling berries. Cover tightly. After several minutes, you may if you want turn each dumpling speedily and carefully. Recover immediately and continue boiling until light and fluffy.

When the dumplings are done, take out and top each with a spoonful of butter or margarine. If any dumplings remain for second helpings, place them in a separate hot dish so they won't become soggy. Spoon the hot berries over the ones you're eating. Pour on some milk or cream if you want. And see what everyone's idea is about dessert for the following meal.

GROUND CHERRY

(Physalis)

Ground cherries, close relations to the tomato but not even distant cousins of the cherry family, grow in all parts of the country except Alaska. Also known as strawberry tomatoes and husk tomatoes, they have long found their way into occasional markets, being raised commercially in some localities. They are also found in fields, waste places,

GROUND CHERRY

and in open country, but particularly in recently cleared and cultivated ground, where they ripen from July through September.

This rapidly growing annual takes up a lot of room, its single or forked branches many times sprawling over several feet of ground, but it seldom grows more than a foot high. The pointed leaves have broadly and roundly indented edges. The decorative flowers, which make one hardy perennial of the family, the Chinese lantern plant or winter cherry, a flower garden favorite, resemble tiny yellow funnels. Their five petals later greatly expand, completely enclosing the round yellow berry in a tiny papery husk.

These large yellowish coverings so protect the single golden fruits that when, as often happens, they fall early, they still ripen on the ground. Too, if you will store the encased berries dry. they will continue to become more sugary for several weeks. But in some areas you have to beat the game birds and some of the game and fur animals to them.

One of the first pies I ever remember eating was made of ground cherries, and it must have been good to stay in my memory all these years. A bit of lemon brings out the flavor, and a little nutmeg enhances it. Combine 4 cups of cleaned fruit, 1¼ cups sugar, ½ teaspoon nutmeg, 2 tablespoons lemon juice, and 2 tablespoons melted butter or margarine. Pour into an uncooked 9-inch pie shell and top with another thinly rolled sheet of dough, venting this last. Cook in a moderate oven, preheated as always, 45 to 55 minutes, or until the crust is golden. This pie is runny, and you'll probably have to finish up with a spoon, but the flavor is all the better for that.

Ground cherries are very easily put up. Just make a syrup by boiling 6 cups water, 3 cups sugar, and the juice of 3 lemons for 5 minutes. Spoon in enough ground cherries to come to the top of the syrup. Simmer until the fruit is tender and clear, pour into hot sterilized jars, and seal.

The raw berries, which are very refreshing when you're out for the day, make a pleasant dessert with sugar and milk. Or try them with vanilla ice cream sometime. They're good with this, too, after they've been blended as for pie and stewed.

The jam, too, is really scrumptuous. Crush 4 cups of fully ripe fruit, a layer at a time, so that each berry is reduced to pulp. Add 4 tablespoons lemon juice and a package of pectin. Bring the mixture quickly to a boil, stirring occasionally. Then put in 4 cups sugar. Bring back to a hard boil for 1 minute, continuing to stir. Remove from the heat and skim off any foam. Let cool for 5 minutes, stirring occasionally, for better consistency. Then pour into hot sterilized glasses and seal at once as usual.

RUM CHERRY

(Prunus)

Some fourteen native species of wild cherries, ranging in size from shrubs to large trees, are widely distributed across the United States and Canada. Game birds and songbirds feast on their fruit summers and falls when it ripens, and even before, and animals feed on the cherries that have dropped to the ground. Deer, elk, moose, and mountain sheep are among those supplementing their diet with the foliage, twigs, and tasty bark of wild cherries. Chipmunks often store large quantities of the seeds for their winter food supply.

The rum cherry, often known as the wild black cherry, is the most important member of the group. This tree is found in woods and open places, particularly along old walls and fences where its seeds have been dropped by birds. The rum cherry is native from Nova Scotia to Minnesota and the Dakotas, south to central Florida and eastern Texas. A slightly different variety grows in the mountain canyons of Arizona and New Mexico.

Rum cherries, sometimes 50 to 60 feet and occasionally 100 feet tall, grow into one of the most highly valued timber trees of the continent. The strong wood, which turns as dark as mahogany upon exposure to air, is popular for cabinet work and for veneering.

The bark, pleasantly aromatic with the odor of bitter almonds, is an old-time home remedy for coughs. The reddish, scale-covered outer bark is first removed. Then the greenish layer, best when young and thin, is stripped off and dried. A teaspoon of this is steeped in a cup of boiling water. One or two cupfuls are drunk cold a day, a large mouthful at a time.

The shining leaves of the rum cherry are narrowly oval to oblong lance-shaped, with broadly rounded or wedge-shaped bases and long, pointed tips. Measuring from two to five inches long, and from three-fourths to one and a half inches wide, they have edges that are finely indented with incurving teeth. The short stems, one-half to one inch long, have a pair of reddish glands at their tops.

The long clusters of white flowers start drooping from the ends of branches while the leaves are still growing. The roundish berries ripen to a bright black or dark purple in August and September, varying from tree to tree in size and quality. Their bittersweet, richly winy juic-

RUM CHERRY
Top left: blossom. *Top right:* branch with leaves and fruit. *Bottom:* branch with leaves and blossoms.

iness, although usually puckery, makes them popular, at least among young boys, wherever they grow.

Rum cherries got their name from being used by old-time New Englanders to mellow rum and other brandies, as well as whiskies. The procedure was to sweeten the strained and simmered juice of crushed rum cherries with an equal bulk of sugar, then add it to taste to the raw liquors. The process was favored because, in addition to its soothing effect, it also thriftily stretched the available supplies of the ardent spirits.

Cherry bounce still works out well with rum cherries, the proportions being 1 quart fruit and ½ pound sugar to a pint of whiskey. Clean and stem the fruit. Start by covering the bottom of a wide-mouthed jar with a thick layer of cherries. Top these with a single layer of sugar cubes. Some connoisseurs then sprinkle on small amounts of clove, cinnamon, nutmeg, and allspice. Continue this process as long as the fruit and sugar last. Then pour in the whiskey. Seal, put away in a dark place, and go about other matters for at least 2 months.

Brandied rum cherries, also popular during the early trading days of New England, can be made by boiling 2 cups of sugar in a quart of water until a clear syrup is formed. Pour this over 2 quarts of cleaned rum cherries and let stand overnight. The next day, drain the syrup into a pot, bring it slowly to a bubble, carefully add the cherries, and simmer for 10 minutes. Then scoop out the fruit with a slotted spoon and pack them into sterilized hot glass jars. Cover them temporarily while boiling the syrup until it is thick. Stir in a pint of rum or other brandy, pour immediately over the cherries, seal, and put away to age.

You can't buy rum cherry sherbet at the store, but you can make a very refreshing version at home. Just squeeze enough ripe cherries to give 2 cups of juice. Bring this to a simmer along with 2 cups of water and 2 cups of sugar. In the meantime, whip the whites of 3 eggs until they are stiff. Pour the hot mixture over these and beat thoroughly. After this has cooled, transfer it to your freezing compartment.

Although they lack pectin, rum cherries make rich dark jelly when combined with apples. The latter should be sour and preferably green. Quarter them whole, put in a kettle with just enough water to cover, and simmer until tender before straining off the clear juice. Mash the cleaned and washed cherries, add ½ cup hot water, and simmer to a pulp, stirring to prevent scorching. Then place in a jelly bag which has been dipped in hot water, and squeeze out the juice. Or you can strain this by pressing the berries in a large sieve lined with facial tissues.

Get 2 cups apiece of both juices boiling together. Then add 4 cups sugar, stirring only until dissolved. Boil rapidly until a large spoon of the mixture runs off in a sheet. Remove from the heat, pour into hot sterilized glasses set on a towel, seal with melted paraffin, cool, and store in a dark, cool, dry place.

Rum cherry jelly can also be made with added pectin instead of apples, and you may very well disagree with us and like it even better. Simmer the crushed ripe berries, which vary quite a bit in juiciness, with ½ cup hot water for 20 minutes and then strain. You'll need 3½ cups of juice.

Return this to the heat, mix in 1 package of pectin, and, stirring, let come to a boil. Add 4½ cups sugar and, continuing to stir, bring to a full boil for no more than a minute. Remove from the heat, skim, immediately pour into hot sterilized glasses, top at once with melted paraffin, cover, cool, and store as before. Incidentally, any wild jellies that are to be kept in a damp place, or mailed as personal gifts, should be put instead into vacuum-sealed or screw-topped jars.

The rum cherries that grew along the orchard walls of my grandparents' farm in western Massachusetts seemed particularly plump, and when I went there as a boy my Grandmother Adams used to prepare me a special dessert of them. She started this the morning before by pitting a small pail of fruit that I had picked early.

She stewed this awhile with a very little water, sweetened it carefully to taste, and then poured the hot juice and berries over thin slices of bread; first bread, then fruit, then another slice of bread, and so on, finally filling the deep dish with what was left of the fruit. She then covered this and, when it was cool, set it in the ice compartment of her ice box. That night I would enjoy it with fresh thick cream and maybe a little more sugar.

CHOKECHERRY

(Prunus)

Perhaps the most widely distributed tree on this continent, the chokecherry grows from the Arctic Circle to Mexico and from ocean to ocean. Despite their puckery quality, one handful of the small ripe berries seems to call for another when you're hot and thirsty. The fruit, which is both red or black, also makes an enjoyable tart jelly.

Often merely a large shrub, the chokecherry also becomes a small tree up to twenty-five feet tall with a trunk about eight inches through. It is found in open woods, but is more often seen on streambanks, in thickets in the corners of fields, and along roadsides and fences. Although the wood is similar to that of the rum cherry, it has no commercial value because of its smallness.

Chokecherry leaves, from two to four inches long and about half as wide, are oval or inversely ovate, with abrupt points. They are thin and smooth, dull dark green above and paler below. The edges are finely indented with narrowly pointed teeth. The short stems, less than an inch in length, have a pair of glands at their tops. The long clusters of flowers blossom when the leaves are nearly grown. The red to black fruits, the size of peas, are frequently so abundant that the limbs bend under their weight.

An attractive and tasty jelly is made by adding 2 parts of cooked applejuice to 1 part of cooked chokecherry juice and proceeding as

CHOKECHERRY
Left: flowering branch. *Center:* branch with leaves and fruit. *Right:* winter twig.

with rum cherry jelly. Too, a pure version can also be prepared with the help of commercial pectin.

Any of these tart wild cherry jellies can be used to flavor pies. Start by lightly beating 3 eggs. Mix 1 cup sugar, ¼ teaspoon salt, and ¼ teaspoon nutmeg, and add slowly to the eggs, continuing to beat. Melt ½ cup of butter or margarine and add that, too. Then thoroughly stir in 1 tablespoon of your jelly. Pour into an unbaked pie crust, that described under strawberry being excellent. Place in a preheated moderate oven for 10 minutes. Then reduce the heat to slow for 15 minutes, or until it firms.

PIN CHERRY

(Prunus)

The pin cherry, also known as the fire cherry and the bird cherry, is the only early and light red native wild cherry. Soon dying when shaded, it grows along the margins of woods, in recently burned regions, in clearings, and along fences and roadsides. It is a northern species, ranging from British Columbia to Labrador, south into the high country of North Carolina, Tennessee, and Colorado.

Despite the sourness and the large stones of the small fruit, they are refreshing when you're outdoors and thirsty. When they are brought indoors, it is mostly for making jelly.

The pin cherry, unlike the rum cherry and chokecherry, has its flowers in small, lateral, roundly flat tufts. The thinly fleshed cherries,

PIN CHERRY
Top left: blossoms. *Right:* branch with leaves and fruit.

about one-fourth inch in diameter, grow similarly, on long stems. They ripen during July and August, depending on the latitude, and even before then the birds do not seem to mind their tartness.

The leaves are oblong and shaped like lances, with rounded or wedge-shaped bases and tapering, pointed tips. With edges indented with fine, sharp teeth, they run from three to five inches long and three-fourths to one and one-fourth inches wide. The thin, short stems, again, have two glands at their tops.

The ruddy, shiny brown bark is smooth, or nearly so, on the younger trees. It frequently peels off in horizontal strips to expose a green inner bark that is pleasantly aromatic but exceedingly bitter. Older trees take on a rougher, curlier shagginess. The gum found on the trunks is often enjoyably chewed. Little more than shrubs in the North, pin cherries sometimes grow forty feet or so tall in the southern Appalachians.

In some parts of the North, pin cherries are boiled down in a small amount of water, strained, simmered with sugar to taste, and then bottled for use on puddings and pancakes.

Their main fame, though, is as a jelly, and for this their flavor is so fine that there is no need to add any other fruit. Like other wild cherries, these vary considerably in juiciness and in the amount of pulp. Be sure to crush and simmer enough, with ½ cup water to every quart, to strain out 4 cups of juice. Return this juice to the heat, add a package of pectin, and bring to a boil, stirring. Then mix in 6 cups of sugar and bring to a boil for 1 minute. Remove from the stove, skim, immediately pour into hot sterilized glasses, and seal at once. Cover and cool as usual, then label, date, and store.

My favorite wild cherry dessert today is a deep-dish pie. Moisten 2½ cups juice pitted fruit with ½ cup water and cook until tender. Add a cup of sugar when almost done. Then pour the hot fruit into a baking dish or casserole.

For the crust, mix 1 cup sifted flour, 1 tablespoon sugar, 1 teaspoon baking powder, and ½ teaspoon salt. Cut in 2 tablespoons shortening. Then quickly stir in enough milk, about ½ cup, to make a soft dough. Spoon this immediately over the fruit. Cut vents. Then get the whole thing at once into a preheated hot oven and bake about 30 minutes, or until the crust is done. Serve hot with vanilla ice cream.

KINNIKINIC

(*Arctostaphylos*)

As for kinnikinic, after you have filled up on the sustaining if blandly dry red berries, you can make yourself a smoke with the leaves. Dried and pulverized, these have been a frontier tobacco substitute for centuries. They are both mixed with dwindling supplies of regular tobacco and smoked alone.

The widely distributed and easily recognizable kinnikinic should be better known, if only for possible use as a sustaining emergency food. Some of the other names that have become attached to it are mealberry, hog cranberry, upland cranberry, arberry, and especially bearberry. In fact, one of the best places to look for black bear after they have come out of northern hibernation in the spring is on a sunny hillside patch of kinnikinic.

Kinnikinic is luxuriant across Canada, Alaska, and the tops of Asia and Europe. Preferring a sandy or gravelly upland habitat, this member of the heath family is found south to Virginia, New Mexico,

KINNIKINIC
Left: with flowers. *Right:* with fruit.

and California. Grouse and other game birds pick its small fat berries. Deer browse extensively on its green, leathery foliage.

Chinook-bared hills around our log-cabin home are green in the very early spring, while snow is still deep in the woods, because of kinnikinic. This trailing perennial shrub with its long fibrous root forms a dense, matlike, evergreen carpet. The alternate egg-shaped leaves are short-stemmed, small, thick, and tough. The pink flowers, which are inconspicuous, grow like tiny bells that sway in terminal clusters. The sometimes pink berries, which are more often dull red with an orange cast, ripen in the fall.

One of the important things about these berries, especially when considered as potentially important emergency food, is that, hard and dry, they cling resolutely to the prostrate shrubs all winter. Otherwise, although mealy, they are rather tasteless. Cooking improves them considerably, however. Too, people depending on wild fruit sometimes gather them in poor berry years and mix them with blueberries.

The odorless green leaves, gathered in the fall and allowed to dry indoors in moderate heat, make a pleasantly bitter and noticeably astringent tea which is regarded in many parts of the Northern Hemisphere as both soothing to the stomach and tonic. You can make it by covering each teaspoonful of dried leaves with a cup of boiling water and allowing to steep 5 minutes. One old sourdough I know, though, claims that the best results are obtained if the leaves are first soaked in just enough whiskey to cover them, then measured and timed the same way.

*vegetables with
the savor
of the wilds*

Wild Greens

IF YOU HAVE ever sat down to a well prepared meal that included wild vegetables, maybe you've noticed that many of them seem to taste better than domesticated varieties. I'll let you in on a trade secret. They are better.

Green leafy vegetables, to give just one example, deteriorate very quickly. Even when purchased as fresh as obtainable from the finest nearby market, they'll already have lost a sizeable proportion of vitamins.

Some of the food values of greens diminish as much as one third during the first hour after picking. But gather them fresh from nature's own garden and eat them while they're at their tastiest, and you'll enjoy the best they have to offer.

DANDELIONS

(Taraxacum)

Gathering wild greens is a happy way to sharpen a satisfactory hunger, even if you go no farther than to collect a bagful of common dandelions. Actually, this familiar vegetable, all too well known because of the way it dots many a lawn, is among the best of the wild greens.

The well-known dandelion of flower beds, lawns, pastures, meadows, roadsides, and other moist, open places, boasts some three species in this country and about twenty-five in the civilized world, over which

DANDELION
Left: Arctic and alpine dandelion. *Right:* ordinary dandelion.

it is widespread. The green leaves are long and narrow, spreading in a rosette at the bottom. Their coarse edges, irregularly lobed and toothed, give this wild edible its name, which means "lion's tooth."

The flowers are yellow, maturing into full white ovals of plume-tailed seeds that later scatter in the wind to make dandelions plentiful and persistent. The hollow and leafless flower stems discharge a bitterish milky juice when bruised or severed, as do the roots when the greens are cut free. These roots are generally thick and deep. Such wildlife as mule and white-tailed deer relish the green foliage, while grouse and pheasant find the seeds delectable.

The tender young leaves, available in the early spring, are among the first wild edibles I gather while bear hunting, trout fishing, or just plain hiking or horseback riding through the greening wilderness. At first they are excellent in salads. Later, when the plants begin blossoming, they develop a toughness and bitterness. Changing the first boiling water into which arey are crammed will remove much of this bitter taste if you want, but we find it clean and zestful. Incidentally, when you can, include as many buds as possible, as they liven both the color and the flavor.

Young, tender dandelion greens can be used to add character and vitamins to scrambled eggs. Mix 4 eggs and 4 tablespoons cold water with salt and pepper to taste. Add a cup of shredded dandelions. Heat 2 tablespoons of butter, margarine, or bacon grease in a frypan just hot enough to sizzle a drop of water. Pour in the egg and dandelion mixture and reduce the heat. When the eggs have started to harden, begin stirring them constantly with a fork. Remove them while they're still soft and creamy.

Although they contain a laxative, *taraxacum*, the roots, when young, are often peeled and sliced, like carrots or parsnips, for boiling as a vegetable. To remove the characteristic tinge of bitterness, you may choose to change the salted water once. Serve with melting butter or margarine. Being particularly nourishing, these roots are a famous emergency food, having saved people from starving during famines.

Although the woods afford a multitude of teas, they are short on coffees. The dandelion will provide one of the latter. Roast the roots slowly in an open oven all afternoon until, shriveling, they resemble miniature dragons and will snap crisply when broken, revealing insides as brown as coffee beans.

Grind these roots and keep tightly covered for use either as regular coffee or for mixing to extend your normal supplies. Dandelion roots may be used the year around for this purpose. Because I generally roast my grind shortly before freezeup in the fall when the roots are near their strongest, I find I only have to use a level tablespoon of this homemade mixture per cup, whereas I prefer a heaping tablespoon of store coffee.

Dandelion wine is famous. If you'd like to make your own, pick a gallon of the flowers early on a dry morning, making sure that no parts of the bitterish stems are included. Press these into a 2-gallon crock. Pour a gallon of boiling water over them and leave for 3 days. Then strain through a cloth, squeezing all the liquid from the blossoms.

Add the juice and the thinly sliced rind and pulp from 3 oranges and 3 lemons. Stir in 3 pounds sugar. Add 1 ounce yeast. Cover the crock with a cloth and let it stand, out of the way, for 3 weeks while the mixture ferments. Then strain, bottle, and cork or cap tightly.

LAMB'S QUARTER

(Chenopodium)

In a lot of homes the acknowledged pick of the edible greens is lamb's quarter. The tender tops of this wild spinach, which has none of the strong taste of market varieties, are delicious from early spring to frost-withering fall.

The entire young plant is good from the ground up. Even from the older ones a quantity of tender leaves can usually be stripped. However, the pale green leaves with their mealy-appearing underneaths and the slim stalks are not the only taste-tempting components of this green, also widely known as pigweed and goosefoot.

Indians long used the ripe seeds, 75,000 of which have been counted on a single plant, for cereal and for grinding into meal. These tiny gleaming discs, which develop from elognated dense clusters of small green flowers, are also handy for giving a pumpernickel complexion to biscuits and breads.

Some twenty of the sixty or more species in this genus, which belongs to the same family as beets and spinach, grow in the United States, thriving in nearly every part of the country. Lamb's quarter is a very common annual which grows from two to seven feet tall. By searching, you can usually find plenty of young plants up to about twelve inches high, and these are best for the table. These young plants have a mealy whiteness to them, but they do not require parboiling. Later, the tender tips alone are excellent. The alternate leaves, which are fleshy and tasty, have long stems and angular margins.

Along with other of the more tender leafy greens, lamb's quarter can be given a bit more taste on occasion with the help of a vinegar sauce. Such a flavorful acid also tends to preserve the vitamins C and A in such vegetables. Alkalies, on the other hand, such as the commonly but inadvisedly used baking soda, destroy an unnecessary proportion of these food values.

For 4 cups of loosely packed greens, take 1 small onion, 4 slices bacon,

LAMB'S QUARTER

¼ cup vinegar, ¼ teaspoon salt, and pepper to taste. Shred the greens if they are large. Dice the onion. Mix. Then chop up the bacon and fry it until the bits become brown and brittle. Put in the vinegar, salt, and pepper and bring to a simmer.

You now have 2 choices. You may pour the sauce over the raw greens. Or you may add the greens to the sauce and cook over low heat until they are limp. In either case, serve immediately. And see what the family's idea is for vegetables for the rest of the week.

STRAWBERRY SPINACH

(Chenopodium)

Strawberry spinach, also known as Indian strawberry and as strawberry blite, is similar to its close cousin, lamb's quarter. The major difference lies in the bright red masses of pulpy fruits which, many a time when I've been moose hunting the Northwest in the early fall, have stained my boots like dye, making this edible easily recognizable. It is common across Alaska and Canada, southward into the northern states.

This annual grows upright, with either a single or a branching smooth stem, from several inches to about two feet high. The thin

STRAWBERRY SPINACH

leaves, longer than they are wide, are broadly triangular with wavy or coarsely indented margins. The inconspicuous little flowers grow in the angles between the leaves and the upper portions of the stem, and often in spikes at the top of the stem. They become dense red masses, with the color and softness of strawberries. They are very nutritious, both raw and cooked.

67

The young stems and leaves, and later the young tender leaves by themselves, may be used like those of lamb's quarter, either raw in salads or cooked like spinach, which they considerably excel in taste, at the same time providing nutritious amounts of vitamins C and A.

PLANTAIN

(Plantago)

Plantain is almost as good as lamb's quarter. Furthermore, plantain is as well known to most of us as are the similarly prepared and eaten dandelions, although not usually by name.

It is the short, stemless potherb whose broadly elliptic green leaves rise directly from the root about a straight central spike. This singular spike blossoms, although possibly you've never noticed it, with minute

PLANTAIN

greenish flowers that later turn into seeds. At any rate, plantain is found all over the world, even growing through sidewalks in New York, San Francisco, and Boston.

Some nineteen kinds of plantain thrive in the United States. One of the more widely distributed of these is the seaside plantain, also known as goosetongue, which grows along such widely separated coasts as those of Quebec, Nova Scotia, New England, Alaska, British Columbia, and California. The natives in Alaska boil this fresh both for eating on the spot and for canning for winter.

Plantain leaves make excellent greens. Fact is, the greener they are, the richer they are in vitamins A and C and in minerals. They are good boiled. What holds for plantain, when it comes to this common if often murderous method of cookery, goes for the other wild greens as well. Unless it means standing over a riled cook with a cleaver, try to see that all these are cooked only until just tender and still slightly crisp. This usually takes a surprisingly brief time.

The simple gimmick with these wild vegetables is to start them in a minimum amount of boiling water and to cook them, covered, as rapidly and briefly as possible. Young plantain and such can be lifted directly from the rinse to the saucepan and cooked without added water.

For two liberal servings of slightly older greens, ½ cup water and ½ teaspoon salt will do the job. When the greens become tougher, a full cup of water may be required. Any of the vitamin- and mineral-rich fluid remaining should be used, as in soups, gravies, sauces, and the like, unless there's some reason against this such as unusual bitterness. Me, I drink it.

Plantain, also called ribwort and soldiers herb, is mildly astringent. During pioneer times, and even today in some backwoods localities, the fresh leaves are mashed and applied to cuts, scratches, and wounds. The leaves are also used for tea, ½ handful being dropped into a cup of boiling water and allowed to steep for ½ hour.

SOW THISTLE

(Sonchus)

This very well-known weed, introduced from Europe where it is used as a potherb, has become common throughout most of the cultivated regions of the world including those of North America. It is so familiar, as a matter of fact, that the tendency is to disparage it. However, in parts of California where dandelions are largely absent the similar sow thistle can be used as an early season green in place of these favorites.

SOW THISTLE

Nearly everyone knows this thistle with the prickly or bristly but otherwise dandelionlike leaves, best handled with gloves, which grows close to civilization. Its top clusters of yellow flowers resemble those of the dandelion but are much smaller. They later develop a multitude of seeds that are one of the favorite foods of goldfinches, those cheerful little cousins of pet canaries.

Like the dandelion, the sow thistle is characterized by a milky sap. This sap is bitterish, again like that of the dandelion, and this is a reason why some users prefer to boil the leaves in two changes of salted water. Even when we gather the smaller of these succulent green leaves as late as midsummer, cutting them off close to the thick stalks so they can drop unhandled into a bag, we personally relish this slight bitterness, however. We just drop them into a small amount of boiling salted water, cover, cook very briefly only until tender, and eat hot with melting butter or margarine or, for second choice, with oil and vinegar.

If you catch the leaves young enough, they make a tasty salad along with sliced tomatoes and hard-boiled eggs. For a really top dressing for this, dissolve ½ teaspoon salt in ¾ cup olive or salad oil. Stir in ¼ teaspoon pepper. Then whip. Keep in a bottle in the refrigerator and shake vigorously before using. A way to change the taste at times, particularly effective with this salad, is by beating 1 tablespoon crumbled Roquefort cheese into 4 tablespoons of the dressing.

PURSLANE

(Portulaca)

Purslane, although commonly unnoticed except as a weed, is sometimes the tastiest crop in the home gardens where it widely occurs. This annual also frequently becomes troublesome in fields and waste places throughout the contiguous forty-eight states, in the warmer parts of Canada, and even in Mexico where it is sold in the markets.

The reason for this distribution, which is worldwide, is its tremendous production of seeds, relished by birds and rodents. Although purslane does not become large, 52,300 seeds have been counted on a single plant. Indians in our Southwest used these for making bread and mush.

The trailing, juicy plant which is familiar to almost everyone who has ever weeded a yard, is native to India and Persia, where it has been a food for more than 2,000 years. An early mover to Europe, it has been eaten there for centuries. Introduced to the New World back in colonial days, it has spread into almost every American city and town.

"I learned that a man may use as simple a diet as the animals, and yet retain health and strength. I have made a satisfactory dinner off a dish of purslane which I gathered and boiled," Henry Thoreau noted in Massachusetts over a century ago. "Yet men have come to such a pass that they frequently starve, not for want of necessaries but for want of luxuries."

The semisucculent purslane, also sometimes called pusley, prefers fertile sandy ground over which it trails and crawls, sometimes forming mats. It seldom reaches more than an inch or so into the air, although it often spreads broadly. The jointed stems, purplish or greenish with a reddish tinge, are fleshy and forking. The narrow, thick leaves, scattered in nearly opposite positions, grow up to about two inches long.

Unfolding their six or seven petals and some eleven stamens only on bright mornings, the small yellow flowers peek out from stems lifting from the forkings of the stalk. They produce tiny round seed vessels whose tops, when ripe, lift uniquely off like lids.

There's a trick, incidentally, to gathering purslane for the table. If you'll just nip off the tender leafy tips, they'll rapidly sprout again. This way just a few plants will furnish you with greens from late June until frost.

Purslane makes excellent salads. However, after its usual grittiness is removed by washing, it has most frequently been enjoyed as a potherb wherever we've lived. Just drop it into salted boiling water, simmer for about 5 minutes or until tender and serve with melted butter or margarine. A little purslane goes surprisingly far, as it loses little bulk in cooking.

You can capitalize a little more on its mildly acid taste, though, by first cutting 4 slices of bacon into small shreds and frying them until crisp. Then pour in ½ cup vinegar and ½ cup hot water, along with 2 teaspoons brown sugar and salt and pepper to taste. Mix these thoroughly, bring to a bubble, and pour over a large heap of tender young purslane tips. Fork the greens gently about until they are all well coated. Garnish with chopped, hard-boiled eggs, sprinkled with paprika.

Individuals who don't like okra frequently object to purslane's mucilaginous quality, which can be an advantage, however, for lending consistency to soups and stews. It can be counteracted, on the other hand, by rolling each young tip, still slightly damp from washing, in flour, then dipping it in beaten egg, and finally rolling it in bread crumbs. Fry in deep, hot fat for about 8 minutes, or until brown.

People who like pickles may be interested to know that purslane has been furnishing these for centuries. As might be expected, methods have varied widely over the years, but you won't go far wrong by just substituting tender young purslane stems for cucumbers in your favorite recipe.

Here's one that works well. Mix 1 cup salt, 2 cups sugar, and 1 cup ground mustard. Gradually moistening and vigorously stirring at first, mix with 2 quarts vinegar. Pour over as many freshly picked and washed young purslane stems as it will cover. If you have a large crock, fresh purslane and pickling brine may be added day by day until the crock is full. Then cover with a weighed-down plate and leave for at least several weeks. These really stimulate enthusiastic conversation when friends stop by.

SCURVY GRASS

(Cochlearia)

Scurvy has gathered more explorers, pioneers, trappers, and prospectors to their fathers than can ever be counted, for it is a debilitating killer whose lethal subtleties through the centuries have too often been misinterpreted and misunderstood.

Scurvy, it is known now, is a vitamin-deficiency disease. If you have it, taking Vitamin C into your system will cure you. Eating a little Vitamin C regularly will, indeed, keep you from having scurvy in the first place. Fresh vegetables and fruits will both prevent and cure scurvy. So will the long misused lime juice and lemon juice but, no matter how sour, only if they, too, are sufficiently fresh. The vitamin C in all these is lessened and eventually destroyed by age, by oxidation, and incidentally, by salt.

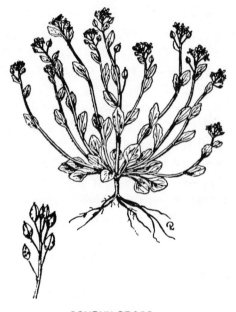

SCURVY GRASS
Bottom left: seed pods. *Right:* entire plant with flowers.

Scurvy grass, of which there are several species belonging to the *Cochlearia* family, was one of the first wild greens used by frontiersmen, explorers, and gold diggers across the northern portions of this continent from Alaska to Newfoundland to combat scurvy; hence the name. It so happens, too, that other greens throughout the New World have been similarly used and similarly named, this being one reason for the use of distinguishing Latin names in this book.

This widely distributed scurvy grass, which has the strong horse-radishlike odor and flavor of cress, has small white flowers whose 4 white petals are arranged in a cross. These grow in long clusters atop branching stems, a few inches high, that rise from grouped leaves. These delicate little blossoms produce flattish, oval pods that become filled with seeds.

The lower leaves, shaped like broad-based spoons up to about an inch long, group together in narrow rosettes. Fleshy and nearly veinless, they have both smooth and toothed edges. These lower leaves have short thin stems, whereas the upper leaves grow directly from the stalks.

Scurvy grass is not only succulent in spring and early summer, but young lower leaves can also be found in the fall. Although it has a distinctive deliciousness whether eaten raw or after being briefly simmered in a small amount of water, scurvy grass furnishes the utmost in nourishment when served in salads or eaten raw between slices of buttered bread. Or for something really different, spread the bread with cream cheese.

Raw young scurvy grass combines well with freshly cooked white rice. Mix 2 cups cooled rice with the juice of a whole lemon, a tablespoon of olive oil, and salt and pepper to taste. Stir in a cup of scurvy grass leaves that have been torn into fine pieces.

Or try this version. Mix 2 cups hot cooked rice with 2 tablespoons melted butter or margarine and 1 tablespoon powdered parsley. Add 1 cup shredded scurvy grass. Season the savory result with salt to taste and serve.

Scurvy grass is also good by itself in a salad, especially when topped with a dressing made of olive oil, vinegar, salt, and pepper. Dissolve ½ teaspoon salt in 4 tablespoons of malt or tarragon vinegar, blended half and half if convenient. Drop in ¼ teaspoon of preferably freshly ground pepper and stir well. Then whip in ¾ cup olive oil. Shake vigorously each time before using.

ROSEROOT

(Sedum)

Roseroot is another of the wild greens that is known as scurvy grass because of the often life-saving amounts of Vitamin C it has provided for explorers, trappers, prospectors, sailors, and other venturers on this continent's frontiers. It is also sometimes known as stonecrop and rosewort. Seen in rocky ground, on cliff walls and ledges, in damply rich mountain soil, and on the vast northern tundras, it may be found from Alaska and British Columbia across Canada to Labrador and Newfoundland, south to North Carolina.

Easy to recognize, it becomes unmistakable when you scrape or bruise the large thick roots, as these then give off the agreeable aroma of expensive rose perfume.

ROSEROOT
Bottom left: root. Right: stems, leaves, and flowers.

The numerous stems of roseroot grow from four to six inches to about a foot high. They are thick with fleshy leaves, ranging in color from pale green to pinkish, that are either oblong or oval, smooth-edged or toothed. Dense tufts of reddish purple to yellow blossoms crowd the tops of the stems. Up to about two inches broad, these are composed of dozens of little flowers, each of which has four petals. These blossoms produce red and purple seed-filled capsules that have four or five prongs.

Good from summer to fall, the perennial roseroot and some of its close cousins are relished both in North America and in Europe as a boiled vegetable and as a salad plant. The succulent young leaves and stems, which are at their tenderest before the plants flower, become pretty tough by the time the seed vessels appear.

But then, where the plants are abundant, you can boil up a feed of the big rough roots, season them with butter and pepper and a little salt, and enjoy them with your meat or fish. When they are young, the juicy stems with the leaves attached lend pleasant overtones to other wild greens, both raw and cooked.

GLASSWORT

(Salicornia)

Also called beach asparagus, glasswort bears the additional names of chicken claws and pickle plant. It is also known on this continent as samphire because of its use for pickles, as is a similarly named coastal plant in Europe.

At least four species grow in saline regions from Alaska and Labrador southward along the Pacific and Atlantic Coasts and around the Gulf of Mexico. Typical of shores, brackish marshes, and glistening tidal flats, these members of the beet and spinach family also pop up on the alkaline mud flats rimming western lakes. All in all, they thrive in salty surroundings, taste salty, and appropriately are also called salt-worts.

Because the raw tops remain tender and tasty from spring until fall, and especially because these wild edibles are so very easy to identify, the glasswort can be a life-saving food in an emergency. Canada and snow geese nibble on its greenness early in the season, while in the fall pintails and other ducks seek the seed-rich tips, even though these have reddened with age.

These fleshy, somewhat glassy cousins of lamb's quarter have apparently leafless stems, generally branching from near the base, that are juicily green in summer. As cold weather approaches, however, they redden from the ground up. The stems ascend in series of very noticeable joints, where what are actually leaves appear as minute scales which conceal the even less evident flowers and later the seeds.

Glasswort is particularly delicate when it pokes up early in warm weather in beds of bright green shoots only a few inches tall, although the distinctively briny tops will do a lot for a salad until frost-withering fall. It is both good alone, served with a spicy but not salty dressing, and chopped up with other greens. Salt should be added very discreetly. It is pleasant to chew while walking, unless drinking water is far away.

For some, it loses its singular sprightliness when cooked as a potherb, although this is done in Europe. To prepare it this way, just drop it in boiling fresh water, letting it provide its own salt, and simmer for 5 minutes or until thoroughly tender. Melt butter or margarine over the individual servings.

There are several ways of making glasswort pickles. You can boil young portions of the stems and branches in a very small amount of fresh water until a fork slips through them easily. Then transfer them to jars and cover them with cider or white wine vinegar that has been spiced to taste by boiling it no more than 6 minutes with a large grated onion, a kernel of garlic if desired, and a tablespoon apiece of nutmeg, cloves, and allspice. Seal and let stand for a month.

Or if the glasswort is tender enough to begin with, gather it in the proper lengths, clean, and stack directly in the jars. Make the same spiced vinegar as before, and while it is still bubbling, turn it to overflowing over the greens. Seal as before and let stand for at least a month before sampling. If you find you can spare enough of these for company, they make conversation-stimulating hors d'oeuvres.

WILD CUCUMBER

(Streptopus)

Wild cucumber, also known as liver berry and twisted stalk, thrives across the northern part of the continent and is common around our cabin in British Columbia. The fresh young shoots impart a cucumberlike taste to a mixed salad, real cucumbers generally being scarce commodities in the wilderness.

This perennial has branched stems which grow up to about four feet tall. The green leaves, which clasp alternate sides of the stem, have parallel ribs and are thinly longer than they are broad, being widest near their bases. The single pinkish or greenish flowers, shaped like tiny bells, droop from minute stalks growing from the junctures of the leaves and the stems.

They become small pulpy berries that, when ripe, range in color from whitish yellow to orange and scarlet. When parched from hunting in Maine and New Brunswick, I've sometimes let one or two linger refreshingly in my mouth. However, despite their deceptive cucum-

WILD CUCUMBER
Left: branched stem with fruits and flowers. *Right:* young shoots.

berlike flavor, they should be used sparingly, as they are cathartic. For this reason, they are known as scoot berries in some localities.

Wild cucumber salad is something we like on hot spring days. Shred tender young wild cucumber shoots and leaves into very small pieces, enough to fill 4 cups. Pile these loosely into a bowl and cover with very thin slices of a large sweet onion. Pour a heaping cup of sugar over everything, stir well, and allow to stand in a cool place. Then add ¼ cup of preferably mild vinegar, salt and pepper to taste, and serve.

The young plant is tasty, too, with gelatin. Add a cup of boiling water to the contents of a package of lemon Jello. Stir until completely dissolved. Then pour in a cup of cold water and start to chill. When it has started to set, mix in 1 cup finely shredded young wild cucumber, 1 teaspoon grated onion, ½ cup mayonnaise, and salt and pepper to taste. This may be poured into individual molds or spooned, when set, from a bowl. It goes well with a savory catch of sizzling fish.

NETTLES

(Urtica)

Don't overcook your wild vegetables. Even with such a formidable green as young nettles, which, like prickly pears, are best gathered with leather gloves and a knife, once the salted water has reached the boiling point and the dark green nettles have been dropped in, they'll be tender almost immediately and ready for that crowning pat of butter or margarine as soon as they are cool enough to eat.

Nettles, which regrow in the same places year after year across Canada and the states, are for the most part erect, single-stemmed greens which sometimes grow up to seven feet tall. The opposite leaves are coarsely veined, egg-shaped to oblong, with heartlike bases, and roughly and sharply toothed. Both stem and leaf surfaces bristle with a fuzz of numerous, fine prickles containing irritating formic acid. Very small green flowers, which, like those of plantain, are easy to overlook, appear in multibranched clusters between leaves and stalk.

Nettle leaves may be gathered in the spring and early summer. These unlikely but delectable edibles are among the first wild vegetables available near our log cabin when greenery begins thrusting up like spring fire, but even so early in the season the presence of stinging bristles makes it necessary to wear gloves while harvesting them. If the skin should be irritated, maybe at the wrists, alcohol can be administered. The Indians of southeastern Alaska, several hundred miles west of our homesite, relieve the stinging by rubbing the irritated skin with the dryish, rusty, feltlike material that covers young ferns or fiddleheads.

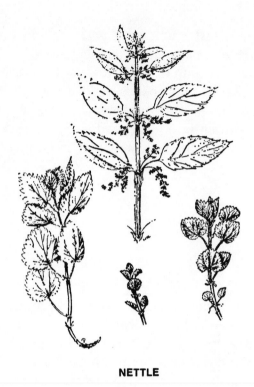

NETTLE

When young, nettle leaves and the small entire plants quickly lose their stinging properties when boiled. They have such a delicate flavor that they are good by themselves. Topped with butter or margarine, they are far more subtly delicious than spinach and are excellent sources of vitamins A and C and some of the minerals.

Because they are so easily and positively identified, nettles may be an important emergency food. Too, in a pinch, the stems of the older plants will yield a strong fiber, useful for fish lines.

CLOVER

(Trifolium)

Everyone who as a youngster has sucked honey from the tiny tubular florets of its white, yellow, and reddish blossoms, or who has searched among its green beds for the elusive four-leaf combinations, knows the clover. Some seventy-five species of clover grow in this country, about twenty of them thriving in the East.

Clovers, which are avidly pollinated by bees, grow from an inch or so to two feet high in the fields, pastures, meadows, open woods, and along roadsides of the continent. Incidentally, when introduced into Australia, it failed to reproduce itself until bumblebees were also imported.

The stemmed foliage is usually composed of three small leaflets with toothed edges, although some of the western species boast as many as six or seven leaflets. This sweet-scented member of the pea family provides esteemed livestock forage. Red clover is Vermont's state flower. White clover is all the more familiar for being grown in lawns.

CLOVER

Quail are among the birds eating the small, hard seeds, while deer, mountain sheep, antelope, rabbit, and other animals browse on the plants.

Bread made from the seeds and dried blossoms of clover has the reputation of being very wholesome and nutritious and of sometimes being a mainstay in times of famine. Being so widely known and plentiful, clover is certainly a potential survival food that can be invaluable in an emergency.

The young leaves and flowers are good raw. Some Indians, eating them in quantity, used to dip these first in salted water. The young leaves and blossoms can also be successfully boiled, and they can be steamed as the Indians used to do before drying them for winter use.

If you're steaming greens for 2 couples, melt 4 tablespoons of butter or margarine in a large, heavy frypan over high heat. Stir in 6 loosely packed cups of greens and blossoms, along with 6 tablespoons of water. Cover, except when stirring periodically, and cook for several minutes until the clover is wilted. Salt, pepper, and eat.

The sweetish roots may also be appreciated on occasion, some people liking them best when they have been dipped in oil or in meat drippings.

Clover tea is something you may very well enjoy. Gather the full-grown flowers at a time when they are dry. Then further dry them indoors at ordinary house temperatures, afterwards rubbing them into small particles and sealing them in bottles or jars to hold in the flavor. Use 1 teaspoon of these to each cup of boiling water, brewing either in a teapot or in individual cups, as you would oriental tea.

MUSTARD

(Brassica)

Mustard, which flourishes wild over most of the globe, is universally recognizable because of its brilliant yellow flowers that become almost solid gold across many a field and hillside. Five species are widely distributed over the United States. Most important of these is black mustard, an immigrant from Europe and Asia, which has become so much at home on this continent that it now grows over most of the United States and southern Canada.

This annual ordinarily grows from two to six feet tall, although in California I have seen it as tall as a telephone pole. A relative of cabbages, turnips, cauliflowers, radishes, brussel sprouts, and similar cultivated vegetables, black mustard grows erect with widely spreading branches. The leaves on the young plants, which are the ones to pick, are rather fuzzy and feel stiffly hairy. The finely toothed lower leaves are deeply indented at the bases of the stalks and less indented as they ascend. These lobes do not appear on the upper, small, extremely bitter leaves that grow, nearly stemless, from the flower stalks.

The sunny yellow flowers are small but numerous. Typically for mustard, each has four petals and six little upright stamens, four long and two shorter. The blossoms mature during the summer into small, short pods. These are filled with dark, minute, zestfully pungent seeds.

One way this pleasantly edible plant can really start the mouth tingling is in a cream of wild green soup—especially when you come in dehydrated from a day of fishing or spring bear hunting and get that first sniff of it, all steaming and savory. To go with 2 cups of chopped or scissored young mustard greens, start slowly heating a quart of milk, not allowing it to boil.

MUSTARD

Meanwhile, melt 2 tablespoons of butter, margarine, bacon drippings, or any other edible fat in a saucepan over low heat. Gradually stir in 1½ teaspoons salt, ⅛ teaspoon pepper, and 2 tablespoons flour. Add a finely minced small onion. Then pour in the hot milk bit by bit. Cook gently for 5 minutes.

Drop in the greens and, stirring occasionally, continue to heat just below the boiling point until these are just tender. To be at its best, mustard requires more cooking than most greens, something like a half hour. You'll need a lot, too, as it shrinks considerably. When the soup is ready, sprinkle with paprika. Serve at once.

Mustard, whether used in soup or elsewhere, is most agreeable when it first appears. The young stalks are not hard to identify, particularly as older mustard is often standing in the same patch. The slightly peppery young leaves are enjoyable raw. So are the young flowers with their then subtle pungency. The entire young plant goes well cooked with fish and meat.

Later on, the profusion of golden flowers can be capitalized upon to make a broccolilike dish. When you pick these over, it is best to eliminate any of the small upper leaves because of their bitterness. The blossoms boil up quickly in salted water. Bring them to a rapid boil, then let them stand away from the heat, tightly covered, for 5 minutes. Drain, spread with melting butter or margarine, and sprinkle with a little vinegar. Besides being colorful and delicious, this repast is full of vitamins and protein.

The easily gathered seeds of wild mustard, even after it has grown old and tough, are hard to equal for garnishing salads, adding to pickles and such for that extra seasoning, giving a final authority to barbecue sauces, and lending a wisp of zip and zest to stews. Mustard's very name comes from its seeds, being a corruption of must seeds, which harks back to ancient Roman-occupied Britain, where these were processed by saturating them in a solution of grape juice, or *must*, as it was sometimes called.

Table mustard can be made by finely grinding wild mustard seeds, between two stones, if you're in camp, or in the family food chopper, if you're at home, and adding enough water or vinegar to make a paste. After that, it's up to you. Commercially prepared condiments often contain such additional ingredients as flour, salt, turmeric, and other spices. If you choose to modify your raw mustard with up to an equal bulk of flour, brown this latter slowly and lightly in an oven first to take away the starchy taste. The vinegar may be diluted, depending on its strength, up to half and half with water. Occasionally, the blender likes the added flavor of horseradish. This white-flowered member of the mustard family, with the pungent white roots, likewise grows wild.

A lot of us remember, back when we were growing up, the application of mustard plasters to cold-congested chests and sore backs. These famous old remedies, still highly regarded in many households, can be easily homemade. Just mix ground mustard seeds with an equal bulk of ordinary flour, then stir in enough tepid water to make a paste. Sandwich this sparingly between two cloths and tape into position while still warmly wet. Leave some 20 minutes, or until the recipient, with skin that starts to redden in about 5 minutes, begins to complain too vociferously of the increasing warmth.

WATERCRESS

(Nasturtium)

Watercress grows over much of North America. Available the year around except when the waters in which it flourishes are frozen, this has long been used in many lands and is cultivated here and in Europe. That which I have seen in markets has been comparatively expensive.

Watercress prefers clean cold water, but with civilization spreading the way it is, you can't always be sure that those streams, pools, wet places, and even springs are not contaminated. A reasonable precaution is to soak the well-washed leaves and tender shoots, including those from the store, in water in which a halazone tablet or so has been dissolved, using two of the little pills to a quart of water and letting stand a half hour. Halazone may be very inexpensively obtained from almost any sporting goods or drug store. These minute tablets work by releasing chlorine gas and therefore should be fresh. A bottle of 100 usually sells for less than 50c and should be kept tightly closed in a dark, dry place.

Be sure, too, that you are just gathering watercress, as the poisonous water hemlocks, which somewhat resemble the carrot plant but with taller stems whose lower leaf stalks have three primary forkings, often grow nearby. The familiar edible, rooting at its stem joints, usually sways and floats in the water. However, it is sometimes found creeping at the edges of cold brooks and springs.

The glossy green leaves grow with three to nine segments, the biggest of which is at the base. The minute white flowers blossom on a succession of tiny stems attached to a longish stalk. They produce needlelike pods up to about an inch long which, if tender to the bite, are tasty, too. Gatherable wherever it can be reached, the whole plant has the characteristic peppery flavor of mustard, to which family it belongs.

Although watercress is good both cooked and in its native state, we prefer it raw. However, there is generally plenty where it grows, and it cooks up admirably either by itself in a small amount of boiling salted water or mixed tastily with blander greens.

You owe it to yourself, too, to try it with scrambled eggs. To every 2 eggs to be scrambled, add 2 tablespoons cold water, ¼ teaspoon salt, and ½ cup chopped watercress. Beat well together. In the meantime, be heating 2 tablespoons butter or margarine in a frypan just hot

WATERCRESS

enough to sizzle a drop of water. Pour in the egg mixture and reduce the heat. When the eggs have started to harden, begin stirring them constantly with a fork. Remove while they're still creamy and soft.

Watercress soup is also memorable. For one variety which we have found to be exceptional, heat 3 cups fresh milk with 1½ teaspoons salt. In the meantime, run enough cold watercress through the meat grinder to fill 1 cup. Add this to the hot milk and simmer 5 minutes, keeping the pan covered as much as possible. Just before sitting down to eat, beat until smooth and add 1 cup of fresh milk or cream. Serve as soon as heated thoroughly, topped with sprinkled paprika and fresh sprigs of cress.

There's a wonderful way out if someday you make too much green salad, predominated by watercress and liberally dressed with oil and vinegar. Empty a can of mushroom soup into your blender along with the salad and dressing and end up with a thick puree. Let this simmer an hour in the top of a double boiler, stirring it occasionally. You may have to vary the fluid content to obtain the desired thick soup. Decorate this with vitamin-teeming paprika.

Watercress will also somewhat similarly solve the problem of left-over cooked partridge or chicken. Cup up 2 cups of the meat and drop it into your blender, along with 1½ cups of the broth, 2 cups watercress, and 2 cups light cream. Run at top speed until you have a smooth liquid. Once more, heat this in the top of a double boiler, salting it to taste. Sprinkle with paprika and serve hot.

The succulent shoots and tender leaves of watercress have made it a favorite garnish and salad staple since olden times. In fact, the flavor of nearly every salad can be enhanced by the addition of this edible. Too, watercress is famous sandwich fodder, either plain or chopped and blended with chopped hard-boiled egg. As if that weren't enough, you can make a nutritious tea by steeping a teaspoonful of the mineral-swarming leaves or roots in a cup of boiling water.

SHEPHERD'S PURSE

(Capsella)

Shepherd's purse is valuable to wild food seekers in that it is one of the more common of the wayside weeds, being found throughout most of the year in gardens, lawns, vacant lots, cultivated fields, and paths throughout most of the world where civilization has moved. It is quickly recognizable, and the tender young leaves, which, like others of the mustard family, are pleasingly pepper, may be enjoyed either raw or cooked. Indians even made a nutritious meal from the roasted seeds.

This wild green is familiar because of its flat triangular or heart-shaped seed pods which, their broad bases uppermost, ascend the top parts of the stalks on short stems. A favorite food of blue grouse, these diminutive pouches develop from long clusters of tiny white flowers, each with twin pairs of opposite petals. Long green leaves, both smooth-edged and roughly toothed, grow in a rosette near the ground.

Growing so near to the earth and in such accessible places, these leaves are apt to pick up a lot of dust and grit, so it is best to gather them young and then wash them well, afterwards drying them in a towel. Otherwise, the dressing will slip off and form a pool in the bottom of the salad bowl. Tear, don't cut, these greens into bite-size pieces and toss them lightly with enough oil and vinegar, mixed 4 parts to 1, to coat them thoroughly. Arrange contrasting red tomato slices

SHEPHERD'S PURSE
Top: stalk with leaves and flowers. *Bottom:* rosette.

for trim. Incidentally, these tomatoes tend to become too watery if tossed with the greens. Serve without delay.

These young greens, which vary considerably in size and succulency according to the richness of the soil where they grow, can also be carefully gathered, washed, and then placed in a frypan where a little bacon has been cut fine and partly fried. Some sour cream is added, but the cooking is slight; just enough to wilt the leaves. Spoon out hot and divide the sauce over the servings.

Although the concentration of vitamins is greater in the green leaves, some people prefer the delicately cabbagelike flavor shepherd's purse takes on when blanched. Where, as so often happens, these edibles grow profusely near your home, you can experiment with blanching by anchoring paper bags over small groups of the young plants to exclude the sunlight.

The leaves, so bursting with vitamins but so low in calories, toughen as shepherd's purse matures. They then can be relegated to a small amount of boiling salted water, cooked until just tender, and dished out with the usual butter, margarine, vinegar, oil, hard-boiled egg, or other supplements.

Shepherd's purse, sometimes known as shepherd's heart and as pickpocket, is also used as a tea, 1 teaspoon to a cup of boiling water, 2 cups of which daily are said to stimulate sluggish kidneys. Too, pioneers sometimes soaked a handful of the leaves in water and used the latter to wash painful bruises.

MINER'S LETTUCE

(Montia)

Stems and leaves of the well-known miner's lettuce—whose unmistakable feature is the way a pair of leaves grow together part way up some of the short stems and form a cup through whose middle the stalk continues—are estimable salad food when young and a better-than-average spinach substitute when older.

Miner's lettuce, also known as Indian lettuce and Spanish lettuce and in Europe as winter purslane, is one of the most abundant springtime edibles of the Pacific regions from British Columbia to Mexico, extending eastward to North Dakota. It grows from a dainty plant several inches high to a foot tall in moist shaded areas in woods, orchards, pastures, vineyards, fields, gardens, and along stream banks.

The succulent leaves differ considerably in shape, from the easily recognizable round leaves that encircle the tasty stems to form disks or cups to fleshy long-stemmed leaves that are sometimes triangular or even kidney-shaped. At the bottom, furthermore, clusters a spread of longish, more slender leaves through which several stems often arise. These are tougher than the others.

The plant is topped with small, edible, white or pinkish flowers that nod in loose bunches. These develop into shiny black seeds that furnish food for such upland game birds as dove and quail.

Hard-boiled eggs in particular bring out the subtle flavor of miner's lettuce, but these former objects should not be the leathery articles that are often served to unsuspecting diners. Instead, get enough water boiling in a pan to cover the eggs by 1 inch. Place the eggs in the pan with a spoon and let the temperature immediately drop to a simmer, keeping it that way until the eggs are done. Keep the eggs simmering, completely covered, for 8 to 10 minutes. Then remove from the heat and plunge into cold water. If the shells are cracked slightly before the eggs cool, peeling will be easier.

MINER'S LETTUCE

For a miner's lettuce salad for 2 hearty appetites, mix 4 cups of miner's lettuce, any stems chopped, with 2 chopped, hard-boiled eggs. Moisten liberally with 4 parts oil, preferably olive, and 1 part tarragon vinegar. Salt and pepper to taste, with freshly ground black pepper if you have it. Sit down to this at once, as the dressing will take the crispness out of the greens all too quickly.

When the Forty-Niners stampeded up California's streams and into its deserts and mountains in their search for gold, the lack of fresh food brought scurvy to some camps. It was the Indians and Spanish who helped some of these argonauts cure the vitamin-deficiency disease by introducing them to the succulencies of miner's lettuce. Those miners who didn't care for salad, or who gathered the edible so late in the season that it was tough, settled for boiling it, ideally briefly in a small amount of salted water.

WILD CELERY

(Angelica)

Wild celery, also known as seacoast angelica, is even juicier and tastier than the celery you buy in stores. It grows in damp fields, beside moist roadsides, and along rocky or sandy coastlines from New England and eastern Canada to British Columbia and Alaska. It is at its best in late spring and early summer, while still tender.

The erect green stalks of this perennial, which are hollow, are coarse with many oil veins and often sticky patches. Growing up to about four feet tall, they are topped with numerous umbrellalike clusters of flowers, the individual members of which are small with five green or whitish petals. These eventually develop into small, angular, ribbed, dry fruits.

Wild celery is leafy, with the leaves growing in three thick groups of leaflets from stalks whose spreading bases sheathe the main stem. The

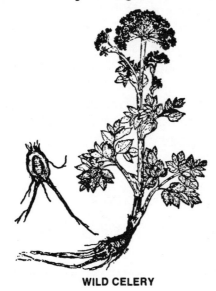

WILD CELERY

roughly and unevenly toothed green leaflets, from one to three inches long, are thickly egg-shaped and have the odor of fresh celery.

Both the stems and leaf stalks are gathered when young, peeled, and their juicy interiors eaten with the same relish that is accorded the choicest celery. They are often boiled, too, sometimes in two changes of water if the user prefers a more subdued taste. Wild celery also imparts a piquant flavor to boiled fish. You'll probably like it, too, in soup. Besides these ordinary ways of preparing wild celery, there are rather more complicated but delectable methods of bringing out the best of this succulent wild edible.

Creamed wild celery tastes like more. Melt ¼ cup butter or margarine, add ½ cup flour, and cook slowly for 5 minutes. Meanwhile heat 3 cups milk, not allowing it to boil. Pour this bit by bit into the flour mixture, stirring and cooking about 15 minutes until everything is smooth. Add ½ teaspoon salt, several shakes of pepper, and ½ cup grated cheese, which should be as snappy as you like it. Continue stirring as the cheese melts. The result may be poured over just boiled wild celery stalks and stems which have been peeled before cooking.

Braised wild celery is well worth the trouble, especially when you're famished from a windy afternoon along the shores. Peel the young stalks and stems, cut them into easily handled lengths, and halve them lengthwise. Lay them atop a base of thinly sliced onions in a shallow pan, cover with warm water in which 2 chicken or beef bouillon cubes have been dissolved, and simmer in the oven for about 15 minutes, or until very tender.

In the meantime, gently sauté some finely chopped onion with a generous amount of butter or margarine in a frypan until it has reached a golden brown. Soften the taste with a little red wine if you want. Then remove the wild celery to a baking dish. Pour the sauce over it. Sprinkle liberally with Parmesan cheese and return to the oven for baking until the cheese has melted.

SCOTCH LOVAGE

(Ligusticum)

Scotch or sea lovage, another of the wild celeries, grows in wind-swept sandy and gravelly stretches along northern seacoasts from New York to Alaska. It has long been a favorite green and cooked vegetable among the coast-dwelling Scots, who early discovered it here during their excursions to the New World. Rich in vitamins A and C, it is particularly tasty with fish. It also can be made into a better than passable confection.

Although its leaves and flowers resemble those of the previously described wild celery *(Angelica)*, Scotch lovage grows more like domestic celery in that its long-stalked leaves rise directly from the base of the perennial instead of growing from a main stem. Each of these leafy stalks, which clasp the plant with broadly sheathlike bases that

SCOTCH LOVAGE

are reddish or purplish, ends in three oval, roughly toothed, shiny leaflets from one to three inches long.

The white or pinkish flowers grow in flattish, umbrellalike clusters on the ends of thin stems up to about two and one-half feet high. They produce short, tan, dryish, oblong fruits. The roots are stout and deep.

The fresh young stalks and leaves are best before the plant blossoms. Although I do not find Scotch lovage's flavor resembling celery's as closely as does the wild celery of the *Angelica* family, it can be used interchangeably, either raw or cooked, in the recipes suggested for the former vegetables. One often finds stalks that have been blanched by being partially covered with wind-driven debris, and these have a blander flavor that many people enjoy more in salads and hors d'oeuvres.

Scotch lovage goes well with hard-boiled eggs. This recipe takes a little work but is worthwhile, especially if you are having company and want to make a special effort.

Halve the eggs, which have been simmered in a covered pan for 10 minutes and then plunged into cold water to ease the peeling. Remove the yolks, which, cooked this way, should be firm and mealy. Mash them and add 2 tablespoons mayonnaise, a few sprinkles of vinegar, and salt and pepper to taste. Mix in an equal bulk of tender young Scotch lovage and sweet pickles, chopped up in equal amounts. Refill the halved whites.

Scotch lovage will also provide a unique and spicy candy. Boil conveniently short sections of root or young stalks until a fork penetrates them easily. Then simmer, covered, for 15 minutes in a syrup made in the proportions of 1 cup of sugar to each cup of water. Although it isn't necessary, you can, if you want, give added crunchiness to the finished products by rolling them in granulated sugar before laying them aside to cool and dry.

MOUNTAIN SORREL

(Oxyria)

Mountain sorrel is a green we've enjoyed in such diverse places as New Mexico, British Columbia, and the green-sloped White Mountains of New Hampshire. This member of the buckwheat family, which grows from Alaska and Greenland to Southern California, is also widely enjoyed in Europe and Asia. It is known in different parts of this country as sourgrass, scurvy grass, and Alpine sorrel.

The perennial mountain sorrel springs from a few inches to two feet high from a large, thick, deep, fleshy root. The small leaves, growing one or two on stems that for the most part rise directly from the rootstock, are smooth and either round or broadly kidney-shaped. Scarcely noticeable greenish or crimson flowers grow in rising clusters on long,

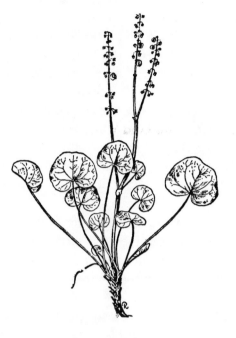

MOUNTAIN SORREL

full stems that extend above the mostly basal leaves. These blossoms turn into tiny reddish capsules.

The juicy leaves, which are at their best before the plant flowers, have a pleasantly acid taste which somewhat resembles that of rhubarb. In fact, mountain sorrel looks to some like miniature rhubarb, although it so happens that the leaves of domestic rhubarb, whether raw or cooked, are poisonous. Those of mountain sorrel, on the other hand, are delicious for salads, potherbs, and purees. Where this wild edible grows in the Arctic, Eskimos both in America and Asia ferment some of it as a sauerkraut. The tender young leaves will also give a zip to sandwiches.

Mountain sorrel leaves can be turned into a puree by simmering them for 20 minutes, then pressing them through a colander or mashing them, and adding butter or margarine, salt, and pepper. You'll save vitamins, flavor, and time, though, if you use a meat grinder or kitchen blender on these juicy greens, then quickly cook and add them to a piping hot base.

For a memorable cream soup, pour a quart of rich milk into a pan and set over low heat. When it starts to bubble, add 3 cups of mountain sorrel puree and salt and pepper to taste. Simmer for 5 minutes, stirring. Then gradually pour 3 beaten egg yolks into the mixture, stirring energetically until the color is even. Remove from the heat and, using a fork, blend in 4 tablespoons of butter or margarine. Serve immediately.

You can capitalize on the excellent way mountain sorrel combines with the delicate flavor of fish by making a thick fish stock, slowly bringing the heads, tails, bones, fins, and even the scales, if any, to a boil in cold water to cover, and simmering all afternoon along with a chopped onion and, if you want, a kernel of garlic. You'll need about ⅓ pound of such remnants for each individual, so wait until the fishing has been good.

Just before you're ready to sit down to the table, heat in proportional amounts for each diner 1 cup strained fish stock, ¼ teaspoon salt, and a sprinkling of black pepper. Stir in an equal amount of mountain sorrel puree, simmer for 5 minutes, and serve hot with a liberal pat of butter or margarine spreading atop.

Mountain sorrel adds a pungency to green salads, especially when about one-fourth as much watercress is added to contrast with its flavorsome sourness. We usually prefer a plain oil dressing, carefully touched up with a very little salt to taste. It's doubtful if you'll want any vinegar. Such salads go especially well with fish, crabs, and lobsters.

Boiled, mountain sorrel combines well with other greens, its acidity giving them added flavor. Because of this acidness, it is best to season gradually to taste and, in most cases, to omit the usual vinegar or lemon juice. A complement of hard-boiled eggs and crisp bacon, both thinly sliced, goes well with these greens.

Always welcome is this robust soup, individually seasoned. For 4 fishermen, the procedure is to start it by dicing about ½ pound bacon and, starting with a cold frypan, slowly bringing this to a sputter. Let the bits become crisp by tilting the pan so that the grease will run to one side. Then spoon them temporarily onto a plate.

Have 8 medium-sized potatoes, 2 onions, and 4 cups of mountain sorrel leaves chopped and mixed. Add these to the bacon fat and stir occasionally until the potatoes start to tan. Then return the bacon, flatten out everything in the pan, cover with water, stir, and simmer until a fork penetrates the potatoes easily. By this time none of us has ever been able to wait any longer.

PASTURE BRAKE

(Pteridium)

When I attended college in Maine, we used to see fiddleheads regularly displayed for sale in the spring in the Lewiston markets. Later, I used to feast on them while spring bear hunting in New Brunswick. We have relished them many times, more recently, in the West and Far North. They are the young, uncoiled fronds of the fern family's brakes, so called because in this emerging state they resemble the tuning ends of violins. They are also known in many localities as croziers because of their resemblance to the shepherd's crooklike staffs of bishops, abbots, and abbesses.

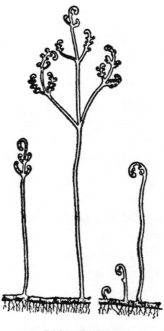

PASTURE BRAKE

Although some other similar fronds are edible, it is the fiddleheads from the widely familiar and distributed pasture brake, *Pteridium aquilinum,* that are most commonly enjoyed. These grow, often luxuriantly, through the Northern Hemisphere, in Europe and Asia as well as in North America. They are found, sometimes in waving acres that brush your knees as you ride through on horseback, from Alaska

97

across Canada to Newfoundland, south through the states to California and Mexico.

These are edible, however, only while still fiddleheads and therefore young. They are then good both raw and cooked. Later, the full-grown fronds toughen and become poisonous to cattle as well as humans. While still in the uncurled state, on the other hand, they are found very acceptable by some of the wildlife, including the mountain beaver.

Pasture brake is known to different people as just plain brake, bracken, hog brake, bracken fern, eagle fern, brake fern, and Western bracken. It decorates often shady roadsides, dry open woods, pastures, clearings, and may often be seen adding welcome green to recently burned forests.

It is a coarse, perennial fern with a blackish root, so favored by the Japanese for thickening and flavoring soups that laws had to be passed there to prevent its extinction. Early in the spring, these roots send up scattered fiddleheads. These later uncoil and stretch into long, erect stalks with typically fernlike leaflets, whose greenness takes on a straw to purplish-brown color with maturity. The widely triangular fronds, which may be from one to three feet across, are distinctively separated into three usually broadly spreading branches.

The fiddleheads, too, are noticeably three-forked. They are easily recognized, also, because of the fact that they are often found near the tangled previous year's bracken, perhaps flattened by snows. They are best when not more than five to eight inches high, while still rusty with a woolly coating. Break them off with the fingers as low as they will snap easily, remove the loose brown coatings by rubbing them between the hands, and they're ready for eating. If you like vegetables which, like okra, are mucilaginous, you'll probably enjoy a few of these raw.

The rather pleasant ropy consistency of this delicately glutinous juice is changed to a certain extent by cooking, but the sweetish fiddleheads are still reminiscent of okra. One way to enjoy fiddleheads is simmered in a little salted water until tender, then salted and peppered to taste, and eaten hot with plenty of melting butter or margarine.

Or bedeck them with a mayonnaise, perhaps homemade. You can very satisfactorily prepare this in a soup plate, if you don't happen to have a flat-bottomed bowl, by dropping in 2 egg yolks and stirring them vigorously with a fork. Then add a cup of oil, preferably olive, although any good cooking oil will do, pouring it in bit by bit and continually mixing with a fork until both ingredients, thoroughly mixed, stiffen. Blend in a tablespoon of good wine vinegar, then salt and pepper to taste. Spoon liberally over the hot fiddleheads.

A supper of fiddleheads on hot buttered toast sets just right for people who don't feel like eating much. When served this way, the little wild vegetables retain more of their delicate flavor when steamed. After they are cleaned and washed, drop them into 2 tablespoons boiling water in the top of a double boiler. Cover the utensil, place over boiling water, and cook for 30 minutes. The best way to keep on retaining the distinctive flavor is just to salt each serving lightly to individual taste, then top with a generous slab of butter or margarine.

Tender young fiddleheads can also add a lot to a mixed green salad. Oil seems to bring out the taste more in these, and we like it mixed 4 to 1 with preferably a wine vinegar, although lemon juice is good, too.

In cold regions such as Alaska, fiddleheads are often canned for opening as a winter vegetable. They delectably thicken soups. It may be well to remember, too, in case of a possible emergency, that the long rootstocks can be roasted, peeled, and if you want, powdered Indian fashion, after which the nourishingly starchy insides may either be eaten as is or used as flour.

DOCK

(Rumex)

The more than a dozen docks thriving on this continent from the Arctic coast of Alaska southward throughout the United States provide hearty greens which were widely eaten by the Indians, some tribes of which used the abundant seeds in grinding meal. The Eskimos still put up quantities for winter use. This wild edible, also eaten in Europe and Asia, has a more rugged flavor than some of the other wild vegetables. Having overtones of both sourness and bitterness that vary with the different species, it is often preferred mixed with other greens.

The docks as a whole have certain distinctive characteristics that are easy to identify. Furthermore, they are well known as edibles in many areas, sometimes as wild spinach, and are even cultivated in some

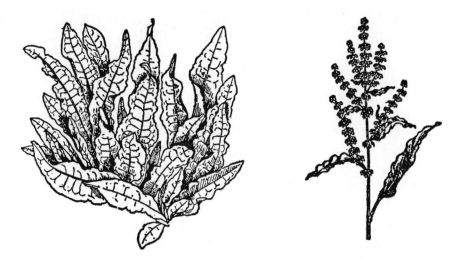

DOCK
Left: leaves. *Right:* stalk with flowers.

regions. They are often troublesome in cultivated fields, pastures, vacant lots, alongside roads, and with provoking frequency in lawns.

Docks are stoutish plants, bearing their leaves sometimes two feet long or occasionally heart-shaped, with smooth undersides, mostly around their bases. Where the fleshy leafstalks are attached to the stem, papery membranous sheaths wrap themselves around the joints.

The numerous tiny flowers, greenish or tinted with purple, crowd together on insignificant stems on long batonlike stalks up to about five feet tall. The erect dry stalks can be seen in the fall, rusty with multitudinous seeds that are ready to be scattered on thin, ribbed wings by the wind.

If dock is picked young enough, it makes a better than average salad, although I prefer to add it to such other greens as dandelion, mustard, and watercress, when these are available. Because of its somewhat lemonish flavor, you may prefer to skip the vinegar, using oil, salt, and pepper alone.

Dock to me is best rapidly boiled in a small amount of salted water only until tender, then served at once with butter or margarine. It does usually gain a certain amount of bitterness with age, however, and people who object to this should change the boiling water once or twice. However, the less these green leaves are cooked, the richer they are in vitamins and minerals.

The delicately bitter, lemonlike flavor of dock makes a lot of seasoning unnecessary, although, like other wild greens, it is often cooked with ham, bacon, or salt pork. However, steamed with something as mild as butter, dock is excellent.

Some docks lose considerably more bulk in cooking than others, but depending on what you're using, you'll need about 6 cups of shredded dock, washed and drained, for 2 liberal servings. Melt 2 level tablespoons butter in a large, preferably heavy frypan over high heat. Stir in the dock, add 2 tablespoons of water, and cover. Stirring occasionally, cook for 2 or 3 minutes, or until the greens are wilted. Sprinkle with salt and serve.

You can also capitalize on the way dock's unique flavor blends with sea food by making a steaming clam soup. Brown 1 large chopped onion only until softly tan, not black, in 4 tablespoons butter or margarine. Then scatter in 2 cups finely shredded young dock leaves and stir for about a minute until they wilt. Add 2 cups cleaned clams, either fresh or canned, and 2 cups rich milk. Bring to a slow simmer for not more than a minute, as cooking toughens clams. Dust with pepper. You probably won't want any salt. For 2 persons, there should be enough for seconds.

COMMON CHICKWEED

(Stellaria) (Alsine)

You can find this meek little member of the pink family blooming almost everywhere in the central United States every month, although its deeply notched white flowers open only in sunshine. It grows in fields, gardens, waste lands, cultivated grounds, woods, and in moist places generally throughout this country and most of the world.

Easily recognized and therefore a good emergency food for stranded and hungry people, this annual is unique in that it begins growing in the fall, survives the severities of cold even in the North, starts blossoming in late winter, and often finishes its life cycle and valuable seed production in the springtime, These numberless tiny seeds in their papery capsules, and the plant's tender leaves, are enjoyed by many game birds. Mountain sheep also eat them.

Botanists have different ideas about this family, not only as to its name, *Stellaria* or *Alsine,* but also as to the number of immediate relations. There may be as many as some seventy-five different species according to some counts, about twenty-five of which grow in this country. Only one of these, however, is important as a human and wildlife food.

COMMON CHICKWEED

Common chickweed is a low, sprawling plant with weak and brittle stems up to about a foot long. Leaves grow in opposite pairs on numerous slender branches. These leaves, which are smoothly oval and rather sharply pointed, are attached directly to the upper parts of the branches but grow from hairy stems along their lower portions.

The small white flowers, clustering at the leafy ends of the branches or stemming from where other leaves meet the branches, have five petals that are so deeply cleft that at first glance they may seem to be ten narrow ones. These develop into papery capsules that are filled with tiny seeds that some people gather for their appreciative canaries.

There's nothing fancy about common chickweed, but it is an abundant green that boils up wholesomely in a little salted water and, topped with an extra amount of butter or margarine, has none of the disagreeable taste that many people find in spinach. If only the top stems and leaves are used, these will become tender in a very short time. Use vinegar, chopped bacon, or both to pep up the delicate taste when guests find it a little too bland. Or, when you can, mix common chickweed half and half with dandelions, mustard, or water cress.

Besides eating this plant, pioneers used to crush the fresh leaves and use them as poultices, replacing them once or twice daily. An ointment was made also by bruising new leaves in fresh lard and using this as a cooling application for skin irritation.

WINTER CRESS

(Barbarea)

The yellow mustardlike flowers of the winter cress—also known as yellow rocket, Belle Island cress, scurvy grass, bitter cress, spring cress, and upland cress—are familiar sights in fields, gardens, meadows, pastures, and along roadsides, especially in the East where three of this country's four species occur. There are two closely related, look-alike cousins, *Barbarea verna* and *Barbarea vulgaris,* which share the same seasons, are equally good to eat, and are often seen growing together.

The clusters of small four-petaled golden blossoms, resembling tiny Maltese crosses, show that these edible herbs belong among the numerous species of native and European mustards. As a matter of fact, winter cress is cultivated both here and abroad both as a winter salad green and as a potherb.

These sunny little flowers, growing in groups between the upper leaves and the stalks, and at the tops of the angled stems, evolve into narrow, rather acutely four-angled pods up to three inches long. The smooth stems, usually growing one to two feet high, become thick with long, glossy, green leaves that have none of the hairiness of some of the other mustards.

The main importance of winter cress lies in its unusual aptitude for growing robustly during mild winter weather where the ground is clear of snow. In fact, its Latin name *Barbarea* recognizes that new young leaves and stems are often ready for the table on St. Barbara's Day which arrives every December 4. Actually, if the initial rosettes of long, dark green, smooth leaves are not gathered when they first spread di-

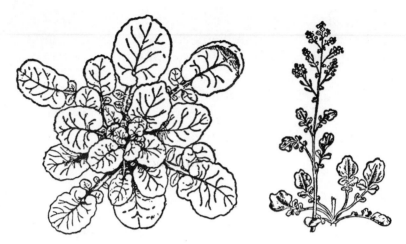

WINTER CRESS
Left: mature rosette. *Right:* early rosette and stalk with flowers.

rectly from the perennial and biennial roots during winter and early spring, they become overly bitter. Besides, this early seasonableness of winter cress gives you an additional reason to enjoy balmy winter periods out of doors.

This first of the year's greens in many localities gives character to mixed salads and, when freshly gathered, is far richer in healthful vitamins than any of the artificially fertilized, sprayed, and much handled greens you can buy in the store. Try it, too, in a smothered salad.

Just before you are ready to eat, shred enough young leaves to provide 3 cupfuls. Chop 3 young green onions, including the tops, into fine pieces and mix thoroughly with the winter cress. Add 1 teaspoon sugar and salt to taste. Pour 2 tablespoons vinegar over everything.

In the meantime, cut 6 slices of bacon into thin strips, put in a cold frypan, and fry slowly until crisp, tilting the pan so that the grease will run away from the meat. Then add the bacon to the salad and pour the hot drippings over it. Toss and serve while everything is fresh and crisp.

Winter cress also provides estimable boiling greens. During the cold seasons while still young, it is no more bitter than some lettuce. Later, though, you may prefer to simmer it in 2 waters, pouring out the first. Early in the season I prefer it with just butter or margarine melting on top, but a little later on vinegar seems to bring out the somewhat radishlike flavor better.

It's true that the leaves take on too much bitterness for enjoyable eating when winter cress finally blooms, but then the buds have a broccolilike savoriness. These grow in clusters at the top of the flowering stalks, making for quick and easy gathering. As with dandelions, the inclusion of a few open flowers does not hurt the taste. However, if you'd prefer to make the flavor a little more subtle, first pour boiling water over the harvest and allow it to stand a minute before draining.

Then, in any event, immerse the buds in a small amount of boiling water, simmer for about 4 minutes, and then drain at once. Be sure not to overcook, or the buds will become mushy. We like these topped with just a melting daub of butter or margarine. They are good with a few dashes of vinegar and a frosting of finely chopped onion, too.

FIREWEED

(Epilobium) (Chamaenerion)

Fireweed, which in summer gives an unforgettable amethyst hue to vast fire-blackened stretches below some of my favorite sheep and goat ranges west of the Alaska Highway, is another wild vegetable difficult to mistake. Thousands of square miles of burned lands from the Aleutians and Greenland to Mexico soften the magenta annually, so showily do these tall perennials flame into spikelike clusters of flowers.

Two species of fireweed enhance most of the northern wooded sections of the continent from the Far North south to California, Kansas, and the Carolinas. These gaunt, pink-to-purple-flowered members of the evening primrose family spring up in otherwise unsightly areas bared by logging operations, forest fires, and road clearings, stretching skywards from one to eight feet.

The showy flowers, which grow loosely in terminal spikes, begin blossoming at the bottom of the single stem and slowly climb upward. The lance-shaped leaves resemble those of the willow. As the warm weather proceeds, the flowers evolve into small pods which later become shaggy with white-tufted seeds that fill air and streams in the fall.

Fireweeds, with their profusion of small magenta blossoms, are valuable honey flowers, and beekeepers sometimes move their hives to the vicinity of recent logging operations to capitalize on them. Around our log cabin in northern British Columbia, I have often seen moose browsing on the plants. Deer eat them, too.

Try cutting the young stems into sections and boiling them in a small amount of salted water until tender. This way they resemble asparagus. In fact, where I was hunting on the Gaspé Peninsula in Quebec one

FIREWEED

time, the local French Canadians called this wild edible *asperge*—wild asparagus.

More mature stalks can be peeled and their sweetish interiors either eaten raw or cooked into thick soup. Young fireweed leaves cook up into satisfactory greens. But even if you can't get to these until fall, all is not lost. Steep them for tea.

Young fireweed is good on occasion pan-steamed with butter. These plants grow so abundantly that you shouldn't have any trouble in picking a quantity of the small, tender leaves. For 2 diners, measure 4 loose cups of these. Then melt 2 tablespoons butter or margarine in a large, preferably heavy frypan over high heat. Stir in the greens and 3 tablespoons of water. Cover and, stirring periodically, cook about 2 minutes, or until the fireweed is wilted. Salt and pepper to taste. Eat while still hot and savory.

WILLOW

(Salix)

This favorite browse of deer, elk, and moose is included here because, being so widely distributed and so easily identified, it is a food that in an emergency could save your life.

Between 200 and 300 varieties of willow grow in the world, about one-third of them thriving all over this country. They prefer damp fertile bottomlands, stream edges which they often hold in place, and lake and pond rims, but some are also seen in high, rocky country. They vary from big graceful trees to tiny shoots and shrubs, only a few inches high, in arctic and alpine regions.

Often the first spring source of Vitamin C, the buds and sprouts of these latter species provide the main subsistence of ptarmigan. Several species of grouse look to willow buds and tender portions of the twigs for food, while rabbits and many of the hoofed browsers seek twigs, foliage, and bark for nourishment.

It is not hard for the average individual to distinguish a willow from other trees and shrubs, especially when varieties become downy with the well-known pussy willows. The willows have alternate, or very occasionally opposite, leaves with smooth or toothed margins. Most species have long and narrow, or oblong lance-shaped leaves with short stems.

The twigs are slim, round, pliable, and often brittle at the base. The buds, usually very flat on the side next to the twig while bulging roundly on the outer side, are covered with a solitary scale apiece. The majority of the willows are shrubby. The bark of many species is bitter with salicin, used in medicine as a tonic and to reduce fever.

Young willow shoots can be gathered at the beginning of warm weather, peeled of their outer bark, and their tender insides eaten raw. The tender young leaves, some of which have been found to be up to ten times richer in Vitamin C than oranges, are also edible raw.

WILLOW
Left: branch with leaves. *Right:* winter twigs.

So is the thin layer of inner bark which, after the outside bark has been removed, can be scraped free with a knife. This is tastiest at the start of the growing season. Bitterish in many species of willow, in others it is surprisingly sweet. Too, this inner bark is sometimes dried and ground into flour.

WILD RICE

(Zizania)

The two native varieties of wild rice, which are tagged with probably surprisingly high prices in the corner market but which flavorwise are worth nearly every penny of it, grow free for the eating throughout much of the East from southern Canada to the Gulf of Mexico. This notable Indian food reaches it most opulent abundance in the north country from Maine and New Brunswick to the eastern reaches of the prairies and in lush freshwater marshes along the Atlantic seaboard. It has also been widely transplanted as a duck food, often successfully where soft, deep mud and gently circulating water are present.

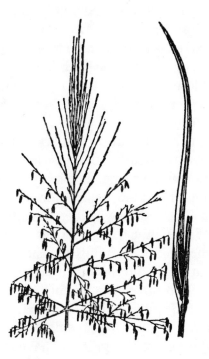

WILD RICE
Left: stalk. *Right:* leaf and stem.

This coarsely large, plume-topped grass grows luxuriantly on mucky or silty bottoms in shallow water where there is enough circulation to prevent stagnation. Black ducks, canvasbacks, mallards, pintails, redheads, wood ducks, and snow geese are among the waterfowl who seek it out in swamps and marshes, and often where it grows in great stands along the rivers, lakes, and ponds that are favorites of sportsmen.

Growing from four to ten feet tall, with a stout stem nearly half an inch through at the bottom, it will hardly be mistaken for anything else. The leaves are long and narrow, averaging between one and three feet long and close to an inch wide. The plants are tipped with long clusters of flowers that are of two different kinds, pollen-bearing below and seed-bearing toward the top. The slender seeds become dark and rodlike, expanding in husks that are stiffly tipped with a hairlike growth.

These husks are loose, however, and not difficult to remove. The secret is to spread the rice in a warm shelter, perhaps on newspapers in the attic, until it is dry. Then parch it in a moderately warm oven for three hours, reaching in a hand and mixing it occasionally, so it will dry evenly without burning. The husks can then be freed by beating or, if you have only a small amount, by rubbing the seeds between the palms. The easiest way I know of to blow away the chaff is by pouring the rice back and forth between two receptacles in a good breeze. Store in a dry place in well-closed containers.

A more important consideration is harvesting the crop during the latter half of summer or in early autumn when, depending on the local climate, it will be ripe and waiting. The mature seeds soon fall from the plants, but on the other hand they adhere too tenaciously for easy gathering while still green. The Indian way of getting in wild rice is still a good one. This consists of spreading a large canvas over the bottom of a canoe, paddling among the plants, bending the stalks over the canoe, and beating the seeds out on the tarpaulin with a stick.

The only drawback to this delicacy, unless you harvest it yourself for free, is the expense of the purple-black seeds with their smoky sweetness, so excellent with game and poultry. Incidentally, if wild rice is not well washed in cold water before using, it will have too much of this smoky flavor.

Although it is too precious to be used indiscriminately, wild rice will improve any recipe I know of calling for the domestic grain. To start off with, why not just stir 1 cup of the wild product into 1½ cups boiling water, seasoned with a teaspoon of salt. Do this so slowly that the bubbling does not stop. Cover and simmer without stirring for about 30 minutes, or until you can bite smoothly through a test kernel. If you're not pressed for time, put the rice in a sieve and set this in the emptied pot over the heat to dry in the rising hot air. Enjoy the different taste hot with butter, cream, or both.

Then maybe you'd like to try some wild rice croquettes, particularly if there is some game to serve them with. Cook a cup of rice with 1½ cups of already bubbling chicken or similar broth in a double boiler for 50 minutes, or until fluffy. Then put in a pan with 3 tablespoons white bread crumbs, 1 beaten egg, 4 tablespoons melted butter or margarine, and salt and pepper to taste. Mix well and then shape into small balls. Roll these in 3 tablespoons flour, then in a whipped egg, and finally in 4 tablespoons of bread crumbs. Fry in deep, hot fat for 2 or 3 minutes until golden brown. Eat at once.

Fried wild rice can be good, too. Start by boiling 1 cup of the smoky seeds until tender. In the meantime, melt ½ pound butter or margarine in a large frypan. Add 2 small chopped onions, a cup of minced ham or other cooked meat, and a minced clove of garlic. Then add the strained rice, salt and pepper to taste, and sauté another 5 minutes, stirring constantly.

You can even have popped wild rice. Place a small quantity of your best, newly gathered, still unwashed seeds in a fine sieve. Immerse this in deep hot fat until the kernels pop. Drain on paper towels, salt, and serve. This goes particularly well evenings with some of the cool wild fruit juices.

Wild Roots And Tubers

INSTEAD OF POTATOES, carrots, parsnips, radishes, beets, and turnips as we now know them, Indians often relied on wild roots and tubers, especially in those parts of the arid West where the lack of rainfall made gardening nearly impossible. When pioneers, prospectors, and others later began daring the plains and deserts, many of them starved amidst abundance, because they didn't know what to eat or how to prepare it.

The tuberous roots of the arrowhead, sometimes stumbled over by starving men where it grows in marshy ground, were relished by a number of tribes. Jerusalem artichokes, distinctively flavored tubers of a native wild sunflower long cultivated by the Indians, became so popular among early settlers that they were introduced into Europe. During colonial days, too, the still widely used sassafras roots became in great demand in England and on the European continent.

Many of the first settlers in Virginia became fond, through necessity, of the sweetish young roots of the cattail. The venturesome Swedes who early brought their log cabins to the Delaware River depended on groundnuts because of the lack of bread.

GROUNDNUT

(Apios)

The Pilgrims, shown the groundnut by friendly Indians, relied on them to a large extent their first rugged winter in Plymouth. Other Indians along the eastern seaboard regularly ate these potatolike vegetables. They thus became known to early white settlers, many of whom found them very acceptable substitutes for bread. Today they can provide interesting supplements to the most modern of meals, while in an emergency they can still prevent starving.

The perennial vines of this member of the pea family twine across low damp places and along the edges of swamps and streams, climbing where they can. They are found from New Brunswick to Florida and the Gulf of Mexico, west to Ontario, Kansas, and Texas. Growing up in New England where the groundnut is still comparatively well known, I was introduced to it early. Other names include Indian potato, bog potato, and wild bean.

You can smell the memorable sweetness of the flowering vine well before you reach it. The abundant brownish or purplish flowers, growing late in the summer in thick clusters from the junctures of the leaves and the soft vines, resemble those of garden beans and peas. The small, slender pods, in turn, look like those of garden beans. When you can collect enough of them, the seeds inside may be prepared like peas. Alternate leaves, each with five to nine egg-shaped leaflets from one to three inches long growing from its stalk on very short stems, angle out from the vines, which have a milky sap.

The groundnuts grow in a chain of tuberlike enlargements, sometimes as big as eggs, on the long roots. Lying in strings just beneath the surface, these can be easily uncovered by hand unless the ground is frozen.

Edible raw, groundnuts are better cooked. Incidentally, their taste

GROUNDNUT

either way has more overtones of turnips than of potatoes. To cook them, just drop them into salted boiling water, simmer them until a fork passes through them easily, and then eat them unpeeled with melting butter or margarine. If any are left over, slice and fry these, as they lack both taste and tenderness when cold.

ARROWHEAD

(Sagittaria)

Indians from the Pacific to the Atlantic ate the potatolike roots of the arrowhead, usually either boiling them or roasting them in the hot ashes of campfires. Related species are also enjoyed in Europe, and in Asia, where some Chinese cultivate them along the damp rims of rice paddies. In fact, when numerous Chinese moved into California, where this common wild plant is known as the tule potato, they quickly adopted it, and it is sometimes seen in the nearby markets.

In other words, the arrowhead is one of the most valuable native food plants and, nutritious and delectable, is well worth eating. Today, however, it is mostly idly observed by fishermen whipping their lines along the edges of ponds and sluggish streams from the southern half of Canada, throughout most of the United States, to deep into Mexico. Starving men, too, sometimes stumble over it where it grows in fresh, marshy ground.

There are some twenty or more species of *Sagittaria,* all bearing edible tubers, scattered in wet, non-saline places throughout the continent. About seven of these have large starchy bulbs. The differences in the plants are usually minor, and there is no need to try to separate them. Other names include arrowleaf, duck potato, and swan potato, as well as the Indian cognomens of wapatoo and katniss. Ducks, geese, and muskrats feast on the tubers when they are not too large or buried too deeply. Ducks also eat the small flattish seeds.

ARROWHEAD
Top: stalks, leaves, and flowers. *Bottom:* tuber.

Despite the name, all the leaves of this five- to thirty-six-inch-tall member of the water plantain family are not arrow-shaped. Growing from four to twelve inches long atop clusters of long erect stems, which thrust up directly from the fibrous roots, these are sometimes long and uniform in width and occasionally lance-shaped.

The white flowers, blooming from July to September, are readily recognized. Fragile and three-petaled, they usually appear in groups near the top of a naked spire that sometimes extends one or two feet above the leaves. The golden-centered, uppermost blossoms are male. Lower down, green-cored female flowers await fertilization pollen from other plants. Rounded heads of flat, winged seeds are later produced.

The hard little tubers, looking much like potatoes and varying from the most used size of eggs to that of BB shot, grow at the ends of often long subterranean runners, sometimes a few feet beyond the plant. Mature after midsummer and in the fall, they are also toothsome throughout the winter.

During these seasons, wading Indians used their toes to dislodge the bulbs, which then readily floated when freed of root and mud. However, you can generally find these native perennials growing thickly along the muddy edges of nearby swamps and shallow ponds where, perhaps wearing boots, you can speedily and repeatedly dig all you can use with a vigorously wielded hoe.

Arrowhead tubers can be eaten raw in an emergency, but they taste better cooked. They can be enjoyed baked, boiled, creamed, roasted, French-fried, and scalloped just like new potatoes, which, in our opinion, they excel, having a unique smoothness and sweetness. They require more cooking than white potatoes of the same size, and they are the better for peeling afterward.

Our favorite arrowhead repast, which we usually enjoy several times every fall, is a cooked salad. For use as a hearty main dish for 2 people, scrub and boil 5 heaping cups of the tubers, removing them from the salted water after 25 minutes while they are a little hard. Peel as sparingly as possible so as to preserve the utmost flavor and nourishment. Hard-boil 6 eggs at the same time; then plunge them under cold water and peel them.

Slice some of the hot arrowhead into a large bowl. Slice some eggs atop it. Now pour on a liberal amount of olive oil or salad oil. Douse on about ¼ as much vinegar. Salt and pepper. Sprinkle on a very small amount of powdered garlic, if desired. Paprika and dried parsley will add eye and taste appeal. Repeat until you've used all the tubers and eggs. Cover so that the flavor will permeate everything.

Preparing this salad half a day or more ahead of time will give the best results. Take off the lid once or twice and carefully, so as not to break up the eggs and tubers, spoon the mixture around a bit to redistribute the oil and vinegar. The superbly harmonizing taste of arrowhead always manages to give this treat that special something.

CHICORY

(Cichorium)

Chicory, millions of pounds of whose roots have been used as an adulterant and as a substitute for coffee, also provides greens for salads and for cooking whose excellence gives them prime positions on the vegetable counters of many local markets. Long popular in Europe, too, chicory is an escapee from that continent and from Asia. It now grows throughout most of the United States and across Canada from British Columbia to Nova Scotia.

Resembling the dandelion both in appearance and taste, it has, however, usually bright blue flowers which, except in cloudy weather when they may stay open all day, generally open only in the morning sunshine and shut by noon. These beautiful wheel-like blossoms, which sometimes spread like soft blue mist along roadsides and across grassy pastures and fields, also give the plant its other common name of blue sailor. It is also known as succory.

This rigid perennial with its angular branches grows from a long, deep taproot and reaches a height of from one to five feet. As in the familiar dandelion, the leaves nearly all grow at the bottom of the plant, starting underground and spreading in a rosette just above the surface. They are narrowly long and coarsely lobed or toothed. Smaller, clasping leaves ascend the stem. The flowers, which often grace the landscape from July to October, are occasionally whitish or pink and are made up of at least two uneven ranks of strap-shaped petals whose ends are toothed. Chicory's sap is bitter and milky.

We use the basal chicory leaves just as we do those of the similar dandelion, although when gathering them in the early spring, we take pains to dig deeply enough to uncover the delicate white portions that grow underground directly from the deep root. You can also upend paper bags over groups of plants and bleach the entire lengths of the

CHICORY
Top: branch with flowers. *Bottom:* rosette.

leaves. Although only pleasantly bitter at first and hard to equal for salads, maturing and toughening chicory leaves all too soon become excessivley bitter even when boiled in several changes of salted water. So get them well before they flower.

Much of the chicory root used in this country as a coffee substitute, stretcher, and flavorer, is imported from Europe, but exactly the same thing grows right here at home. If you'd like to make your own, just dig some of the long roots, scrub them with a brush, and then roast them slowly in a partly open oven until they will break crisply between the fingers, exposing a dark brown interior. Then grind and store in a closed container for brewing as a coffee substitute, in lesser amounts, as it's stronger, or for blending with your regular supply of the bean.

JERUSALEM ARTICHOKE

(Helianthus)

Jerusalem artichokes, distinctively flavored tubers of a native wild sunflower, were cultivated by Indians and much used by early settlers. Besides still growing wild, they are also raised for today's markets, all of which indicates how well worth finding they are.

They have no connection with the Holy City. Soon introduced into Europe following Columbus' voyages to the New World, they became popular along the Mediterranean and were called *girasole* in Italian and *girasol* in Spanish. These words, denoting sunflower, became corrupted in English to *Jerusalem*. The artichoke part of the name stems from the fact that even centuries ago the flower buds of some of the edible sunflowers were boiled and eaten with butter like that vegetable.

About ninety species of sunflowers occur in the world. Some two-thirds of these grow in the United States, among them these tall perennials whose roots are such a delicacy. You have to like them, of course. We've learned to prepare them so that we do.

Wild Jerusalem artichokes, which should be harvested no sooner than fall, are native to the central parts of the United States and Canada. Their popularity among Indians and arriving Europeans, plus their cultivation in different parts of the country, helps explain why this native has long since escaped its original bounds and is now often found in abundance elsewhere—such as east of the Appalachians, where it has moved to usually moist soil along ditches, streams, roadways, fence rows, and in vacant fields and lots.

These perennial sunflowers grow with thin stalks commonly five to ten feet tall. The rough leaves, whose tops are hairy, develop sharp points from oblong or egg-shaped bodies that are broadest near their bases. The frequently numerous flowers are yellow. From two to three inches broad, and maturing on slender stems that rise from where the higher leaves meet the stalk, these blossoms lack the purplish and brownish centers of those sunflowers that yield edible, oil-rich seeds. But the tubers, which are attached to the thickly creeping roots, more than make up for this deficiency.

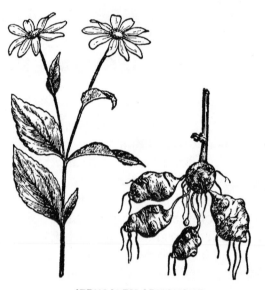

JERUSALEM ARTICHOKE
Left: **stalk with leaves and flowers.** *Right:* **tubers.**

History is all in favor of these delicacies whose somewhat sweetish juiciness, however, may take a bit of getting accustomed to. On the other hand, Jerusalem artichokes are nutritious and easily digestible enough to be regarded as a favored food for invalids. Here are a couple of hints that may help along your enjoyment. Dig them late in the year, even in winter if the ground is not too frozen, previously noting their whereabouts when they are conspicuously in bloom. Secondly, take care that they are not cooked too long nor at too high temperatures, as both toughen them.

Your cooking efforts may be as simple or as elaborate as you want them to be. The long, somewhat flat tubers are good just scrubbed, simmered in their skins in enough water to cover until just tender, and then peeled and served like potatoes, either with salt and butter or margarine or with a cream sauce. They then afford a by-product, too. When cold, the water in which they were boiled becomes jellylike, providing a flavorful and substantial foundation for soup.

Or, if you want everything all ready when mealtime arrives, wash and scrape the Jerusalem artichokes. As you finish with each one, drop it into acidulated water, made by stirring 1 teaspoon vinegar with a quart of cold water, to prevent it from darkening in the air. Slice or dice. Then cook, covered, in a small amount of boiling salted water 15 to 30 minutes, or until tender. Drain well. Serve with salt, pepper, and butter or margarine, or cream.

The non-starchy Jerusalem artichokes also make memorable salads. One way is to boil them first, then mix 4 cups with 1 finely diced small onion, 1 cup chopped celery, ½ teaspoon salt, a sliced cucumber, and a cup of mayonnaise. Stir together lightly, lifting from the outside in, season, and serve cold.

However, we usually prefer the crisp sweetness of the peeled tubers, which have somewhat the same texture as that of cabbage stalks, just sliced raw and added liberally to tossed salads.

Although not mealy like potatoes, Jerusalem artichokes can be substituted in many recipes for that common vegetable. For instance, fried slices of the wild edible have a flavor and consistency of their own. When in a hurry I've frequently cooked them in camp this way, sautéing them 8 to 10 minutes with bacon drippings in an already warm frypan and turning them several times during the process. When you have more leisure, they're even better rubbed with oil and baked. Or just add them to a mulligan when it's about half an hour from being done.

When someone in the household is a little under the weather, they may especially enjoy Jerusalem artichokes simmered in milk. Peel about a pound of these healthful tubers and dice them. Drop these small pieces into ¼ cup hot milk, stirring to moisten them well. Cover and cook just below the boiling point for 10 minutes. Then mix in 1 teaspoon salt and 2 tablespoons ground parsley. Sprinkle with paprika and serve while still steaming.

BURDOCK

(Arctium)

This member of the thistle family marched across Europe with the Roman legions, sailed to the New World with the early settlers, and now thrives throughout much of the United States and southern Canada. A topnotch wild food, it has the added advantages of being familiar and of not being easily mistaken.

The somewhat unpleasant associations with its name are, at the same time, a disadvantage when it comes to bringing this aggressive but delicious immigrant to the table. Muskrats are sold in some markets as swamp rabbits, while crows find buyers as rooks. But unfortunately in this country burdock is usually just burdock, despite the fact that varieties of it are especially cultivated as prized domestic vegetables in Japan and elsewhere in the Eastern Hemisphere.

BURDOCK

Burdock is found almost everywhere it can be close to people and domestic animals—along roads, fences, stone walls, and in yards, vacant lots, and especially around old barns and stables. Its sticky burrs, which attach themselves cosily to man and beast, are familiar nuisances.

The burdock is a coarse biennial weed which, with its branches, rapidly grows to from two to six feet high. The large leaves, growing on long stems, are shaped something like oblong hearts and are rough and purplish with veins. Tiny, tubular, usually magenta flowers appear from

June to November, depending on the locality, the second year. These form the prickly stickers, which actually, of course, are the seed pods.

No one need stay hungry very long where the burdock grows, for this versatile edible will furnish a number of different delicacies. It is for the roots, for instance, that they are grown by Japanese throughout the Orient. Only the first-year roots should be used, but these are easy to distinguish as the biennials stemming from them have no flower and burr stalks. We get all we can use from the sides of our horses' corral, where they are easily disengaged. When found in hard ground, however, the deep, slender roots are harder to come by, although they are worth quite a bit of effort.

The tender pith of the root, exposed by peeling, will make an unusually good potherb if sliced like parsnips and simmered for 20 minutes in water to which about ¼ teaspoon baking soda has been added. Then drain, barely cover with fresh boiling water, add a teaspoon of salt, and cook until tender. Serve with butter or margarine spreading on top.

If caught early enough, the young leaves can be boiled in 2 waters and served as greens. If you're hungry, the peeled young leaf stalks are good raw, especially with a little salt. These are also added to green salads and to vegetable soups and are cooked by themselves like asparagus.

It is the rapidly growing flower stalk that furnishes one of the tastier parts of the burdock. When these sprout up the second year, watch them so that you can cut them off just as the blossom heads are starting to appear in late spring or early summer. Every shred of the strong, bitter skin must be peeled off. Then cook the remaining thick, succulent interiors in 2 waters, as you would the roots, and serve hot with butter or margarine.

The pith of the flower stalks has long been used, too, for a candy. One way to make this is by cutting the whitish cores into bite-size sections. Boil these for 15 minutes in water to which ¼ teaspoon baking soda has been added. Drain. Heat what you judge to be an approximately equal weight of sugar in enough hot water to dissolve it, and then add the juice of an orange. Put in the burdock pieces, cook slowly until the syrup is nearly evaporated, drain, and roll in granulated sugar. This never lasts for very long.

The first-year roots, dug either in the fall or early spring, are also used back of beyond as a healing wash for burns, wounds, and skin irritations. One way to make this is by dropping 4 teaspoons of the root into a quart of boiling water and allowing this to stand until cool.

TOOTHWORT

(Dentaria)

These slender members of the mustard family flourish in moist woods and along streams. The medium-small white or pinkish flowers grow in clusters, their four petals sometimes arranging themselves in the shape of crosses. The smooth stems, six to fourteen inches high, support leaves with toothed margins. The crisp, whitish roots taste like peppery water cress and mild horseradish. Some dozen species grow, often abundantly, across the continent, one western variety whitening the meadows of the Coast Range in the springtime when it blooms.

TOOTHWORT
Left: root. *Right:* stem with leaves and flowers.

Cut-leaved toothwort, *Dentaria laciniata,* blossoms from April to June from Quebec and Minnesota south to Louisiana and Florida. The one-half- to three-fourths-inch white or pinkish flowers, nodding together in terminal groups of some six to eight blossoms, rise on stems seven to twelve inches above the ground. These produce slim seedpods about an inch long. The toothed or lobed leaves, a trio of which encircle the stalk below the flowers, are deeply indented into three to five divisions. The name toothwort comes from the little scales or teeth on the long, easily disjointed root. Both this native perennial and its first cousin, just below, are also known as crinkleroot and as pepper-root.

The two-leaved toothwort, *Dentaria diphylla,* spreads its peppery goodness over much the same range. Again, its four-petalled flowers, which are white and about half an inch long, grow in clusters of six to eight atop a stalk sometimes a foot high. They bloom in May. The main difference is in the leaves which, growing opposite or nearly opposite one another, number two. They are also a bit larger and lighter green than those of the above species, and they have shorter stems. The roots are long and wrinkled.

We often eat the long, crisp roots of these two species, many times just nibbling their refreshing pepperiness while walking or fishing. They also make very palatable additions to meat sandwiches, whose salt helps bring out their flavor. Chopped, they give character to green salads.

Some day when you're having company and want an elegantly nippy cocktail-hour dip, or a sauce to go with a special boiled beef or venison dinner or succulent roast, whip a cup of heavy cream. Then fold in a teaspoon of freshly grated apple and les   f   gra
toothwort root.

We make a camp version of this by melting 2   ons butter margarine, blending in 2 tablespoons flour, a   adding a cup of milk. Cook, preferably in the top of a doub   ring cons until thick. Then add 2 tablespoons grated to   ort root, ½ te salt, and a sprinkling of pepper. Cook 5 minutes more, stir casionally.

Or when you're too busy with other things, just scrape or grate a couple of tablespoons or so of these pungent, fleshy rootstocks, moisten with a little vinegar, and set on   table in a small covered cup. You haven't lived until you try this sometimes with fat roasted or boiled moose.

SPRING BEAUTY

(Claytonia)

You sometimes come upon thousands of frail little spring beauties, a very close cousin of the succulent miner's lettuce, carpeting sunny stream banks and moist open woods from Alaska to Nova Scotia, south to Florida and Texas. The individually delicate and inconspicuous little flowers, which together make such a spectacular display, range in color from white to pale rose and measure less than an inch across. Their pinkish-veined heads stay open only in sunlight.

These six-to-ten-inch high members of the purslane family, which grow in a number of similar, small-flowered species, are also known as fairy spuds because of their starchy edible roots, which were a favorite Indian food.

SPRING BEAUTY
Left: root. *Right:* stalk with leaves and flowers.

The grasslike to broadly ovate leaves, depending on the species, are also edible, in salads when young and when older, boiled briefly in a small amount of salted water and served as greens. Both ways they are excellent sources of vitamins A and C. The five-petaled flowers, each of which has five tiny stamens, grow in clusters on long weak stems that are often so overweighed that they lie on the ground.

The spring beauty grows from small, potatolike roots that lie several inches below the surface and require a certain amount of digging, although where they are abundant you can amass a respectable number with just a pointed stick. These roundish tubers range in diameter from one-half to two inches, becoming more and more irregular in shape the larger they grow. The best way we have found to clean them is by scouring them with a brush. Because they are boiled with the jackets on, though, this is not too critical a task.

Fifteen minutes of boiling in salted water usually does the job, although if some of the tubers are the larger ones, up to 5 extra minutes may be required. They're done when a fork shoves through without any difficulty. Then just peel and eat, dipping each first into a pool of melted butter or margarine. To me, they taste like particularly choice little potatoes with overtones of chestnut.

EVENING PRIMROSE

(Oenothera)

The usually bright yellow, but occasionally pink to white, flowers of this fragrant wild edible are familiar to many because of the way they open at dusk, carrying on their activities in the near darkness when their odor and light color attract the night-flying moths, upon whom they depend for fertilization. These showy but short-lived blossoms close their four petals for good the next morning, remain wilted a day or so, and then fall off.

This native food of mule deer, pronghorn, and other North American wildlife has a wide range that extends across the continent from British Columbia to Labrador, south to Texas and Florida. Preferring open, gravelly locations, the evening primrose is common to dry fields and waste places. Its abundant fleshy roots, sweet and nutritious when boiled, caused it to be transplanted to Europe as a food even before the Pilgrims set sail for the New World.

One of the names it has gained through the centuries is king's cure-all, partly because its somewhat astringent qualities have caused it to be used for coughs resulting from colds. A dose is a teaspoonful of the plant, cut small, to a cup of boiling water, drunk cold during the day, a large mouthful at a time. Too, an ointment made from it is said to be beneficial in treating minor skin irritations.

This native biennial grows only a round, broad rosette of leaves with toothed or wavy margins the first year. These leaves are from one to six

EVENING PRIMROSE
Left: rosette. *Right:* stalk with leaves, flowers, and seed capsules.

inches long, often lance-shaped, pointed, thickish, and with obvious midribs. The one- to five-foot flower stems, terminated by one- to two-inch loose-spiked blossoms, do not thrust up until the second year. The seed capsules are about an inch in length, oblong, and hairy. After producing them, the plant dies.

The stout, branching roots are good only the first year, before the evening primrose flowers. Their growth varies with the climate, and so do the times in spring, summer and fall when they are at their mildest and best. A little local experience, therefore, is usually necessary. But it's worthwhile, for peeled and then boiled in 2 changes of salted water until tender, then served hot with butter or margarine, these roots explain why the evening primrose was one of the first wild American edibles taken back to the Old World for cultivation.

We also like to boil ½ dozen good-sized roots in 2 changes of salted water, to remove the pepperiness, until the tines of a fork pierce them easily. Then peel them, slice them lengthwise, and lay them in a baking dish. We then simmer 1 cup brown sugar and 5 tablespoons butter or margarine in ½ cup water until syrupy. This is poured over the roots which go into a moderate oven for 20 minutes, or until candied.

Evening primrose French-fries, too, always seem to be popular with company. Get enough of the roots for 4, for example, peel them, and then slice each lengthwise and cut into pieces as you would for French-fried potatoes. Boil in 2 changes of salted water until a fork will pierce them with a little difficulty. Then drain and cool.

In the meantime, beat 2 eggs and ¼ cup milk. Season 1 cup flour with 1 teaspoon salt and ⅛ teaspoon pepper. Roll the sections in this, dip in the egg mixture, and finally roll in bread crumbs, patting on all of these that will adhere easily. Fry in shallow butter or salad oil until golden brown, drain briefly on absorbent paper, sprinkle with salt, and serve while hot.

CATTAIL

(Typhaceae)

Who does not know these tall strap-leaved plants with their brown sausagelike heads which, growing in large groups from two to nine feet high, are exclamation points in wet places throughout the temperate and tropical countries of the world?

Although now relatively unused in the United States, where four species thrive, cattails are deliciously edible both raw and cooked from their starchy roots to their cornlike spikes, making them prime emergency foods. Furthermore, the long slender basal leaves, dried and then soaked to make them pliable, provide rush seating for chairs, as well as tough material for mats. As for the fluff of light-colored seeds, which enliven many a winter wind, these will softly fill pillows and provide warm stuffing for comforters.

Cattails are also known in some places as rushes, cossack asparagus, bulrushes, cat-o'-nine-tails, and flags. Sure signs of fresh or brackish water, they are tall, stout-stemmed perennials with thin, stiff, swordlike, green leaves up to six feet long. These have well-developed, round rims at the sheathing bases.

The branched rootstocks creep in crossing tangles a few inches below the usually muddy surface. The flowers grow densely at the tops of the plants in spikes which, first plumply green and finally a shriveling yellow, resemble long bottle brushes and eventually produce millions of tiny, wind-wafted seeds.

These seeds, it so happens, are too small and hairy to be very attractive

CATTAIL
Left: leaves, head, and flower spike. *Right:* basal leaves and root.

to birds except to a few like the teal. It is the starchy underground stems that attract such wildlife as muskrat and geese. Too, I've seen moose dipping their huge, ungainly heads where cattails grow.

Another name for this prolific wild edible should be wild corn. Put on boots and have the fun of collecting a few dozen of the greenish yellow flower spikes before they start to become tawny with pollen. Husk off the thin sheaths and, just as you would with the garden vegetable, put while still succulent into rapidly boiling water for a few minutes until tender. Have plenty of butter or margarine by each plate, as these will probably be somewhat roughly dry, and keep each hot stalk liberally swabbed as you feast on it. Eat like corn. You'll end up with a stack of wiry cobs, feeling deliciously satisfied.

Some people object to eating corn on the cob, too, especially when there is company. This problem can be solved by scraping the boiled flower buds from the cobs, mixing 4 cups of these with 2 cups buttered bread crumbs, 2 well-beaten eggs, 1 teaspoon salt, ⅛ teaspoon pepper, and a cup of rich milk. Pour into a casserole, sprinkle generously with paprika, and heat in a moderate oven 15 minutes.

These flower spikes later become profusely golden with thick yellow pollen which, quickly rubbed or shaken into pails or onto a cloth, is also very much edible. A common way to take advantage of this gilded substance, which can be easily cleaned by passing it through a sieve, is by mixing it half and half with regular flour in breadstuffs.

For example, the way to make pleasingly golden cattail pancakes for 4 is by sifting together 1 cup pollen, 1 cup flour, 2 teaspoons baking powder, 2 tablespoons sugar, and ½ teaspoon salt. Beat 2 eggs and stir them into 1⅓ cups milk, adding 2 tablespoons melted butter or margarine. Then rapidly mix the batter. Pour at once in cakes the size of saucers onto a sparingly greased griddle, short of being smoking hot. Turn each flapjack only once, when the hot cake starts showing small bubbles. The second side takes only about half as long to cook. Serve steaming hot with butter and sugar, with syrup, or with what you will.

It is the tender white insides of about the first 1 or 1½ feet of the peeled young stems that, eaten either raw or cooked, lends this worldwide delicacy its name of cossack asparagus. These highly eatable aquatic herbs can thus be an important survival food in the spring.

Later on, in the fall and winter, quantities of the nutritiously starchy roots can be dug and washed, peeled while still wet, dried, and then ground into a meal which can be sifted to get out any fibers. Too, there is a pithy little tidbit where the new stems sprout out of the rootstocks that can be roasted or boiled like young potatoes. All in all, is it any wonder that the picturesque cattails, now too often neglected except by nesting birds, were once an important Indian food?

*desserts
that grow
on trees*

Wild Nuts

SOME OF THE most fun I've ever had in the woods, both as a youngster and as an adult, has been when I've gone nutting. If, when leaves are blazing and days are crisp, you've never gathered beechnuts, walnuts, butternuts, or other of the numerous edible wild nuts with which North America is so liberally endowed, then you've never really lived.

The highly nutritious oiliness of nuts causes them to keep best when protected from air, moisture, and warmth. To prolong freshness, store them in a cool, dry place or, ideally, in a refrigerator or freezer. Unshelled nuts last the longest. Nut meats should be kept in well-sealed containers or in moistureproof wrappings. Large pieces stay fresh longer, so it is best not to break, chop, grate, or grind nuts until you are ready to use them.

BLACK WALNUT

(Juglans)

Six of the world's dozen species of *Juglans* are native to this country. In addition to the common black walnut, whose range extends throughout most of the East and partway into the prairies, there are two species of black walnut in the Southwest and two more in California. Since early colonial days, this leading gunstock wood has been the king of the American cabinet woods. The hulls which enclosed the nuts dyed the homespuns of many of the first settlers.

BLACK WALNUT

The black walnut is a strong and durable tree, often fifty to a hundred feet in height, with a close-grained trunk from two to six feet in diameter. The prominently ridged and furrowed bark is a rich, dark brown. The large compound leaves, one to two feet long, are composed of up to fifteen to twenty-five leaflets, with what would be the topmost one often missing. These somewhat ovally lance-shaped leaflets, from two to four inches long and about half as wide, have pointed tips and sharply toothed edges. Yellowish green on top, they are lighter and generally downy underneath.

During the summer the nuts, covered with a greenish and warty husk, become two to three inches in diameter. Growing alone and in pairs, they ripen about October and soon fall from the widely spreading branches. Underneath this husk is the familiar globular nut, varying up to about two inches in diameter. Sculptured bony shells, as everyone knows, surround the deeply corrugated, furrowed, sweet, four-celled meats.

If you don't buy your walnuts at the store, the hardest part about gathering and using them is getting off the husks with their indelible brownish dye. When we were kids we didn't mind this and, just stamping on the husks and breaking them off with bare fingers, we collected stained hands that defied parental scrubbing for weeks. Today gloves are a more usual precaution. A knife will remove the green hides. Some pioneers also early found out that if they spread the freshly gathered nuts in the sun until they partially dried, the husks were easily shucked off. The wetly stained nuts were then spread out to dry and to lose bitterness until they were ready to be cracked open.

Those of the sweet and somewhat oily kernels that are not eaten on the spot are much in demand for cakes and candies because of their strong and distinctive taste. You no doubt have your own recipes, but here are a few that have become our favorites over the years.

One of the best of these is a nut bannock which even comes out well in a camp oven if you happen to be hunting in the fall where walnuts abound. For a hot loaf large enough for 2 hungry people, thoroughly blend 2 cups flour, ½ cup sugar, 3 teaspoons baking powder, and 1 teaspoon salt. To avoid any unnecessary loss of the leavening carbon dioxide gas from the baking powder, mix in ½ cup broken walnut meats at this time. Stir an egg into a cup of milk. Add this to the dry ingredients, rapidly forming a dough.

Get this without delay into a buttered pan and into a preheated moderate oven. Bake about 45 minutes or until a straw inserted into the loaf comes out clean. If any is left over, it will provide memorable sandwiches for the next day. Although walnuts excel in this baking powder bread, other wild nuts can be substituted.

People who live in the vicinity of both fresh walnuts and dates can combine both to make a most delicious dessert. Cut 2 cups dates into small bits. Add 2 tablespoons butter or margarine and 1 teaspoon baking soda. Pour 2 cups boiling water over everything. Blend well 2 well-beaten eggs, 1 teaspoon vanilla, 2 cups sugar, and 2 cups sifted flour, and stir well into the above mixture. Then fold in 1 cup walnuts, which have been broken into small pieces. Spread out in a greased pan. Bake 40 minutes in a moderately slow oven. Cut into squares and served with whipped cream, this is something to liven the conversation.

If you like walnut fudge, give this recipe at least a try. Melt a ¼-pound stick butter or margarine and 2 ounces bitter chocolate. Sift

WILD
NUTS

together 1½ cups sugar, ½ cup cake flour, and ⅛ teaspoon salt, and add it to the above. Stir 3 well-beaten eggs, 1 teaspoon vanilla, and a cup of walnuts, broken into fine pieces, into the mixture. Bake in a moderate oven for 25 minutes. Then cut into squares and make up your own mind.

Eating your first walnut pie is sort of like it used to be to put on your first pair of long pants or high heels. Melt ¼ pound butter or margarine and stir into it 1 cup sugar, 1 cup corn syrup, and 1 teaspoon cinnamon. Beat 3 eggs and add these. Cover ⅓ cup walnuts with a cloth and pound and mash the meats into a pulp. Stir in these, along with 2 tablespoons boiling water. Pour everything into an un-cooked 9-inch pie shell and bake in a moderate oven for 50 minutes. This is surprisingly good either hot or cold, although we prefer the former.

BUTTERNUT

(Juglans)

Confederate soldiers and partisans were referred to as butternuts during the Civil War because of the brown homespun clothes of the military, often dyed with the green nut husks and the inner bark of these familiar trees. Some of the earliest American settlers made the same use of them. As far back as the Revolution, a common laxative was made of the inner bark, a spoonful of finely cut pieces to a cup of boiling water, drunk cold. Indians preceded the colonists in boiling down the sap of this tree, as well as that of the black walnut, to make syrup and sugar, sometimes mixing the former with maple syrup.

The butternut thrives in chillier climates than does the black walnut, ranging higher in the mountains and further north. Otherwise, this tree, also known as white walnut and oilnut, closely resembles its cousin except for being smaller and lighter colored. Its wood is comparatively soft, weak, and light, although still close-grained. The larger trees, furthermore, are nearly always unsound.

Butternuts grow from the Maritime Provinces to Ontario, south to the northern mountainous regions of Georgia and Alabama, and west to Arkansas, Kansas, and the Dakotas. They are medium-sized trees,

135

ordinarily from about thirty to fifty feet high, with a trunk diameter of up to three feet. Some trees, though, tower up to ninety feet or more. The furrowed and broadly ridged bark is gray.

The alternate compound leaves are from fifteen to thirty inches long. Each one is made up of eleven to seventeen lance-shaped, nearly stemless leaflets, two to six inches long and about half as broad, with sharply pointed tips, sawtoothed edges, and unequally rounded bases. Yellowish green on top, these are paler and softly downy underneath. The catkins and the shorter flower spikes appear in the spring when the leaves are about half grown.

BUTTERNUT

The nuts are oblong rather than round, blunt, about two to two and a half inches long, and a bit more than half as thick. Thin husks, notably sticky and coated with matted rusty hairs, enclose the nuts whose bony shells are roughly ridged, deeply furrowed, and hard. Frequently growing in small clusters of two to five, these ripen in October and soon drop from the branches.

The young nuts, when they have nearly reached their full size, can be picked green and used for pickles which bring out the flavor of meat like few other things and which really attract notice as hors d'oeuvres. If you can still easily shove a large needle through the nuts, it is not too late to pickle them, husks and all, after they have been scalded and the outer fuzz rubbed off.

Put them in a strong brine for a week, changing the water every other day and keeping them tightly covered. Then drain and wipe them. Pierce each nut all the way through several times with a large needle. Then put them in glass jars with a sprinkling of powdered ginger, nutmeg, mace, and cloves between each layer. Bring some good cider vinegar to a boil, immediately fill each jar, and seal. You can start enjoying this unusual delicacy in two weeks.

A noteworthy dessert can be made with butternuts by mixing ½ cup of the broken meats with 1 cup diced dates, 1 cup sugar, 1 teaspoon baking powder, and ⅛ teaspoon salt. Beat 4 egg whites until they are stiff and fold them into the above mixture. Bake in a greased pan in a slow oven for 20 minutes. Serve either hot or cold with whipped cream. This is also good, particularly when hot, with liberal scoops of vanilla ice cream.

Butternut and date pie is something special. Chop a cup apiece of dates and nuts. Roll a dozen ordinary white crackers into small bits, too. Mix with 1 cup sugar and ½ teaspoon baking powder. Then beat 3 egg whites until they are stiff. Sometimes, if the nuts are not as tasty as usual, we also add a teaspoon of almond extract. In either event, fold into the nut mixture and pour into a buttered 9-inch pie pan. Bake ½ hour, or until light brown, in a moderate oven. Cool before cutting. Ice or whipped cream is good with this, too, but it is also delicately tasty alone.

Butternut brownies, eaten by the nibble and washed down with draughts of steaming black tea, are one of the ways I like to top off my noonday lunches when hunting in the late fall. Just blend together 1 cup sugar, 1 teaspoon salt, ½ cup melted butter or margarine, 2 squares bitter chocolate, 1 teaspoon vanilla, and 3 eggs. When this is thoroughly mixed, stir into it 1 cup finely broken butternuts and ½ cup flour. Pour into a shallow greased pan and bake in a moderate oven 20 minutes.

HAZELNUT

(Corylus)

Three species of hazelnuts are natives of the United States and Canada. Two grow in the East, making these nuts available from Newfoundland all the way across Canada to British Columbia, south to Georgia, Tennessee, and Florida. Another grows in the mountains of California. Incidentally, the filberts sold in stores are cultivated hazelnuts.

The low-spreading thickness of hazelnut bushes provides useful cover and nesting sites wherever these thickets occur along streams, the edges of woods, pasture slopes, fences, and roadsides. Squirrels and chipmunks feast on the nuts. Grouse pick off the catkins, while deer, moose, and rabbits browse on the plants themselves.

The three varieties of this many-branched shrub are much alike, although the nuts differ some. Those of the *Corylus Americana,* growing in open husks, have brown shells that are usually thick and hard. The beaked hazelnut, also of the East, has an exceedingly bristly husk that, instead of likewise flaring at the top, is contracted into a long neck about one and a half inches long. The shell of this nut is more whitish brown and is comparatively thin. The nuts of the California species are larger but similar.

HAZELNUT
Top: beaked hazelnut. *Bottom:* American hazelnut.

The *Corylus Americana,* to describe one of these species, grows in clumps whose widely spreading branches reach a height of six or seven feet. The young brown growth, which later becomes smooth, is initially furred with pinkish bristles. The alternate short-stemmed leaves, which resemble those of the yellow birch and alder, are egg-shaped or widely oval, with sharp tips and toothed margins.

Slender catkins, which sway in the breezes, make their appearance in early spring before the new leaves burst forth, and grow three or four inches long. The inconspicuous fertile flowers appear in scaly buds near the tips of the branches. The nuts are usually sweet and ripe in August and if not bothered, cling to the shrubs until late in the fall.

If you should want to remove the inner skin from hazelnuts, this can be done without softening them. Just spread them in a pan and heat in a moderate oven 20 to 30 minutes. Do not brown. Let them cool. Then rub off the loosened skins with a towel.

Hazelnut macaroons come alive in your mouth. Chop up 3 cups of hazelnuts or, easier, grind them in an electric blender at high speed until very fine. Beat 5 egg whites with ⅛ teaspoon salt until they stand in peaks. Then gradually beat in 2 cups sifted confectioners' sugar and ½ cup sifted flour. Thoroughly stir in the nuts and 1 teaspoon baking powder. Drop, ½ teaspoon at a time, about 1½ inches apart, on a greased shallow pan or cookie sheet. Bake in a slow oven 15 minutes, or until the edges take on a golden tinge. After they have cooled, keep the 5 dozen or so cookies in a closed container for as long as they last, which isn't likely to be long.

There are many delicately flavored candies you can make with hazelnuts. One of the best of these can be made without cooking. Just mix 1 egg white and 2 cups sifted confectioners' sugar. Add 2 teaspoons butter or margarine and continue to blend until creamy and smooth. Then thoroughly work in 2 cups finely chopped hazelnuts and form into balls. And see who wants to go nutting again tomorrow.

HICKORY

(Carya)

Hickories are probably our most important native nuts. The Indians used them in great quantities for food, and the settlers soon followed suit, even tapping the sweet sap in the spring for syrup and sugar. Today the nuts are familiar in the stores of this country.

The shellbark hickory, also called the shagbark, is the leader of the clan, although there are from twenty to twenty-two other species, depending upon the botanist. All are edible, although the taste of some is not appealing. There are the sweet hickories, including the above, in which the husk splits into 4 parts when the nuts are ripe. There are the pignuts, often bitter but sometimes delicious, in which the thin husk splits only above the middle, or, sometimes late in the season, all the way to the base. There are also the familiar pecans.

The stout twigs and the gray bark which loosens in shaggy narrow strips, attached at the middle, distinguishes the shellbark and the shagbark, actually two different species, from all other trees. The leaves, from seven to fourteen inches long, are composed of usually five but sometimes seven leaflets. Dark yellowish green above, these are lighter and often downy beneath, with fine sharp teeth marking the edges.

HICKORY
1 Shagbark   2 Pignut.   3 Bitternut.

Hickories grow slowly, and the shellbark does not produce nuts until about eighty years old. It becomes a large stately tree, reaching a height of up to 180 or more feet and a trunk diameter of one to three feet. Its wood is used for such things as bows, skiis, and ax handles, while hickory-smoked hams and bacon are famous. Wood duck, ring-necked pheasant, bobwhite, and wild turkey compete with man for the nuts. Black bear, raccoon, squirrel, and rabbit eat both nuts and bark, while the white-tailed deer relishes both these and the younger twigs.

The shellbark, which leafs out later than most other trees and sheds its bronze foliage earlier, ranges from Maine and Quebec west to the Great Lakes and Minnesota, and south to northern Florida and eastern Texas. The fruits, varying a great deal in size, are on the average from one to two inches in diameter, nearly round or somewhat oblong, and depressed at the top. The husks, which are about a quarter inch thick, split into four pieces at maturity. The familiar white or tawny nuts are a bit flattened with four ridges, an easily cracked thin shell, and large sweet kernels.

You can have an enjoyable time with just a heap of hickory nuts and a stone or hammer. But the pleasant, slightly aromatic meats also excel in the kitchen.

They can even be cooked with vegetables. Sometimes when you have gathered a bushel or so of nuts, probably from a noble tree in an open field or along the rim of a wood where its branches can stretch far into the sunlight, try cooking some with corn. Whip 2 eggs to a froth. Stir in a teaspoon salt, a tablespoon flour, and a cup of chopped hickory nuts. Add a cup of milk and 2 cups corn, fresh, canned, or frozen. Bake the mixture in a greased dish in a moderate oven until it is firm.

It is in the desserts, though, that the sweet-meat members of the clan are surpassingly good. For instance, it is difficult to outdo the following simple cookies. Just whip the whites of 2 eggs until they are stiff. Beat 2 cups of brown sugar into this. Then add 2 cups nuts that have been broken into small pieces. Drop from a teaspoon, about 1½ inches apart, onto a shallow greased pan or a greased baking sheet. Bake in a slow oven for 35 to 45 minutes or until light brown.

When we are in hickory country, nut balls have become traditional with us for the Christmas season, when neighbors are always dropping in to exchange cheer. You have to crush 2 cups of nuts for this by pounding, rolling, or, most easily, by running through a food grinder. Then blend a cup of butter or margarine with 4 tablespoons sugar and 3 teaspoons vanilla until creamy. Thoroughly mix the nuts with 2 cups sifted flour and stir into the preceding mixture. Shape the dough into little balls slightly larger than marbles. Place on a greased shallow pan or cookie sheet. Bake in a slow oven 45 minutes. Frost by rolling in confectioners' sugar while hot and again when cool. Store those that aren't snatched up immediately in a closed container.

The following pie is delectable with pecans but even better with shellbark hickories. Beat 3 eggs until light. Add 1 cup sugar, 1 cup white corn syrup, a melted ¼-pound stick of butter or margarine, 1½ teaspoons vanilla, and finally, 1 cup shopped nuts. Bake in an uncooked 9-inch pie shell in a moderate oven for about 40 minutes. We don't know of a tastier way to usher in the nutting season.

BEECH

(Fagus)

The first dawn I ever went deer hunting in New Brunswick, my friend, Sandy Macdonald, saw to it that we were stalking into the wind along the top of a beechnut ridge by the time the late fall sun was wheeling above the horizon. He was right, too. Whitetails, black bear, wood duck, ruffed grouse, and other wildlife vie with man for this important crop which, as Indians and early settlers well knew, is one of the most flavorful products of our northern forests.

The now largely cleared beechnut forests of the Middle West were once the gathering places of the also departed passenger pigeons, which subsisted to a large extent on the nuts. Our single native species of this tree grows from the Maritime Provinces to Ontario and Wisconsin, southward to eastern Texas and northern Florida. The large handsome trees, with their bright emerald foliage that oxidizes to a magnificent copper or gold in the autumn, are also planted for shade and landscaping. Unfortunately, however, the nuts are by far most numerous only where the trees grow in the northern states and in Canada.

The beech is readily identified throughout the year by its smooth, attractively dappled, bluish-gray bark, which in frequented places, especially when the trunks are two to three feet through, often invites the carving of initials. The trees, up to 100 feet tall, have greatly forked branches that end in numerous delicate gray twigs.

The oblong or oval alternate leaves, almost twice as long as they are wide, have pointed tips and rounded or wedge-shaped bases. Straight-ribbed and coarsely toothed, they are thin and somewhat papery, smoothly emerald green above and yellower and paler beneath. Their short stems, one-fourth to one-half inch long, have a somewhat hairy silkiness.

Both sterile and wind-pollinated fertile blossoms grow on the same tree. The former appear in balls that dangle on long stems. The latter grow in pairs where the upper leaves meet the twigs, developing into small, four-part burrs, softly bristling with recurved hairs. Easily opened by the thumbnail when they mature in October, these contain two triangular, somewhat concave, brown nuts that are nutritious and sweet.

Mostly, I've gathered beechnuts in New England and the Maritimes after heavy frosts have dropped them to the ground. They are so small

BEECH
Left: winter twig. *Top center:* branch with mature leaves and burrs. *Bottom center:* nut. *Right:*
branch with early leaves and sterile and fertile blossoms.

and delicious that we've always eaten a large proportion of them raw, but they are good cooked, too. Although I've never tried it, a friend of mine at Seven Mile Lake in New Brunswick roasts and grinds them for a beverage which he says tastes like coffee. The young leaves may be cooked as a green in the spring. The inner bark, dried and pulverized for bread flour in times of need in Europe, is an emergency food to remember.

Beechnut and date cakes taste just as good as they smell. Stir 1 teaspoon baking soda into 2 cups boiling water and pour over 1 cup chopped dates. Let stand 10 minutes. Then mix 3 tablespoons butter or margarine, 2 eggs, 3 cups flour, and 2 cups sugar. Stir well into the date mixture. Fold a cup of broken nut meats into all this. Spread in a greased pan and bake 40 minutes in a moderate oven. Cut into squares. Serve those you don't eat on the spot with whipped cream.

When we're East, we try to have beechnut pie several times each autumn. One cup of beechnuts will do for this, too. Thoroughly whip 3 eggs. Then slowly beat into them a ¼-pound stick of melted butter or margarine, 1 cup white corn syrup, and ¾ cup sugar. Turn into an uncooked 9-inch pie shell and bake in a slow oven for 35 minutes. Remove the pie long enough to cover it quickly with nuts. Then return it to the oven, turn up the heat to moderate, and bake another 15 minutes. The only trouble with this is that it encourages you to rush through the rest of your meal to get at it.

143

flavorful
wilderness teas
and coffees

Wild Beverages

INDIANS DEPENDED LARGELY on edible wild plants for their beverages. When the first settlers arrived, and for centuries afterward as they were pushing their way westward, they followed suit. If these wild drinks had not been rich in Vitamin C, a vitamin which the body cannot store and which is necessary for the prevention and cure of scurvy, many pioneers could not have lived to open our frontiers.

At the time of the American Revolution, even in the communities where stores were well stocked, many chose wild drinks rather than continue to use oriental tea, tinged with an English tax. When the Civil War tore the country apart, many northerners and southerners alike had to turn again to the wilds for their teas and coffees.

The earlier described wild fruit juices are all refreshing. So are the previously mentioned wild teas brewed from roses, strawberry leaves, raspberry leaves, blackberry leaves, kinnikinic, wintergreen, fireweed, plantain, clover, shepherd's purse, and watercress. This holds true, too, for the coffee substitutes made from dandelion roots, chicory roots, and beechnuts. Then there are the following excellent wild beverage sources.

SPEARMINT

(Mentha)

Spearmint, the source of the familiar chewing gum flavor and a boon to cookery from ancient times to the present, can be found along damp roadsides and waterways and in wet places from Nova Scotia to British Columbia, south to the Gulf of Mexico and California. The long, creeping roots of this aromatic perennial spread it rapidly.

About twelve to twenty inches high, the spearmint is branched and has oblong or lance-shaped green leaves growing opposite each other. These are stemless or nearly so, 1 to 2 inches long, toothed, pointed,

SPEARMINT

veiny, and wrinkled. Tiny, light purple or almost white flowers encircle slender, leafless spikes in the summertime.

Wild mints, as a whole, are quickly identified by their square stems, opposite leaves, and familiar aroma. This characteristic fragrance may be lacking if just a few plants grow together, but you've only to crush a single leaf between your fingers to catch it.

You can find wild mint almost anywhere. I'll never forget the time I took a southern friend of mine hunting in a remote section of British

Columbia, two days north of the nearest railhead. Charlie was pretty tired and thirsty by the time we had set up camp by a mountain lake in the late afternoon, especially as the last part of the trip had been made on horseback.

However, he let himself be persuaded that now was a good time of day to see if anything was stirring. We'd no sooner cut some grizzly tracks beside the water, though, than we ran into what must have been an acre of wild mint. The unmistakable odor ended the hunt right there, bear tracks or no, and in less than a half hour Charlie had us back by our tent sipping improvised mint juleps.

Wild mint sprigs also give a welcome piquancy to instant iced tea made with one of the dehydrated powders. Or if you want something really special for a hot day, make 3 cups of double-strength tea. When this is ready, pour it over a tablespoon of mint jelly and stir until the latter is dissolved. Chill. Fill glasses half full of tea. Add crushed ice, and then fill to the rims with cold ginger ale. Garnish with mint sprigs.

Wild mint vinegar has an agreeableness all its own. You can make it by filling a jar loosely with fresh green sprigs of wild mint. Cover with ordinary cider vinegar. Then close the jar and place on a sunny windowsill for 3 weeks. At the end of this time, strain and rebottle.

For a mint sauce to serve hot over lamb or well-done roast venison still sizzling from the oven, mix a tablespoon of sugar with ½ cup mild cider vinegar, diluted with water, if too strong. Pour this over ½ cup torn mint leaves and let stand ½ hour over low heat. Or if you're going to use it cold, just bring the sugar and vinegar to a bubble, add the leaves, let boil up briefly, and then set aside to cool.

Mint jelly is something we particularly like when we're living in the woods and eating lots of meat. Wash and quarter 4 quarts unpeeled and uncored apples, put in a kettle, barely cover with cold water, and simmer until soft. Then mash, drain through 4 thicknesses of dampened cheesecloth, and measure. Add an equal volume of sugar. Bring again to a bubble, add ½ cup fresh mint leaves and 2 tablespoons lemon juice, and boil until a spoonful runs off the side of the spoon in a sheet. Strain into hot glasses and cover immediately with melted paraffin.

A quicker method is boiling 3 cups apple cider with ½ cup fresh mint leaves for 15 minutes and then straining through a sieve. Stir a package of pectin into the juice and, continuing to stir, bring to a boil.

Now gradually add 4 cups sugar and continue stirring until a full rolling boil is reached. Boil 2 minutes. Then remove from the heat, stir in 4 tablespoons cider vinegar, skim, and pour as usual into hot sterilized glasses, sealing these at once with hot paraffin. To avoid losing track of fruit if you put up very much, label and date all batches.

OSWEGO TEA

(Monarda)

Early settlers found this family of native perennials an excellent substitute for tea, especially in the backwoods where supplies were limited and in populated regions during the American Revolution. We have also used the minty leaves as a flavor in cooking. The fragrant plants with their showy flowers are also known as beebalm, wild bergamot, and horsemint. They grow from Quebec to British Columbia, south to Tennessee and Georgia.

OSWEGO TEA

The Oswego teas are rather coarse plants two to three feet tall, with beautiful large flowers that vary in color from scarlet to lavender. In fact, their beauty enhances the occasional garden, and some species brought from Europe have gone wild. Their square stems, opposite leaves, and the aroma of their crushed foliage identify them as members of the mint family. The dark green, aromatic leaves, two to six inches long, are sharp-toothed. The very pretty blossoms, almost two inches broad, adorn these mints from July to September.

To brew Oswego tea, use ½ to 1 teaspoon of the dried leaves, according to taste, for each cup of boiling water. If you are using fresh leaves, double the quantity. Let steep 5 minutes. We prefer this plain, but some of our friends like to add sugar, milk, or both.

Incidentally, the best way to dry the wild teas is at room, never oven, temperature. Just hang a bagful near the ceiling for a few weeks. Then store in closed jars and keep in a cool dark place, so as to retain as much of the volatile aroma as possible.

WILD COFFEE

(Triosteum)

Wild coffee has also collected the names of feverwort, tinker's weed, and horse gentian. The three species of this coarse perennial grow in open woods and along roadsides, slopes, walls, and fences from New England to Nebraska, south to Alabama and Missouri. They are more of the wild plants used as beverages during colonial days.

Wild coffee has rather hairy stems up to three or four feet high. The opposite leaves, which narrow abruptly at their bases, often encircle the stem. The reddish or orange berries, which are egg-shaped to nearly spherical and about half an inch long, grow in small clusters in the joints between leaves and stems. Each contains a trio of large seeds.

Dried, roasted, and ground, these berries may be used instead of coffee. Put into fresh cold water, using 2 level teaspoons for every cup of water. Amounts can be varied, of course, for a stronger or weaker brew. Set this on the heat. Watch it carefully. As soon as it boils up once, lift it off to take on body for 5 minutes. Then settle the grounds, if you want, with a couple of tablespoons of cold water and start pouring.

WILD COFFEE

KENTUCKY COFFEE TREE

(Gymnocladus)

Roasted and ground, the seeds of the Kentucky coffee tree were used by early settlers in the New World as a substitute for coffee. Some of the Indians roasted them and ate them like nuts. The trees, often planted today for shade and for landscaping, range from New York to southern Minnesota, south to Tennessee and Oklahoma.

Usually a medium-sized tree, reaching a height of forty to ninety feet and a trunk diameter of from one to three feet, the Kentucky coffee tree ordinarily branches a few feet above the ground into three or four limbs which climb almost vertically to form a narrow crown.

The dark green leaves, which remain on for only about half of the year, are sometimes almost three feet long and two feet wide. They are composed of up to forty or more short-stemmed leaflets. Long clusters of greenish-white flowers appear in June. These develop into reddish-brown pods from four to ten inches long and from one to two inches wide. Each

149

KENTUCKY COFFEE TREE

contains six to nine large, oval, flat, hard brownish seeds encased in a dark sweetish pulp.

You can roast these seeds slowly in the oven, grind them, and brew them like coffee. They have none of the caffeine of regular coffee, and the resulting beverage agrees with some people better.

SWEET FERN

(Myrica) (Comptonia)

The fragrant leaves of the sweet fern were used as a tea as far back as the American Revolution. This plant is actually a shrub, partial to open fields and upland slopes where trees are sparse or absent, often forming solid stands in such habitats. It is also found to a lesser degree in open woods. Deer browse on it, and game birds and rabbits sometimes seek it out for food. It grows from the Maritimes to Saskatchewan and Minnesota, south to North Carolina, Georgia, Tennessee, and Indiana.

This sweet-scented shrub, growing from one to three feet tall, has fernlike leaves that give it its name. These are deeply divided into many roundish sections, the edges of which are usually sparingly toothed. The male flowers, about an inch in length, grow in clusters at the ends of the slim branches in catkins approximately one inch long. The female flowers grow in egg-shaped catkins. The resulting bristly round burrs envelop hard, glossy, brown little nuts. If you don't mind getting your thumbnail yellow, these are easily exposed and enjoyed, especially during June and early July while they are still tender.

The dried aromatic leaves of the sweet fern, a teaspoon to each cup of boiling water, make a very pleasant tea. When you use them fresh, just double the amount.

SWEET FERN
Left: **branch with leaves.** *Right:* **burr.**

We've also brewed this in the sun by filling a quart bottle with cold water, adding 8 teaspoons of the fresh leaves, covering the glass with aluminum foil, and setting in the sun. The length of time required depends, of course, upon how hot the sunlight is. The several times I tried this in New Hampshire, about 3 midday hours were needed before the brew became sufficiently dark. Made this way, wild teas have no bitterness of acrid oils extracted by other methods. You can then strain it, dilute it to individual taste, and serve it with ice.

SASSAFRAS

(Sassafras)

There is just one species of the familiarly fragrant sassafras that is native to North America. Ours is a small or medium-sized tree, growing from New England to Ontario, Iowa, and Kansas, south to the Gulf of Mexico.

This member of the laurel family, which also includes several trees whose bark is powdered to provide cinnamon, is found along fences and roads, in abandoned fields, in dry woods, and in other open and semi-open places. Thickets often spring up from the roots. Famous for its supposed medicinal qualities soon after Columbus voyaged here, sassafras is now employed commercially mainly as a flavor. Privately, though, it is still widely used for everything from jelly to gumbo.

SASSAFRAS
Left: **flowers.** *Right:* **twig with leaves and fruit.**

The very limber twigs and young shoots of the easily recognized sassafras are bright green and mucilaginous. The leaves, aromatic when crushed, grow in three shapes as shown in the drawing, all varieties sometimes stemming from the same twig. Also mucilaginous, they oxidize in the autumn to beautiful reds and oranges. Greenish-gold flowers, which have a spicy odor, appear with the leaves in the spring, the sexes on separate trees. Birds flock to the dark bluish fruits, nearly half an inch long, when they ripen on their thick red stems in the fall.

Sassafras tea, famous for centuries on this continent, where many people still drink it as a spring tonic, can be made by putting a palmful of preferably young roots into a pot with cold water and boiling them until the rich red color that you've learned by experience you like best is reached. Second and third extractions can be made from the same roots.

For drying and storing some of the makings, use just the bark of the young roots. Older roots can be employed, too, but it is best to scrape off the usual hard, rough covering first.

We like this tea sweetened. Only moderate amounts should be used, in any event, as an overdose of the oil may have a narcotic effect. But you can drink too much ordinary tea, too.

With the help of lemon juice, commercial pectin, and sugar, spicy jellies are made of strong sassafras teas. The dainty green winter buds are delicious, and later the young leaves will add flavor to a salad.

In the South, soups are flavored and thickened by the dried leaves, the veins and hard portions of which are first discarded. If you like the wholesome thickness and smoothness of gumbos, why not try this for yourself? The easiest way to go about it is by drying the young tender stems and leaves, grinding them to a fine powder, sifting this through a sieve to remove the hard parts, and pouring the remainder into a large saltshaker for everyone at the table to use according to his own pleasure.

SPICEBUSH

(Benzoin)

The young leaves, twigs, and bark of the spicebush provide another of the wild teas much used on this continent, especially in the early days when remoteness and wars made oriental blends scarce commodities. They provide a pleasant drink, especially if you happen to prefer your tea with milk and sugar.

Two species of the aromatic-leaved spicebush are native to North America, both being common undergrowths in swampy woods, along stream banks, and on moist bottomlands. The northern species is found from Maine to Michigan, south to Georgia and Kansas. A similar species, but with downy branches and leaves, grows in the southern states. Like other familiar wild edibles, these cousins of the sassafras have a variety of local names including spicewood, spice, snapwood, wild allspice, and Benjamin bush. Sometime in the past, feverbush and feverwood were added because of the use of this tea in pioneer days to reduce fever.

The spicebush is a shrub, up to some fifteen feet tall, with smooth bark and slim, brittle twigs. Its dark emerald leaves—short-stemmed, thin, smoothly edged, oval or oblong, from three to five inches long, prominently veined, and pointed—change to gold in the fall. The dense

SPICEBUSH
Left: **branch with leaves.** *Right:* **branch with flowers.**

clusters of yellow flowers, whose spicy fragrance precedes the leaves in the spring, grow like those of the sassafras with one sex to a shrub. Ring-necked pheasant and bobwhite quail relish the spiciness and oiliness of the oval reddish fruits, each of which contains a single large seed of similar shape.

A handful of young twigs, leaves, or bark simmered for 15 minutes in 4 cups of water makes an aromatic tea. Some people use the berries for this purpose, too. Dried and powdered, these also provide a substitute for allspice. If you become thirsty and dry while outdoors, chewing the pleasantly flavored young bark is an enjoyable way to start the saliva flowing again.

SUMAC

(Rhus)

Sumac "lemonade" is just the thing to take the edges off a hard afternoon. Pick over a generous handful of the red berries, drop them into a pan and mash them slightly, cover with boiling water, and allow to steep away from any heat until this is well colored. Then strain through 2 thicknesses of cloth to remove the fine hairs. Sweeten to taste, and serve either hot or cold.

Some Indian tribes liked this acid drink so much that they dried the small one-seeded berries and stored them for winter use. Many settlers followed suit.

The rapidly growing staghorn sumac, also called the lemonade tree and the vinegar tree, is one of the largest species of the cashew family, commonly reaching ten to twenty feet in height. It is easily recognized at any season because of the close resemblance of its stout and velvety twigs to deer antlers while these are still in velvet. It ranges from the Maritime Provinces to Ontario, south to Georgia and Missouri.

The bark of these shrubs or small trees, which often form thickets, is smooth. The satiny and often streaked wood, sometimes used commercially for such small objects as napkin rings, is green to orange in color. The fernlike leaves, about fourteen to twenty-four inches long, are composed of eleven to thirty-one pointed leaflets from two to five inches in length. Dark green and smooth above, pale and sometimes softly hairy beneath, these flame into brilliant red in the fall.

The tiny, tawnily green flowers grow in loosely stemmed clusters, one sex to a shrub or tree. The male clusters are occasionally ten to twelve inches long. The female blossoms are smaller and extremely dense, producing compact bunches of berries. These are erect and so startlingly red that sometimes I've come upon a lone cluster suddenly in the woods and thought it was a scarlet tanager perched on a branch.

The hard red fruits are thickly covered with bright red hairs. These hairs are tart with malic acid, the same flavorsome ingredient found in grapes. Since this is readily soluble in water, the berries should be gathered for beverage purposes before any heavy storms, if possible.

Incidentally, the berries of the poisonous sumacs are white. However, there are other sumacs in the United States and Canada with similar red

STAGHORN SUMAC
Left: winter twig. *Right:* branch with leaves and fruit cluster.

berries that provide a refreshing substitute for pink lemonade. All these red-fruited species are harmless.

One of them is the smooth or scarlet sumac, *Rhus glabra,* which grows from the Maritimes to Minnesota, south to Florida and Louisiana. This closely resembles the staghorn sumac, except that it is entirely smooth, with a pale bluish or whitish bloom coating the plump twigs.

Another is the dwarf, shining, or mountain sumac, *Rhus copallina,* which grows from New England and Ontario to Florida and Texas. Although similar to the aforementioned species, it can be distinguished from all other sumacs because of peculiar winglike projections along the leaf stems between the leaflets.

Indians made a poultice of the bruised leaves and fruit of the red-berried sumacs and applied it to irritated skin. An astringent gargle, made by boiling the crushed berries in a small amount of water, is still used for sore throats.

BIRCH

(Betula)

The nutritious bark of the black birch is said to have probably saved the lives of scores of Confederate soldiers during Garnett's retreat over the mountains to Monterey, Virginia. For years afterward, the way the soldiers went could be followed by the peeled birch trees.

The black birch may be identified at all times of the year by its tight, reddish-brown, cherrylike bark, which has the aroma and flavor of wintergreen. Smooth in young trees, this darkens and separates into large, irregular sections as these birches age. The darkly dull green leaves, paler and yellower beneath, are two to four inches long, oval to oblong, short-stemmed, silky when young, smooth when mature, with double-toothed edges. They give off an odor of wintergreen when bruised. The trees have both erect and hanging catkins, on twigs that also taste and smell like wintergreen.

BLACK BIRCH

In fact, when the commercial oil of wintergreen is not made synthetically, it is distilled from the twigs and bark of the black birch. This oil is exactly the same as that from the little wintergreen plant, described earlier.

Black birches enhance the countryside from New England to Ontario, south to Ohio and Delaware, and along the Appalachian Mountains to Georgia and Alabama.

A piquant tea, brisk with wintergreen, is made from the young twigs, young leaves, the thick inner bark, and the bark from the larger roots. This latter reddish bark, easily stripped off in the spring and early summer, can be dried at room temperatures and stored in sealed jars in a cool place for later use. A teaspoon to a cup of boiling water, set off the heat and allowed to steep for 5 minutes, makes a tea that is delicately spicy. Milk and sugar make it even better. As a matter of fact, any of the birches make good tea.

You can make syrup and sugar from the sap, too, as from the sap of all birches. I'll never forget my first introduction to this. It was our first spring in the paper birch country of the Far North, and Vena and I were bemoaning the fact that there were no maples from which to tap sap for our sourdough pancakes.

"Birch syrup you can get here in copious amounts," Dudley Shaw, a trapper and our nearest neighbor, informed Vena. "Heavenly concoction. It'll cheer Brad up vastly."

"Oh, will you show me how?"

"I'll stow a gimlet in my pack when I prowl up this way the first of the week to retrieve a couple of traps that got frozen in," Dudley agreed. "Noble lap, birch syrup is. Glorious on flippers."

Dudley told us to get some containers. Lard pails would do, he said, or we could attach some wire bails through nail holes in the tops of several tomato cans. He beamed approval when he arrived early Tuesday morning. The improvised sap buckets, suspended on nails driven above the small holes Dudley bored with his gimlet, caught a dripping flow of watery fluid.

"You'd better ramble out this way regularly to see these don't overflow," Dudley cautioned. "Keep the emptied sap simmering cheerfully on the back of the stove. Tons of steam have to come off."

"Will it hurt the trees any?" Vena asked anxiously.

"No, no," Dudley said reassuringly. "The plunder will begin to bog down when the day cools, anyway. Then we'll whittle out pegs and drive them in to close the blinking holes. Everything will be noble."

Everything was, especially the birch syrup. It wasn't as thick as it might have been, even after all that boiling. There was a distressingly small amount of it, too. But what remained from the day's work was sweet, spicy, and poignantly delicious. What we drank beforehand, too, was refreshing, sweet, and provocatively spicy.

All the birches furnish prime emergency food. Two general varieties of the trees grow across the continent, the black birch and those similar to it, and the familiar white birches whose cheerful foliage and softly gleaming bark lighten the northern forests. Layer after layer of this latter bark can be easily stripped off in great sheets, although because of the resulting disfigurement this shouldn't be done except in an emergency, and used to start a campfire in any sort of weather.

The inner bark, dried and then ground into flour, has often oeen used by Indians and frontiersmen for bread. It is also cut into strips and boiled like noodles in stews. But you don't need to go even to that much trouble. Just eat it raw.

LABRADOR TEA

(Ledum)

Labrador tea, also known as Hudson's Bay tea across much of the North where the Hudson's Bay Company maintains its red-roofed white trading posts, is a pretty evergreen shrub whose robustly aromatic leaves still make one of the most famous teas of the north country. It is found growing densely in woods, muskegs, bogs, swamps, damp mountain meadows, and across the tundras of Alaska and Canada south to New England, Pennsylvania, New Jersey, and the Great Lake states, where it is seen mainly in mountain bogs and swamps. Its leaves were among those gathered for tea during the American Revolution.

Labrador tea is easy to distinguish, being a resinous evergreen shrub, ranging from one to four feet high, which is so attractive that two centuries ago the English brought it back to embellish their gardens. The telltale features are the alternate, dryly leathery, fragrant leaves whose smooth edges roll inward toward densely woolly undersides. These darken from grayish to reddish brown, as the otherwise green leaves age. These very distinctive, thickish leaves are usually less than two inches in length, although I have seen them as long as four inches.

This member of the heath family, which is eaten by moose and deer, blooms with tiny white flowers that, growing on slender individual stems, form showy, umbrellalike clusters at the tops of woolly stalks. These later provide slim seedpods.

Available in winter as well as during the warm months, the spicy leaves of Labrador tea make a palatable and refreshing tea. Although I seldom bother to measure exactly, about 1 tablespoon per cup, heaping or other-

LABRADOR TEA
Left: branch with leaves and budgs. *Center:* branches with leaves and flowers. *Right:* branches with seed pods.

wise, depending on your particular palate, will make a pleasant brew. Drop them into bubbling water and immediately set this away from the heat to steep for 5 minutes.

Old sourdoughs have warned me that drunk in too large quantities this tea may have a cathartic effect. But, using it sparingly over the years, I have never experienced any ill effects. As a matter of fact, I often find it both refreshing and thirst-quenching to chew on a few leaves while hunting or getting in wood.

NEW JERSEY TEA

(Ceanothus)

Possibly the most noteworthy of the native American beverage plants is the widely growing New Jersey tea, also known as redroot because of the color of its roots, which make a fine dye. The leaves of this common shrub, both green and dried, were regularly brewed in the thirteen colonies when, around the time of the Boston Tea Party and later during the Revolution, oriental blends were both in disfavor and scarce. More than one soldier under General Washington's command kept up his spirits with such pleasantly flavored infusions which, even if they lacked the caffeine of the more familiar tea, were at least hot and bracing.

Despite its name, New Jersey tea is found in dry open woods and on sandy or gravelly banks from New England to Manitoba, south to the Gulf of Mexico from Florida to Texas. It is a low shrub with erect

NEW JERSEY TEA
Left: bud and leaf scar. *Center:* stalk with leaves and flowers. *Right:* fruit.

branches, commonly growing in small bunches from the same group of roots, that reach from about one to three feet in height and then die back from the tips downward.

This member of the buckthorn family, also sometimes called wild snowball, has a large root with a thickish red or brownish bark which is sometimes used, a teaspoon to a cup of boiling water, to make a gargle.

The alternate leaves, growing on short stems, are oval and pointed, with edges reminiscent of a blunt fine-toothed saw. Up to about three inches long and somewhat less than half as wide, they have dark green tops and pale undersides that are marked by three very definite ribs. The minute white flowers, which attract quantities of insects when they appear from June to August, grow in very noticeable, long-stemmed clusters on the tops of the branches. The fruit is a dry, three-lobed capsule.

Although the freshly picked leaves make a flavorful enough beverage, this is considerably improved if they are dried first, especially if sugar and cream are added. We gather several small paper bagfuls of the leaves while the plant is still in blossom and hang them near the ceiling for several months. Measure and use like oriental tea.

HEMLOCK

(Tsuga)

Hemlock tea is famous in northern New England and Canada. Drunk hot and black, its taste is reminiscent of the way a Christmas tree smells. More important for trappers, prospectors, and other outdoorsmen, this tea contains the vital Vitamin C.

Of the seven to nine species of hemlocks recognized in the world, four are native to North America. These tall, straight evergreens are typical of cool, damp slopes, ravines, and swamps, generally in northern regions and in the higher mountains. They also spring up after tree-cutting operations, their low dense foliage affording fine winter cover for grouse, turkey, deer, and other wildlife.

The needles grow in spirals, although they often seem to be attached in two ranks. The hanging cones have thin segments which hide a pair of tiny winged seeds that are important food for birds and red squirrels. Hemlocks in New England and the Maritimes are often killed by porcupines eating the bark.

Incidentally, these conifers are no relation whatsoever to the poison hemlock from which Socrates and other ancients brewed their deadly draughts. Those entirely different plants are members of the parsley family.

It doesn't really make too much difference if you mistake one of the

HEMLOCK

other conifers for hemlock. All these members of the pine family provide aromatic and beneficial tea. The bright green young tips, when they appear in the springtime, are best. These are tender and starchy at this time and can also be enjoyed raw. Older green needles will do, too. I just put a handful in a receptacle, cover them with boiling water, and let them steep until the tea tastes strong enough. If you prefer this black as I do, there's no need of any straining. Just narrow your lips on the rim and quaff it down.

The hemlocks and other members of the great pine family, which includes the numerous pines themselves, the spruces, firs, balsams, and all the others, have another feature which, if one is ever lost or stranded, can mean the difference between life and death. The inner bark can be cut off and eaten, either raw or boiled, to provide strength and nourishment.

Part II

More Free-for-the-Eating

Wild Foods

*veritable
forests of
food*

Food That
Grows on Trees

WHEN WOOD SMOKE lifts among poplar in patterns as primitive as those formed there other days by frost crystals, have you sometimes found yourself wishing you could taste peace and quiet and solitude long enough to find out how good they—and you—really are?

Maybe you've even put into words this natural yearning of that portion of our most primitive ancestor which survives within us. Circumstances may conceivably be such for anybody, whether because of misadventure or storm or man-loosed disaster, that tomorrow a man may be alone in the wilderness and compelled to rely solely on his own ingenuity and resourcefulness for survival.

Most individuals worry that, if forced to shift for themselves in the unfrequented farther places, they would starve. Yet there are actual forests of food.

Everyone, of course, knows that trees furnish delectable fruits and nuts, but few people realize that the inner bark and sap of many trees such as the poplar and maple are not only edible but delicious to boot.

Trees offer another dividend, too. Because they provide shelter and food for so many game birds and animals, they often furnish clues to the presence of birds and animals which can supply meat for the table or sustenance during an emergency.

PIÑON

(Pinus)

The soft little nuts from the pinecones of millions of low-spreading conifers in the western United States and Mexico are not only pleasantly sweet by themselves, but they also afford prime flavoring for salads of the edible greens often seen flourishing nearby.

Roast the piñons first, after shelling them with the help of pliers or hammer, by spreading them in a single layer in a pan and placing it for 5 minutes in a moderate 350-degree oven. Shake the pan several times during the process.

Coarsely chop ½ cup of the toasted piñons. Mix these with ¼ teaspoon each of grated lemon peel, tarragon, and salt, and with ⅛ teaspoon cinnamon. Shake well with ½ cup salad oil and ¼ cup vinegar. This salad dressing can be stored, tightly covered, in the refrigerator. Use only about 1½ teaspoons for every cup of greens. As exciting as a honking wedge of geese undulating across the blue evening sky, it will make everything taste new.

Piñon pines have needlelike leaves in clusters of from two to five which persist for two, three, or more years. The flowers appear in the spring, producing an abundance of yellow, sulphurlike pollen which enlivens the wind. Once this fertilizes the pistillate flowers, which are scattered among the new shoots, there develop the familiar cones which take two and occasionally three years to reach maturity and disperse their winged seeds on the breezes. It is only on the innumerable small, low-growing pines in the vast drier mountainous regions of the West that these seeds become large enough to bother with. They are regularly available in stores.

However, if the cones' seeds, no matter how greatly relished by squirrels, turn out to be small, at least there will be nothing unwholesome about them. Romanian cooks grind entire young pinecones and use them to flavor game sauces. Some Indians used to roast the soft centers of green cones by the fringes of their campfires and feast on the syrupy results.

The settlers early learned to gather the inner bark of the pines in the spring, dry it throughout the summer, and then grind it and mix it with regular flour. Next to devouring it raw, though, the easiest way to eat this sweet cambium is first to cut it into thin strips, then cook it like spaghetti. The bland flavor goes well with meat simmered at the same time.

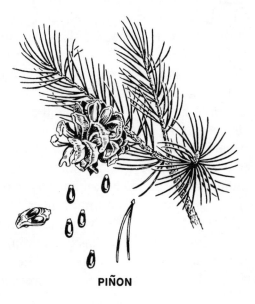

PIÑON

Some of the tribes went to more elaborate preparations, even to making a sort of bread. The squaws mashed the cambium to a pulp in water, then molded this into big cakes. In the meantime, a rousing fire was kindled in a rock-lined hole. The coals were then removed, the cakes set in on green leaves, and the embers raked back over a thick layer of leaves on top. Damp moss covered everything, which was left to smolder for upwards of an hour. The cakes were then placed on pole frames and smoked for a week, after which they could be carried as trail rations. The results were so hard that before use the cake was customarily broken into bits and boiled until soft.

Even pine needles, when they are new and starchy, are pleasantly nutritious to chew on. Some Indians boiled the still firm, spikelike flower clusters, in which the petalless blossoms grow in circular rows on slender stalks, to flavor their meats.

The piñons have also long been important medicinally. Hot pine tea, made by steeping the needles or by boiling gum or pitch, was one of the earliest cold remedies. Chewing the gum was considered soothing to sore throats. Too, the resin was dried, powdered, and applied to sore throats by swabs.

The piñon resin was also used by various Indians, and later by white adventurers and settlers, as a cure for everything from rheumatism and flu to indigestion. Heated, it was applied as a poultice to draw out splinters and to bring boils to a head. This hot resin dressing was also smeared on cuts, burns, sores, abrasions, and insect bites. Applied liberally to a hot cloth, it was used like mustard plasters in treating pneumonia, neuralgia, and general muscular soreness and stiffness.

The pines as a whole hold a position near the peak in importance to wildlife, partly because many birds and mammals feast on the seeds and to some extent because of the year-around cover the trees afford game birds, fur bearers, and both large and small game animals. Grouse, pigeons, doves, quail, prairie chickens, and turkeys eat the needles as well as the seeds. Deer, elk, moose, and mountain sheep browse on the foliage.

If you've ever lived in New Mexico, you'll remember the fragrance of burning piñon enlivening the air, as it has been doing in this country for centuries. The piñon and its cousins, such as the Parry pine and the Digger pine, have long been the most important trees to the Indians in the Southwest. The women still use the nuts in all kinds of cooking, from soups to salads, and a pocketful of their almost airy evergreen flavor goes well at any time.

Incidentally, when you're foraging for piñons in high country, don't overlook the ungainly nests of the pack rat. Indians customarily break each of these rough, large retreats apart, often finding as much as several pints of nuts stored for winter use.

These rich little nuts found in the hearts of pinecones add a subtle sweetness to the already piquant flavor of young dandelions. To go with enough of these greens to serve four, get 3 tablespoons of salad oil sizzling in a frypan. Then stir in ½ cup of piñons, ½ cup of diced black olives, ¼ cup seedless raisins, and a small mashed clove of garlic. After 3 minutes, put in the greens that have been torn to bite size, including a reasonable number of buds if possible. Reduce the heat, cover, and cook only until warm and tender. Season to taste with salt and, if you want, with a dusting of black pepper. Serve hot.

A delicious green sauce, flavorsome over steaming noodles or spaghetti, can be made with piñons and watercress. Start with ½ cup of chopped watercress, ¼ cup piñons, a large chopped garlic clove, and ⅛ teaspoon of salt in the blender. When this is pureed, add ½ cup of freshly grated Parmesan cheese. Conclude by slowly blending in ¼ cup salad oil and ½ stick of butter or margarine. With fruit and perhaps a dry red wine, this makes a perfect meal.

When the Indians taught the early frontiersmen how to obtain nuts from the piñons and related low-spreading pines, they began an adventure in good eating that continues to this day. Piñon cakes are unique and delicious, both hot and cold. You can make them in camp, perhaps where you're gathering the nuts, or at home. In either event, the shelled nuts first must be chopped or crushed, as with a rolling pin, to a coarse meal. The easiest way to go about this, of course, is in the home blender.

If you're cooking over an open fire, just mix each cup of piñon meal with ¼ teaspoon of salt and about ⅓ cup of lukewarm water to make a stiff batter. Get a tablespoon of shortening warming in a large, preferably heavy frypan until it is just short of smoking. Drop the batter from a tablespoon, flattening it into cakes with a spatula. Reduce the heat and tan the cakes slowly on one side before turning them to brown the other.

If you are at home, you can make a little less primitive cake by stirring each cup of piñon meal, then ¼ cup of all-purpose flour, into a well-beaten egg. Drop on a greased baking tin with a teaspoon. Bake in a moderate 375-degree oven about 10 minutes until lightly browned. The flavor of these is even more delicate.

For about three dozen piñon bread sticks of unusual crunchiness and distinctive flavor, stir a package of yeast into a cup of lukewarm water. Once it has dissolved, pour into a mixing bowl. Add ¼ cup olive oil, ¼ cup salad oil, a tablespoon sugar, 1½ teaspoons salt, a slightly beaten egg, and a cup of all-purpose flour. Beat until smooth.

Then add ¾ cup piñons and enough additional flour, about 2¼ cups, to make a stiff dough. Using a floured board or square of plastic, knead this about 5 minutes until it is smooth and elastic, adding flour if necessary. Cover with a damp cloth and place in the refrigerator overnight or, if you are in a hurry, for at least 2 hours. In any event, plan your cooking so that the dough can later rise for another 2 hours, starting this recipe early in the afternoon if you plan to serve the hot bread sticks for dinner.

Divide the chilled dough into 3 parts. Cut each portion into a dozen equal slices. Using your palms, roll each piece into an 8-inch crayon-like strip. Place about ½ inch apart on greased baking sheets, brush with melted butter or margarine, and let rise until about double size. Salt lightly. Bake in a preheated moderate 325-degree oven for about a dozen minutes until crisp and barely golden. Either warm or cold, such crusty tidbits, their outdoorsy flavor becoming more evident with each bite, will really arouse the appetite.

Piñon crops vary in different years, but if you happen to run into a bountiful harvest, you may like to try some cookies. These are simply made in any desired quantity by mixing each cup of chopped piñons with a cup of brown sugar and the beaten white of an egg. Drop small blobs from a teaspoon onto a greased pan or cooky sheet. Bake in a slow 300-degree oven until lightly browned.

Or you can bake more elaborate cookies. In any event, piñon cookies will fill the house with a tantalizing aroma. Start the preparations for these by finely grinding 2 cups of blanched almonds. Lightly beat 2 egg whites. Mix these thoroughly with the almonds and with a cup of sifted confectioner's sugar. You may choose to omit this next step, but we now like to blend in 2 tablespoons of crème de cacao.

Shape the dough into cookies about 1½ inches in diameter. Place apart on a well-greased cooky sheet. Brush the top of each with lightly beaten egg white. Arrange a half-dozen or so toasted piñons atop each cooky. Leave at room temperature all afternoon. Just before dinner, heat your oven to a moderate 350 degrees and cook the delicacies, which will number between 3 and 4 dozen, for about 10 minutes or until they are a light brown.

One of the most splendiferous edibles ever concocted by man is piñon torte. Beat ¼ cup of sugar and a stick of melted butter or margarine into 2 egg yolks. Add 2 tablespoons milk and ¾ cup toasted piñons. Mix together ½ cup all-purpose flour and ½ teaspoon salt, and fold that in. Whip 2 egg whites until they form short peaks. Gradually beat in ¼ cup of sugar and fold that, too, into the batter.

Bake in 2 deep, well-greased, 8-inch layer cake pans in a slow 300-degree oven for 50 minutes. In the meantime whip a cup of heavy cream, sweetened to taste with sugar. Put the cooled layers together with half the whipped cream. Spoon the remaining whipped cream over the dome and garnish it with ¼ cup of the toasted nuts, perhaps arranged in a pine tree pattern.

The flavor of chilled piñon soup is so satisfyingly piquant that this luxury is particularly refreshing on a hot fall evening. The soup is also excellent while still steaming. Because it is better appreciated when served in small portions, the following recipe will make enough for four.

Bring 2 cups of milk, a cup of game bird or chicken stock, a cup of raw piñons, a small diced onion, ⅛ teaspoon dried mint, and ⅛ teaspoon of black pepper, preferably freshly ground, to a simmer. Stirring occasionally, cook for half an hour over heat so low that only an occasional bubble dances to the surface. Then process in the blender until smooth. Either reheat for immediate use or refrigerate for serving cold. A palmful of minced chives scattered on just before bringing to the table helps bring out the savor.

APPLE

(Malus)

"The time for wild apples is the last of October and the first of November," averred an early expert on the subject, Henry David Thoreau. "They then get to be palatable, vivacious and inspiring, for they ripen late.

"To appreciate the wild and sharp flavors of these October fruits, it is necessary that you be breathing the sharp October or November air. The outdoor air and exercise which the walker gets give a different tone to his palate, and he craves a fruit which the sedentary would call harsh and crabbed.

"This noblest of fruits must be eaten in the fields, when your system is all aglow with exercise," Thoreau said, "when the frosty weather nips your fingers, the wind rattles the bare boughs or rustles the few remaining leaves, and the jay is heard screaming around. What is sour in the house a bracing walk makes sweet. Some of these apples might be labelled, 'To be eaten in the wind'."

Apples, natives of Asia and Europe, were not brought to Massachusetts until some nine years after the arrival of the Pilgrims, but they soon escaped into the wilderness. Nearly 200 years ago, the pioneer preacher named John Chapman, better known as Johnny Appleseed, traveled some 100,000 miles between Massachusetts and Missouri planting seeds and seedlings. Apples and crab apples *(Pyrus)* now grow wild in every state of the Union.

Most of these are only occasionally to be relished raw, although they cook up all the better for that. However, as Thoreau noted more than a

APPLE

century ago, "Who knows but this chance wild fruit, planted by a cow or a bird on some remote and rocky hillside, may be the choicest of its kind. It was thus the Porter and the Baldwin grow. Every wild apple shrub excites our expectation thus, somewhat as every wild child it is, perhaps, a prince in disguise."

Everyone knows the apple. Even though your yellow-green find may be little more than an inch in diameter, and hard and sour to boot, very few wild fruits are as quickly gathered, and their very tartness and firmness lend themselves to some of the finest apple dishes you have ever eaten. The flowers of the apple are perhaps the most beautiful of any tree.

The scent of both them and the later developing fruit has a piquancy unequaled in any costly perfume.

Deer, bears, raccoons, and foxes are among the wild animals who seek out apples. Apple buds are a favorite winter sustenance of the ruffed grouse. Pheasant, quail, and prairie chicken dine well on fruit, seeds, and buds.

The Iroquois, employing wild apples and maple syrup, made an applesauce that was all the more flavorsome because the fruit was used unpeeled. With the help of the kitchen blender, you can do an even smoother job of this today. Cut up the apples first, removing the cores. Barely cover with water, bring to a simmer, and cook with only an occasional bubble ascending to the top until the fruit is soft. Transfer at once to the blender, whirling it in this until nothing remains of the peel but the savor and color.

Then add sugar to taste, preferably stopping short of obliterating all the tartness. You may also like what a little cinnamon and lemon juice will do for applesauce. A bit of salt will help bring out the deliciousness, too. Much depends on the particular wild fruit. Many like this best when it is warm, perhaps with a splash of cream.

If you can beat the deer and other forest folk to them, you sometimes come upon wild apples plump and sweet enough for baking. Carefully cut out the cores. Arrange the fruit in a pan. Then fill each hollow as nearly as you can with 2 tablespoons brown sugar, a teaspoon butter or margarine, ⅛ teaspoon nutmeg, and a small pinch of salt. Pour ½ inch of boiling water into the bottom of the pan. Bake in a moderate 375-degree oven, frequently spooning the thickening syrup over the fruit, until a testing fork indicates that the apples are soft. This dish, best hot, calls for either fresh cream or liberal scoops of vanilla ice cream.

Another wild apple dessert that is good hot with cream, although in the woods evaporated milk chilled in a brook will do, is apple slump. This recipe is geared to 6 cups of wild apples, pared, cored, and thinly sliced. The amount of sugar will depend on the tartness of the particular fruit. Start with 1 cup of sugar, also adding a teaspoon of cinnamon and ½ cup of water. Bring to a simmer in a large saucepan with a tightly fitting cover. Now correct the sweetening.

Sift 2 cups of sifted all-purpose flour, 2½ teaspoons baking powder, 1 teaspoon sugar, and ½ teaspoon salt. Using a pastry blender or 2 knives, cut in ⅓ cup of shortening until the texture of the mixture is similar to that of coarse cornmeal. Using a fork, stir in enough milk bit by bit to make a soft dough. Drop this from a tablespoon atop the hot apples, cover tightly, and simmer over low heat without lifting the cover for a half-hour. You may occasionally like to vary this recipe by cutting ½ cup grated sharp American cheese into the flour mixture along with the shortening.

One way to appreciate wild apples with their, according to Thoreau, "wild flavors of the Muse," is in what back in New England natives used to call apple snow. Peel, core, and slice your apples. Simmer them in just enough water to cover until they are soft enough to press through a sieve. Sweeten them to taste with a minimum of white sugar and allow to cool. For each cup of apple, fold in a stiffly whipped egg white. Serve either with cream or whole milk.

For something special in the way of dessert, sift 2 cups of all-purpose flour into a mixing bowl. Press a hollow in the center and add a stick of melted butter or margarine, 2 egg yolks, 3 tablespoons sugar, and ⅛ teaspoon salt. Blend thoroughly, moistening with a little cold water if necessary. Then wad into a ball, wrap in foil or waxed paper or place in a covered bowl, and refrigerate for an hour.

In the meantime, chop 2½ cups pared and cored wild apples. Brown them in a frypan, along with ½ stick of butter or margarine, with ½ cup seedless raisins, 2 tablespoons heavy rum, 1 teaspoon cinnamon, and about a cup of sugar—however much the particular fruit needs.

Then roll out the dough very thinly. Cover it with the fruit and roll it up tightly. Brush it with melted butter or margarine, sprinkle lightly with sugar and cinnamon, place in a well-greased pan, and bake in a moderate 350-degree oven for about a half-hour or until the pastry is done. Cut into slices and, for a taste treat, serve with wild applesauce.

Wild apples really lend themselves to this sour cream pie. Make enough pastry for a 9-inch double-crust pie by sifting together 2 cups of all-purpose flour and a teaspoon of salt. Using a pastry blender or 2 knives, cut in ⅔ cup shortening until the mixture is the texture of large peas. Stir in about ⅓ cup cold water, a bit at a time, until you have a ball of dough. Lightly roll out half of this ⅛-inch thick and line a greased, deep pie pan with it. Slice ½ stick of butter or margarine over this pastry and scatter a tablespoon of sugar and a teaspoon of flour over it.

Core, pare, and chop enough wild apples to fill the pan, about 5 cups. Combine a cup of sugar, 1 teaspoon cinnamon, ¼ teaspoon each of ginger, nutmeg, and salt, and ⅛ teaspoon cloves. Flatten a layer of apples over the bottom, sprinkle with the sugar mixture, and repeat until everything is used. Pour a cup of sour cream over the mound of fruit. Top with ½-inch strips of crust, moistening the rim of the lower pastry with water and pressing the ribbons firmly to it. Slice the remaining ½ stick of butter or margarine over everything.

Bake in a preheated hot 450-degree oven for 10 minutes. Then lower the temperature to a moderate 350 degrees and continue cooking another half-hour or until the apples are tender and the crust is golden brown on top. For that extra touch, serve this with thin, freshly sliced cuts of sharp American cheese.

POPLAR

(Populus)

The poplar's sweetish, starchy sap layer is edible both raw and cooked. This lies between the wood of trunks, branches, and twigs and the outside bark, the latter being intensely bitter with salicin, which for some reason is relished by moose, beaver, and rabbit and is an ingredient in some tonics concocted for the benefit of mankind.

All three animals chaw poplar bark, and poplar trunks and branches are common in beaver dams and houses. Deer, elk, and mountain sheep browse on the twigs and foliage. Grouse, prairie chickens, and quail are among the game birds relying on buds, catkins, and seeds.

One of the most common trees on the continent, the life-giving poplar grows about as far north as any other on the great barrens of Canada. Cottonwoods as well as aspens are poplars. On the other hand, the so-called yellow poplar of the Southeast is not a poplar at all. In numerous northern areas, poplars quickly spring up in burns and clearings.

The poplars, members of the great willow family which has saved more than one man from starving, have alternate leaves with toothed and sometimes lobed edges. The stems are long and slender, occasionally being definitely flattened. The branches are characteristically brittle and, breaking easily from trunks and big limbs, make excellent firewood for lone campfires, burning with a clean, medicinal odor.

Pollen fills the wind when the flowers, growing in drooping spikelike clusters, appear in the first warm weather of spring before the light green leaves blaze forth, like pale green fire crowning the forest. The cottony aspect of the later splitting capsules of seeds, each with its long, fibrous hairs, has brought the name "cottonwood" to some species.

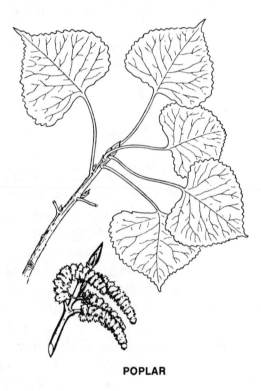

POPLAR

The soft formative tissue between wood and bark can be scraped off and eaten on the spot. One of the modern ways of obtaining such nourishment is in tea. It can also be cut into strips or chunks and cooked like noodles in soups and stews. Dried and powdered, it is a flour additive and substitute. No matter how it is eaten, however, it can by itself keep you going for weeks.

SLIPPERY ELM

(Ulmus)

Pour a cup of boiling water over a teaspoon of the shredded inner bark of the slippery elm. Cover and allow to steep until cool. Then add lemon juice and sugar to taste, and you'll have some of the famous slippery elm tea of pioneer days, still highly regarded as a spring tonic and as a plain pleasant drink in some parts of the country.

The slippery elm—also known as the red, gray, moose, and rock elm—abounds on bottomlands and on rich, rocky inclines in company

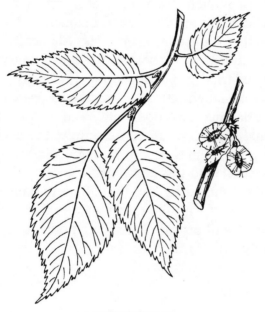

SLIPPERY ELM

with other hardwoods. A medium-sized tree, generally some forty to seventy feet tall with a trunk diameter from about one to three feet, it grows from Maine and southern Quebec to North Dakota, south to eastern Texas and northern Florida. Spreading branches provide broad, open, flattish crowns.

The sharply toothed leaves, scratchy above and downy beneath, grow on short, hairy, stout stems. Growing from woolly, egg-shaped,

179

blunt buds about one-quarter of an inch long, the leaves become unsymmetrical, four to eight inches long, and from two to three inches across the middle, where they are usually broadest. Dark green and dull, lighter on their under portions, they turn to beautiful masses of golden yellow in autumn. The bark is either grayish or dark reddish brown, becoming divided by shallow fissures and mottled by large, loose scales. The hairy twigs, incidentally, turn out to be mucilaginous when chewed.

The inner bark of branches, trunk, and root is extremely mucilaginous. Thick and fragrant, it is still widely gathered in the spring, when because of the rising sap, trees peel more readily. This whitish inner bark is then dried as in a garret or a warm, half-open oven, then powdered as in the kitchen blender. It has demulcent and emollient, as well as nutritive, properties. Medically, it is still sometimes used for dysentery, diseases of the urinary passeges, and bronchitis. For external application, the finely ground or powdered bark is mixed with enough hot water to make a pasty mass and used as a poultice for inflammations, boils, etc., and also in the form of both rectal and vaginal suppositories. More simply, the tea described in the first paragraph is sometimes used for coughs due to colds, one or two cupfuls a day, several cold sips at a time.

Many boys chew this intriguing bark. The Indians used it for food, some of them boiling it with the tallow they rendered from buffalo fat. In an emergency, it will provide life-saving nourishment today, and not at all unpleasantly, either raw or boiled.

ACORNS

(Quercus)

There is no need for anyone to starve where acorns abound, and from 200 to 500 oaks (botanists differ) grow in the world. Some eighty-five of these are native to the United States. Although some of the latter species are scrubby, the genus includes some of our biggest and most stately trees. Furthermore, except in our northern prairies, oaks are widely distributed throughout the contiguous states, thriving at various altitudes and in numerous types of soil.

Abundant and substantial, acorns are perhaps this country's most important wildlife food. The relatively tiny acorns of the willow oak, pin oak, and water oak are often obtainable near streams and ponds, where they are relished by mallards, wood ducks, pintails, and other waterfowl. Quail devour such small acorns and peck the kernels out of the larger nuts.

Pheasants, grouse, pigeons, doves, and prairie chickens enjoy the nuts as well as the buds. Wild turkeys gulp down whole acorns regardless of their size. Squirrels and chipmunks are among the smaller animals storing acorns for off-season use. Black-tailed mule and white-tailed deer, elk, peccaries, and mountain sheep enjoy the acorns and also browse on twigs and foliage. Black bears grow fat on acorns.

Acorns probably rated the top position on the long list of wild foods depended on by the Indians. It has been stated, for example, that acorn soup, or mush, was the chief daily food of more than three-quarters of the native Californians. The eastern settlers were early introduced to acorns, too. In 1620 during their first hungry winter in Plymouth, the Pilgrims were fortunate enough to discover baskets of roasted acorns which the Indians had buried in the ground. In parts of Mexico and in Europe, the natives today still use acorns in the old ways.

All acorns are good to eat. Some are less sweet than others, that's all. But the bitterness that is prevalent in different degrees is due to tannin, the same ingredient that causes tea to be bitter. Although it is not digestible in large amounts, it is soluble in water. Therefore, even the bitterest acorns can be made edible in an emergency.

Oaks comprise the most important group of hardwood timber trees on this continent. A major proportion of our eastern forests is oak. Its dense, durable wood has many commercial uses. Furthermore, oaks are among the most popular shade trees along our streets and about our dwellings.

The oaks may be separated into two great groups: the white oaks and the red oaks. The acorns of the former are the sweet ones. They mature in one growing season. The inner surfaces of the shells are smooth. The leaves typically have rounded lobes, but they are never bristle-tipped. The bark is ordinarily grayish and is generally scaly.

Among the red oaks, the usually bitter acorns do not mature until the end of the second growing season. The inner surfaces of the shells are customarily coated with woolly hair. The leaves have distinct bristles at their tips or at the tops of their lobes. The typically dark bark is ordinarily furrowed.

Indians used acorns both by themselves and in combination with other foods. For example, the Digger Indians roasted their acorns from the western white oak, *Quercus lobata,* hulled them, and ground them into a coarse meal which they formed into cakes and baked in crude ovens. In the East, the acorns of the white oak, *Quercus alba,* were also ground into meal but then were often mixed with the available cornmeal before being shaped into cakes and baked. Roasted and ground white oak acorns provide one of the wilderness coffees.

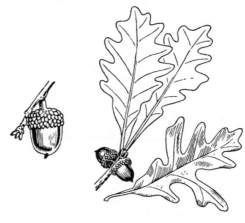

EASTERN WHITE OAK

Indians leached their bitter acorns in a number of ways. Sometimes the acorns would be buried in swamp mud for a year, after which they would be ready for roasting and eating whole. Other tribes let their shelled acorns mold in baskets, then buried them in clean freshwater sand. When they had turned black, they were sweet and ready for use.

Some tribes ground their acorns by pounding them in stone pestles, many of which are found today, and then ran water through the meal by one method or another for often the greater part of a day until it was sweet. The meal might be placed in a specially woven basket for this purpose, or it might just be buried in the sandy bed of a stream.

To make the familiar, somewhat sweetish soup or gruel of the results, all that is necessary is to heat the meal in water. The Indians generally used no seasoning. As a matter of fact, until the white man came they ordinarily had no utensils but closely woven baskets. These were flammable, of course, and the heating had to be done by putting in rocks heated in campfires. Still showing how little one can get along with, the tribe then ate from common baskets, using their fingers.

It's an easy thing to leach acorns today. Just shell your nuts and boil them whole in a kettle of water, changing the liquid every time it becomes yellowish. You can shorten the time necessary for this to as little as a couple of hours, depending of course on the particular acorns, if you keep a teakettle of water always heating on the stove while this process is continuing. The acorns can then be dried in a slow oven, with the door left ajar, and either eaten as is or ground into coarse bits for use like any other nuts or into a fine meal.

To make acorn cakes, mix 2 cups of the meal with ½ teaspoon salt and ¾ cup of water to form a stiff batter. This will be improved if you let it stand at room temperature for about an hour before turning it into the skillet.

Heat 3 tablespoons cooking oil in a large frypan until a test drop of water will sizzle. Drop the batter from a tablespoon, using a greased spatula to shape cakes a bit over 3 inches in diameter. Reduce the heat and tan the cakes slowly on each side. They are good either hot or cold.

For acorn pancakes for two, combine a cup of acorn meal and a cup of regular flour with 2 tablespoons sugar, 3 teaspoons double-action baking powder, and ½ teaspoon salt. Beat 2 eggs, 1½ cups milk, and 2 tablespoons liquid shortening. Get your preferably heavy frypan or griddle hot, short of smoking temperature, and grease it sparingly with bacon.

When everything is ready to go, mix the whole business very briefly into a thin batter. Overmixing will make these tough. For this reason, a slightly lumpy batter is preferable to one that's beaten smooth. Turn each hotcake only once, when the flapjack starts showing small bubbles. The second side will take only half as long to cook. Serve steaming hot with butter or margarine and sugar, maple syrup, or one of the wild jellies.

We think of antibiotics as modern developments, but some of the Indian tribes used to let their acorn meal accumulate a mold. This was scraped off, kept in a damp place, and used to treat sores and inflammations.

MAPLE

(Acer)

The maple leaf, emblem of Canada and a principal reason why northern New England is so colorful in the autumn—especially when frost-hazed nights are succeeded by brisk, smoky days—is known to everyone. The fruits, too, are very characteristic, being made up of a pair of brown wings with the seeds enclosed in the plump juncture.

Maple seeds are edible by humans, some Indians formerly hulling the larger of them and then boiling them. So are the leaves. The inner bark of the maple is one of the more appetizing sap layers and is eaten in emergencies, either raw or cooked. But it is for the sap that the tree has been famous since Indian days.

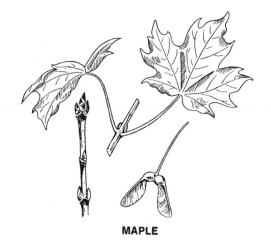

MAPLE

Wild turkeys, quail, grouse, and prairie chickens eat maple buds, twigs, and seeds. Black bears, rabbits, beavers, and squirrels dine on flowers, seeds, bark, and twigs. Incidentally, before they store the seeds for winter use, squirrels often thriftily remove the hulls and wings. Deer, moose, elk, and mountain sheep relish twigs and foliage.

The first settlers to venture along the Atlantic seaboard were introduced to the wild sweet by the red men, who caught the sap in birch-bark containers and in tightly woven baskets and skin vessels. All the maples have sugar-rich sap. So do other trees, for that matter, such as the birch and hickory. But it is the sugar maple, *Acer saccharum,* that is by far the most famous for this characteristic. Incidentally, the tree is perhaps the most prized of the hardwoods in the lumber industry. It is also a highly desirable shade and ornamental tree, so perhaps you have your own private source of maple sugar growing right by your own home.

Groves of maple trees, with the rude sugar houses, are familiar land-marks in many parts of the country, inasmuch as the sugar maple grows from Newfoundland to Ontario and Minnesota, southward as far as Louisiana and Georgia. The trees, often reaching a height of from sixty to almost a hundred feet, are tapped in late winter or early spring, before the buds begin to expand. Sharp frosty nights, followed by mild thawing during the daylight hours, make for the free flow of sap. The sweetness of this varies, but it usually takes between thirty and forty gallons to boil down into a gallon of the high-priced syrup.

Additional boiling makes maple sugar. During early American years, this was about the consistency of present-day brown sugar. In fact, it was used in place of cane sugar by colonists who couldn't afford the then much more expensive sweetening, even when it was available. Maple sugar is still more nourishing than the mass manufactured product, containing the B vitamins, calcium, phosphorus, and enzymes refined from today's sugar beets and sugar cane.

You can buy the necessary spiles and pails for sap gathering. Unless you are going in for sugaring in a big way, though, you can do very well on your own. The Indians used to cut a "V"-shaped gash in the tree, at the apex of which they drove an elderberry spout. The latter was made by cutting straight elderberry limbs in the spring, drying them with the leaves on, and then poking out the soft pith of their interiors with hot sticks.

You may find it more conservative to drill about a two-inch-deep hole with a gimlet, or brace and bit, and to close this with a peg when you're finished. For the spout, just make a single bend in a can top cut off by one of the smooth-cutting openers. Don't try to suspend the pail from this, however. Instead, drive a nail into the tree for this purpose. As a precaution, empty the containers often enough so that the sap doesn't hang too long in the sun and sour.

Then it's just a matter of boiling the sap, and spooning off the characteristic scum as it rises, until some thirty-five or so parts of water evaporate, leaving a clear amber syrup. This you'll want to strain very carefully. Or, for sugar, you'll wish to continue boiling until a test portion of the syrup forms a very soft ball in cold water. Then remove from the fire, beat with an egg beater if you're making only a small amount or a regular sugar beater if you have a large quantity, and pour into dry molds.

One's first sugaring-off party is in the same category as that initial seashore clambake—unforgettable! I remember as a small boy riding out to a hillside maple bush behind two glistening horses in a pung. Syrup was already bubbling in the sugar house with an elusive and marvelous odor, and they gave me a small pitcher of it and an old fork.

Everything must have been ready, for when I strung this amber liquid out in a fine line of fresh snow, it hardened. Even before it was cool enough, I twined the string on my fork and transferred it gingerly to my mouth. This I repeated until all the syrup was gone, and then I got some more. The flavor was indescribable, except that there was the aroma of the forest in its sweetness—the fresh wind blowing, the branches swinging overhead, and all the free, rich wildness of the mountains themselves.

You'll get snow in your boots at a sugaring-off party and there'll be an occasional bit of bark in your sweet. But you won't give either a second thought. It's worth it a dozen times over.

The Indians used to blend their maple syrup and maize, and the marriage is still a happy one. For steaming chunks of maple corn bread, broken from a hot loaf, sift together a cup of all-purpose flour, a cup of cornmeal, 4 teaspoons baking powder, and a teaspoon salt. Stir together 2 beaten eggs, ½ cup melted shortening, and ⅓ cup maple syrup. Now blend the two mixtures as thoroughly and quickly as possible. Pour without delay into a greased pan and bake in a preheated very hot 450-degree oven for about 20 minutes or until a straw inserted in the loaf comes out clean.

Or maybe you'd like some maple muffins. Beat an egg with ¼ cup of milk. Sift together 1¾ cups of all-purpose flour, 3 teaspoons of baking powder, and ¼ teaspoon of salt. Stir into the milk mixture, along with ½ cup of maple syrup, a bit at a time. Then fold in ½ stick melted butter or margarine. Bake in a warmed, greased muffin pan in a preheated moderate 350-degree oven for about 20 minutes or until done.

Maple buns are another possibility. Sift together 2 cups all-purpose flour, 3 teaspoons baking powder, and 1 teaspoon salt. Cut in ½ cup of shortening until everything has the texture of rough cornmeal. Then, taking a fork, stir the mixture gently but quickly into a soft dough with about ⅔ cup milk. Have a muffin pan well greased and each container holding a tablespoon of maple syrup, a scant tablespoon of slivered almonds, and ⅛ teaspoon melted butter or margarine. Fill each ¾ full of dough. Put at once into a preheated hot 425-degree oven and bake about 15 minutes or until golden.

For about 2 dozen maple rolls, sift together 2½ cups all-purpose flour, ¼ cup baking powder, and a teaspoon of salt. Cut in ½ stick of butter or margarine until the mixture is the consistency of cornmeal. Beat an egg and a cup of milk and blend. Knead very briefly, then roll out into a ¼-inch-thick rectangle. Brush with melted butter or margarine and dust with finely crumbled maple sugar. Roll, cut into 1-inch slices, place apart in a greased baking pan, brush again with melted butter or margarine, and bake in a preheated very hot 450-degree oven for about 12 minutes or until golden brown.

Then there is the dessert based on biscuits. Sift together 2 cups all-purpose flour, 2 teaspoons baking powder, ½ teaspoon salt, and ¼ teaspoon cream of tartar. Cut in ¼ cup shortening Add enough milk, about ½ cup, to make a soft dough. Roll this out about ½-inch thick and cut a dozen small biscuits. Place these in a shallow greased pan and top each with several chips of butter or margarine and a slight dusting of cinnamon. Have a cup of maple syrup bubbling on top of the stove. Pour this now over the biscuits. Place at once in a preheated hot 425-degree oven and bake 15 minutes or until done. Serve hot with either whipped cream or with scoops of butter pecan ice cream.

Occasions when you're not hungry enough for any of the above, appetite-stimulating maple toast smells almost as good as it tastes. You can use a toaster if it browns one side of the bread at a time. After the first side is tanned, butter the second, strew it with soft maple sugar, dust with cinnamon, and return it to the heat until the sugar has melted. Otherwise, use the oven.

For a maple sauce with which to top squash, apple, pumpkin, and blueberry desserts, whip a cup of heavy cream into soft peaks. Then tip ¼ cup of maple syrup across the top and carefully fold it in. Season with a scattering of grated nutmeg.

Another maple sauce, one many especially like when it is spreading over hot cereal, is made by crumbling ½ pound of maple sugar, stirring in 3 tablespoons boiling water, and heating at a bubble until all the sugar is dissolved. Add a sprinkle of nutmeg. Then remove from the stove and mix in a stick of butter or margarine.

Maple syrup and cream is always a felicitous combination. Boil a cup of heavy cream with a cup of maple syrup until a sample forms a very soft ball in cold water. Then whip with an eggbeater for 2 minutes. If you are going to use this atop vanilla ice cream, you may like to stir in ⅓ cup of chopped walnuts or pecans.

Or for a simple and delicately flavored candy, boil 2 cups of maple syrup, a cup of whipping cream, and ⅛ teaspoon of salt until a thread forms when a bit is dribbled off the tip of a spoon. Then cool and beat until dense and creamy. Drop the individual candies from a spoon onto waxed paper.

You can make enough frosting for, say, an 8-inch layer cake with either maple sugar or maple syrup. For the first, heat and stir 2 cups maple sugar and a cup of light cream until a test portion forms a soft ball in cold water. Remove from the stove, cool a bit, and then work with an eggbeater until creamy.

For the second, boil 2 cups of maple syrup without stirring until a test portion runs off the tip of a spoon in a long thread. Then pour gradually over 3 stiffly beaten egg whites. Beat until thick enough to apply with a knife. If you want, ½ cup of chopped nuts can be added during the last stage to either of these frostings. Walnuts, pecans, and toasted almonds are tasty. For a real taste thrill, though, try piñons.

For some memorable cookies, sift together 2 cups of all-purpose flour, 2 teaspoons baking powder, and ¼ teaspoon salt. Cream a cup of finely crushed maple sugar with ½ cup of shortening. Beat an egg with ¼ cup of milk. Now mix everything into a dough, ball this, either wrap in waxed paper or foil or place in a covered bowl, and leave in the refrigerator overnight.

The next day preheat the oven to a moderate 375 degrees. Roll the dough out very thin on a floured board, rectangle of plastic, or pastry cloth. Cut and bake on a sparingly greased cooky sheet for 8 to 10 minutes or until lightly browned. These will be dainty and crisp.

If you like ham, you owe it to yourself to bake at least one with maple syrup. First, try a slice an inch thick, parboiled to freshen it. Stud this with cloves and place in a casserole. Mix a cup of maple syrup with 2 tablespoons cider vinegar and 2 teaspoons dry mustard. Pour this over the meat and bake in a moderate 375-degree oven for 45 minutes, occasionally basting with the sauce. Delectable!

*a pantryful
of jellies, desserts,
and seasonings*

Food That
Grows on Shrubs

AS A SOURCE of nutritious food and distinctive seasonings, shrubs are incredibly versatile. Do you want jelly? Then choose from wild plum, hawthorn, and barberry. Are you in the mood for tea? Then try the refreshing beverage made from the sprigs of juniper. Do your soups and stews need a dash of extra savor? Nothing can take the place of the flavor which the leaves of the bayberry add to such dishes.

When it comes to desserts, shrubs really excel. Anyone with a yen for mouth-watering pastry can do no better than sample the taste-tingling delights of wild plum rolls, tarts, and pies, or the zesty tang of barberry tarts. For a really special dessert, try plum graham pudding topped with whipped buffalo berries.

Besides stocking your pantry, shrubs can also help fill your medicine chest. As the Indians and pioneers discovered, a diuretic can be made from juniper berries, a laxative from barberry roots, and a remedy for diarrhea from bayberry roots.

Learning to recognize the shrubs pictured and described below will not only furnish delicacies for the table but will also provide survival insurance for an emergency.

WILD PLUM

(Prunus)

Some fifteen species of wild plums abound throughout the United States and southern Canada, growing from Alaska and California to the Great Lakes and the eastern seaboard, where the fragrant white flowers of the prolific beach plum brighten the springtimes. They are close cousins botanically of the wild cherries, considered at length in Part I.

Wildlife does not use the plum so freely, however, foxes being the most avid diners. On the other hand, scattered thickets afford invaluable shelter for birds and small game. The fruit varies considerably, some of it being delicious straight off the twigs. The chief value of much of the rest is in incomparable jellies, jams, and other kitchen delights.

The beach plum, *Prunus maritime,* is a wild native plum which grows in abundance along the beaches, among the sand dunes, and on the coastal plains from Nova Scotia and New Brunswick to Virginia and inland, as around the Great Lakes. It is very abundant in Massachusetts, on Cape Cod and on the islands of Martha's Vineyard and Nantucket.

Growth and fruiting habits of the beach plum vary, a common trait in seedling plants. It resembles a bush more often than a tree. Some bushes sucker freely from the roots and produce dense thickets. The root systems are coarse, rangy, and deep, as necessitated by the usual bleak and dry habitat.

The fruit, which generally varies between one-half inch and one inch in diameter, varies in color from red through purple to blue and almost black. Yellow-fruited bushes are occasionally found. The natural home of the beach plum is in sandy, light soils or even the pure sand of wind-sculptured dunes. Most beach plums bloom profusely each year but sport a crop only once every three or four years. One reason for this is that they depend on cross-pollination. The weather, which is often very foggy or rainy, dark, cold, and windy during blooming, may greatly reduce or even stop insect flight so that there is no transfer of pollen among the self-sterile plants. Too, it may slow the growth of the pollen tubes so that fertilization fails.

Specifically, the beach plum is a sprawling shrub up to about six feet in height. In does not have thorns, although the oval leaves are sharp with sawtooth edges. The innumerable white flowers burst out before

BEACH PLUM

the leaves start to appear. The fruit, which occupies many thrifty families day after day and finds its way into stores, ripens during the sweltering weather of August and September.

Another wild plum that is often seen in country markets is the *Prunus americana,* a great favorite among the Indians, and a native from Montana to New England, south to New Mexico, Texas, and Florida. Its numerous branches, whose twigs are thornlike, have rough, thick barbs. The oval or oblong leaves, ending in long, tapering points, are sharply saw-toothed like those of the beach plum. The frail white blossoms, again appearing before the leaves in early springtime, are extremely redolent. The red and sometimes yellow plums, appearing in late summer, are about seven-eighths of an inch in diameter, tough-skinned, pulpy, and usually sweet.

In northern California and southern Oregon many families make annual pilgrimages to wild plum orchards in and around the mountains and bring back luscious bushels of richly mottled yellow, red, and purple fruit, especially in the northern part of the range. Here the trees and shrubs are from three to ten feet tall, with ash-gray bark and occasionally spiny branches. The flowers, again appearing before the leaves from March to May, are white, fading to rose. By August and September, the branches are often loaded with the handsome fruit, its colors duplicated in the brilliant autumn foliage.

Here is a way to preserve wild plums that does away with the bitterish taste often found in such cooked fruit. Wash the plums and prick the skins with a sharp fork. Pack in hot, sterilized jars and cover with boiling water. Seal and process for 20 minutes in a boiling-water bath. Then cool, label, and store. When you open a jar, pour off the juice for jelly or punch. Pit the fruit and for each quart of plums mix a cup of sugar with a cup of cold water. Pour this over the plums and let stand half an hour. Then enjoy them whatever way your fancy of the moment dictates.

Such canned plums can be used during the winter to make some delectable rolls. For enough for four, you'll need a pint of the wild fruit. Drain the plums well, transferring the juice to a baking pan. Pit them and chop them into small segments. To the juice in the pan add 2 tablespoons sugar, a tablespoon of butter or margarine, and ¼ teaspoon of powdered ginger. Bring to a boil.

In the meantime, sift together a cup of all-purpose flour, a tablespoon of sugar, 2 teaspoons of baking powder, and ¼ teaspoon of salt. Cut 2 tablespoons of butter or margarine into the dry mixture. Beat an egg with ¼ cup milk and ⅛ teaspoon almond extract and combine with the pastry to make a soft dough. Roll this ½-inch thick. Spread with the chopped wild plums, roll up, slice crosswise into 2-inch lengths, and place carefully in the hot syrup. Bake in a moderate 375-degree oven for about half an hour or until the rolls are done. Vanilla ice cream really touches up the individual servings, especially if you enjoy them hot.

The sharpness and tartness of wild plum compote make it ideal with game. For this recipe, pit a quart of fully ripe plums and cut them into small pieces. Grate the rind from 2 lemons and an orange. Squeeze the juice. Combine plums, rind, juice, 3 cups sugar, a cup of seeded raisins, and ½ cup good sherry. Bring to a bubble in a saucepan and, stirring frequently, simmer until thick. Spoon into hot sterilized jars and seal.

Along Cape Cod there are so many dozens of home stands selling wild plum jelly that many start to enjoy this at an early age. There are two secrets of making this delicacy successfully. First, pick the plums while they are still on the unripe side. Second, unless you have special equipment, make only small batches at a time, about three quarts at once being plenty.

Pick over and wash the plums. Barely cover them with water and bring this to a boil. Then drain, cover with boiling water, and cook about 10 minutes or until soft, mashing and stirring every few minutes. Squeeze either through a sieve or a jelly bag. Measure the juice and return to the kettle. Slowly add an equal volume of sugar, all the time stirring. Boil rapidly until 2 drops form on the edge of a metal spoon, then come together to run off in a sheet. This occurs at 220 to 222 degrees.

Pour to within ¼ inch of the tops of hot sterilized glasses. Have paraffin melting over water, and tip a thin layer atop each nearly filled glass, turning and slightly tilting the container so that the edges will be sealed. Cool, add a second thin layer of wax, cool, cover with a lid or aluminum foil, and store in a dark, cool, dry place. This is excellent with game, lamb, poultry, and especially with rare roast beef.

You may also care to experiment by combining plum juice with other wild juices to make your own blend of wild jelly. A particularly successful combination can be achieved by mixing every ⅔ cup of wild plum juice with ⅓ cup of wild apple juice, then proceeding as above to prepare your jelly.

Wild plum jam is also good. Wash and pit a quart of ripe plums, keeping the fruit as intact as feasible. Put in a large saucepan, along with ½ cup of water, and bring to a bubble. Gradually mix in 4 cups of sugar, all the time stirring. Simmer for 15 minutes or until thick, stirring whenever necessary to prevent sticking. Remove the froth.

Spoon into hot, sterilized glasses. Seal immediately with paraffin. Cover to protect from drafts, which might break the glass, and leave to cool. Label and store in dry, cool darkness. Incidentally, any wild jams or jellies that are to be kept in a damp place, or mailed, should be put instead into vacuum-sealed or screw-topped jars.

Jam and tarts go together. To make enough of the latter for four, cream together a stick of butter or margarine and a 3-ounce package of cream cheese. Using 2 knives or a pastry blender, cut this into a cup of flour, ⅛ teaspoon salt, and a scant ⅛ teaspoon powdered ginger. Chill in the refrigerator. Then roll out in a thin sheet.

Cut into ovals with a glass, knife, or 3-inch cooky cutter. Place on a greased low pan or baking sheet. Bake in a hot 425-degree oven for 15 minutes. Then remove, make a concavity in the centers with the back of a spoon, place a spoonful of your plum jam in each hollow, dust with grated orange peel, and eat hot. These are rich but utterly delicious.

Wild plum pies are apt to be a bit on the tart side, and some like to combine the sliced and pitted fruit with an equal volume of peeled, sliced, and pitted peaches. Fill your uncooked pie shell with the fruit. Mix 1½ cups sugar, ¼ cup cornstarch, and ⅛ teaspoon salt and sprinkle over the fruit. Dust with a teaspoon of grated orange rind and dot with 2 tablespoons of chipped butter or margarine. Spread on a lattice top. Bake in a hot 425-degree oven for about an hour. Try this warm sometime with melting pecan ice cream.

Also sweet and odorous when served hot with ice cream, especially vanilla, is plum graham pudding. For enough for four, you'll need 2 cups of pitted, sliced plums. Mix 2 cups graham cracker crumbs, ½ cup sugar, ½ stick melted butter or margarine, ¼ cup chopped walnuts, ¼ cup cold water, 2 tablespoons grated orange rind, ½ teaspoon nutmeg, ½ teaspoon cinnamon, and ¼ teaspoon allspice. Starting with the crumb mixture and ending with the fruit, place alternate layers into 4 small baking dishes. Bake in a moderate 350-degree oven for a half-hour, if possible arranging for the pudding to come out just when everyone is ready for dessert.

Wild plums, wild rice, and venison—all tasting the same now as they did when man first ventured on this continent—make a rugged, straightforward meal.

Let the venison come to room temperature before consigning it to a slow 300-degree oven for 12 minutes a pound. Lay strips of beef fat over the roast. Baste it every 15 minutes after the first hour, employing a bulb-type baster. For the last half-hour of cooking, add a cup of washed whole plums and ½ cup of water.

When you've finally removed the meat to a hot platter and salted it, press what remains in the pan through a sieve to get a rich sauce which should then be seasoned to taste with salt and pepper and sweetened a bit with brown sugar if this last seems advisable. Bring to a simmer and serve over the sliced rare venison and steaming wild rice.

You can also use wild plums to mellow gin, a process favored by some of the colonists because it thriftily stretched available supplies of the ardent spirit. Wash 3 cups of wild plums, puncture each in a half-dozen places with a fork, and place them in a large jar with a closely fitting top. Add ¾ cup of sugar and a quart of gin. Cover tightly and place in a cool, dark spot for two months, shaking the contents weekly.

At the end of that time, press the mixture through a sieve, return the sieved portion to the jar, cover again, and leave to clear. Then carefully pour or siphon the clear liquid in equal amounts into 2 quart bottles. Fill each nearly to the top with cooled water that has been boiled for 5 minutes if at sea level, and an additional minute for every extra 1,000 feet of elevation. Shake thoroughly, seal, and allow to mature for at least 5 weeks.

JUNIPER

(Juniperus)

Black bear, quail, and band-tailed pigeon are among the game dining on the fruit of the juniper. These evergreen shrubs and shrubby trees with their compact branches, thin shreddy bark, and scalelike leaves pressed closely to the twigs grow from Alaska to Labrador, south as far as New Mexico and California. The usually sprawling evergreens prefer exposed dry slopes and rocky ridges, and many a hunter has lounged in them to glass the country or to watch a game trail. The not unpleasant sharpness of some of their short needles makes one feel warmer on a brisk day.

The fruit, whose flavor and aroma is familiar to anyone who has had contact with gin, is dark blue and has a bloom to it. Growing in large numbers on the shoots of the female shrubs, these berries are to be found the year around. They are the size of peas. The flesh surrounding the large seed is sweetish and resinously aromatic.

Indians used to dry and grind juniper berries and use them for cakes and for mush. The principal individual use today is as a nibble and as a

JUNIPER

woodsy seasoning. A few will take the edge off hunger. Too many, though, are irritating to the kidneys. In fact, a diuretic is made of the berries, a teaspoon of them to a cup of boiling water, drunk cold, a large mouthful at a time, one or two cups a day.

Juniper tea, quaffed in small amounts, is one of the decidedly pleasant evergreen beverages. Add about a dozen young berryless sprigs to a quart of cold water. Bring this to a boil, cover, reduce the heat, and allow to simmer for 10 minutes. Strain and serve like regular tea.

HAWTHORN

(Crataegus)

It is fortunate that it's easy to distinguish the hawthorn from other shrubs and small trees. Even the professionals find it difficult to identify the separate species, the number of which in the United States is estimated to run all the way from about 100 to as high as 1,200. They grow from one coast to the other, making them valuable when survival is a problem. Taste varies considerably, and the only way to determine the edibility of hawthorn you've come across is by sampling. The better of them are delicious raw and when turned into jelly require very little sugar.

These cousins of the domestic apple are also known as thorn apples, thorn plums, thorns, mayhaws, red haws, scarlet haws, haws, cockspur thorn, etc. Wood ducks eat the fruit. Pheasants, grouse, pigeons, and turkeys relish both buds and fruit. Black bears, rabbits, beavers, raccoons, and squirrels include both fruit and bark in their diets. Deer browse on the foliage and the apple-like pomes. In addition to all this, hawthorns provide almost impregnable nesting places.

You can readily identify a hawthorn even in winter, particularly as the long, sharp, usually straight, occasionally slightly curved thorns, ranging in length up to about five inches, are not shared by any of our other native trees and shrubs.

Showy when blossoming in the spring and attractive when colorful with fruit, especially against the snow, hawthorns thrive in sunny

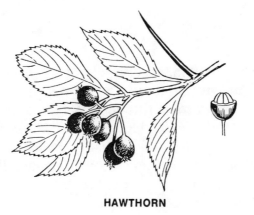

HAWTHORN

locales in clearings, pastures, abandoned fields, and along roads and fences. The white and occasionally pinkish flowers, which have five petals, grow in terminal clusters. The fruit, which is usually red but sometimes greenish or yellowish, looks like tiny apples. Each contains one to five bony, one-seeded nutlets.

The part of the fruit that isn't seed is somewhat dry, and you'll need a lot of it, but the jelly made from hawthorns is golden and intriguing. Cover the berries with water and simmer them until they are soft, stirring them occasionally to prevent their sticking. Add more hot water if they start to run dry. Then put the results in a jelly bag, squeezing this to get out the last drop of juice. Depending on the particular fruit, it will take about 2 pounds of the berries to make the following recipe.

Stir a package of pectin into 4 cups of the juice. Continuing to stir, bring to a boil over high heat. Add 6 cups of sugar and stirring, bring to a full rolling boil for 2 minutes. Then remove from the heat, skim off the foam, and pour to within ¼ inch of the tops of hot, sterilized jelly glasses that are standing on a towel away from drafts. Seal with a thin layer of melted paraffin, carefully tilting each of the glasses so that this will adhere evenly to the sides. When it has cooled, add a second coating. Cool gradually, cover with regular caps or with aluminum foil, label, and store in a cool, dry place.

HACKBERRY

(Celtis)

Homer asserted that the thin, sugary pulp of the hackberry proved so delectable to the ancients that those who ate it forgot their native countries. Eight of the world's some fifty to seventy-five species (depending on the botanist) are native to the United States. These trees and shrubs range over a large proportion of the nation in habitats varying from wet, swampy spots and stream banks to rich, rocky hillsides and hardwood forests. They are frequently planted for shade and decoration. The local name of sugarberry recognizes the pleasant, wholesome sweetness of the fruit.

Wildlife feasts on the fruit of the hackberry, also known as the nettle tree and as the hoop ash. Cedar waxwings flit among the branches as long as the last frost-sweetened drupe remains. Such upland game birds as quail, turkeys, pigeons, and doves become more palatable on a similar diet. So do beavers, opossums, raccoons, and squirrels. Both mule and white-tailed deer browse on the twigs and foliage.

Even the botanist has considerable trouble in distinguishing all the species of the hackberry. Generally they are shrubs or small trees with alternate leaves, typically lopsided at the base. Three prominent veins rise from the top of the short stem. So-called witches'-broom, dense clusters of small twigs, frequently appear in the hackberry, also commonly distinguished by warty outgrowths of a corky nature on the bark.

The flowers, small and inconspicuous, blossom out in the junction between the leaf stalk and the branch at the same time the leaves are developing in the spring. These flowers are followed by berries that are actually drupes; each drupe consists of a sweet, thin pulp covering a large, round seed. About the size of peas, these drupes vary in color from orange-red and yellowish to dark purple.

Ripening in September or October but often persisting on the

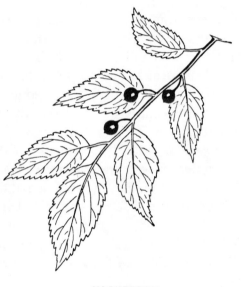

HACKBERRY

branches until well into winter and becoming even more sweet with cold weather, hackberries, although dry, will pleasantly take the edge off hunger. They are an important survival food.

Some Indians, after feasting on the pulp, used to dry the large pits and pound them into fine bits for seasoning meats. The soft white kernels, exposed by cracking the outer shell, are sweet and somewhat datelike in flavor.

BARBERRY

(Berberis)

Depending on which botanist is doing the defining, there are some fifteen species of barberry in this country. These shrubs, common along many a road, generally grow in well-drained upland areas. Deer eat them, despite the thorns of some, and so do elk and mountain sheep. Rabbits and their cousins, the varying hares, nibble on bark, leaves, and twigs. Ruffed grouse and ring-necked pheasants are among the birds devouring the berries.

Barberries, which grow from one coast to the other, become fragrant masses of yellow flowers in the spring, glossy rich green expanses in the summer, and brilliant crimsons and bronzes during the crisp weather of autumn. Berries range from orangy and scarlet to the fine blue of the so-called Oregon grape. In the Southwest, you can sometimes find at little roadside shops neck crosses simply made of the distinctively beautiful yellow wood of the barberry.

The leaves of the *Berberis vulgaris,* a typical barberry shrub, grow, often in clusters, on slender, curved gray branches. Ranging from about an inch to an inch and a half long, they are rounded at their tops and narrowing at the bases. They have stiff, coarse hairs and are toothed around the edges. Triple-tipped spines appear in place of leaves on some of the younger shoots. The quarter-inch flowers, growing in drooping, elongated clusters like those of the lily of the valley, give way to dense, acid fruit.

Both the Indians and the early settlers dried the fruit for winter use, made an agreeably cooling drink from it, and turned much of it into pleasantly tart sauces and preserves. The jelly closely rivals that of the highbush cranberry (see Part I), which to many palates is the best made. Too, housewives used to add the berries to sweeter, blander fruits to give them character.

The tough, hard roots of the barberry were crushed and boiled to make a bright yellow dye for baskets, fabrics, and buckskins. The stems and bark were also sometimes used for this purpose. The Karok Indians pounded the blue fruit of the Oregon grape with other ingredients to make a paint for embellishing their bows and arrows.

The bitter root of the barberry was also used as a tonic and laxative. One of the earlier purgatives of this continent was a teaspoonful of the powdered bark of the root in a glass of water. Taken in small amounts during the day, this concoction was also held to be a tonic and blood purifier. Externally, it was employed as a lotion to treat various skin diseases.

The Indians used to chew the root and use the resulting liquid for wounds. The roots are too bitter for many who nevertheless find that chewing a couple of the pleasantly acid leaves is refreshing when they're

BARBERRY

thirsty and no water is handy. The Indians used to steep these leaves and drink the tea for rheumatism.

You can make straight barberry jelly, extracting the juice from the cooked berries with the help of a jelly bag and then boiling it until it runs from the tip of a spoon in a sheet or your jelly thermometer reads 220 to 222 degrees. This jelly requires no pectin.

Years when the barberry crop is sparse, you may have to add water to the berries when first softening them by cooking. Then if you add apples to make the extraction jell, you may like the results even better. Today, where used, barberry-apple jelly is one of the favorites with game.

To make it, pick over and wash 4 cups of wild barberries. Quarter 4 tart apples, leaving cores and skins but removing the stems and blossom ends. Simmer the berries and apples, along with 3 cups of water, until everything is soft. Then move to a jelly bag. If you do not squeeze this, you'll have a clearer, more sparkling jelly. By the way, if you want the basis for some refreshing drinks in the summertime, just bottle this barberry juice as is for use later with sugar and ice.

Otherwise, bring the juice to a boil, stir in an equal volume of sugar, and heat until 2 drops will come together on the edge of a metal spoon and run off in a sheet, or until your jelly thermometer reads 220 or 222 degrees. Pour into hot, sterile glasses that have been set on a towel, away from drafts. Fill to within ¼ inch of the top. Pour a thin layer of melted paraffin over the top, tipping each glass slightly so that this will adhere to all the edges. Cool, add a second thin layer of wax, cover with a lid or foil, and store in a cool, dry place.

You can also make a rich sauce by combining equal volumes of barberries and molasses, simmering this until the fruit is soft. Then run everything through a sieve to remove the fruit, boil the liquid until about half of it has evaporated, tip in the fruit, bring everything to a boil, and finally pour it into hot, sterilized glasses. Seal these as above.

To go with cold venison sandwiches, there's nothing like cold barberry tarts. For the pastry, cut 1½ cups shortening into 2 cups all-purpose flour until it is the consistency of large peas. Then add a bit at a time enough cold water, about ⅓ cup, to make your dough. Shape this into a ball, wrap in foil or waxed paper or place in a covered bowl, and chill overnight in the refrigerator. When ready to go, roll out ⅛-inch thick and cut into 3-inch squares.

Make your filling by simmering 3 cups of barberries with 1½ cups sugar and ⅓ cup water until the fruit mashes easily. Then press through a strainer. Place a tablespoon of the puree on each square of pastry. Fold together to make a triangle, moisten the edges with cold water, and press together with a fork. Preheat the oven to a hot 425 degrees and bake 25 minutes or until the tarts are a rich brown.

BAYBERRIES

(Myrica)

The shiny evergreen leaves of the bayberry, used in moderation and removed before the dish is brought to the table, will do wonderful things for soups, stew, broths, and steaming chowders. As for the greenish berries, which ripen to white, they have been valued since Colonial days for making soaps and scenting candles.

The bayberry—also called wax myrtle, candleberry, waxberry, and a horde of local names—is essentially a seaboard small tree and stocky shrub, although it follows the broad St. Lawrence River inland to the start of the Great Lakes. Seven species are native to this country and southern Canada, one along the Pacific Coast and the other six in the East. Too, bayberries are widely planted as a part of landscape gardening.

Numerous varieties of birds consume the picturesque berries. These include duck, grouse, turkey, and the scurrying quail. Incidentally, the fruit should not be given to pen-raised quail, as its waxiness interferes with their digestion. Foxes also devour the berries, while deer browse on the twigs and foliage.

The bark of these evergreen shrubs and small trees, with their characteristically stiff branches, is gray. The narrowly oblong leaves, from one to four inches long, are occasionally slightly toothed. The attractive fruit, actually a nutlet, is based on a hard stone that encloses a two-seeded kernel. On the outside of the stone are gunpowder-like grains. Over these is a dryish, pleasantly scented crust of granular, greenish-white wax that once smelled will never be forgotten. The leaves, too, when bruised, give off a memorable aroma.

If bayberries grow near your home, you may choose to pick two or three leaves whenever you're cooking a stew or such. The leaves can also be satisfactorily preserved. Just gather the shiniest and greenest of them, perhaps during that summer or early autumn vacation at the seashore, and bring them home in a bag. Then spread them out and dry them in the kitchen or attic. Pack them in tightly closing jars. Store them in a dark cabinet where they'll be handy. They're apt to become one of your favorite spices.

Growing as it does from Newfoundland to Florida, the bayberry was one of the earliest American plants used for medicine by the settlers venturing up and down the eastern seaboard of the New World. The dried bark of the root, preferably gathered just before winter, was pounded into powder and stored, tightly enclosed, in a dark place. A teaspoonful to a cup of boiling water, drunk cold one or two cupfuls a day, was used to quiet diarrhea. Pioneers also sniffed this powder with reportedly good effect for catarrh and nasal congestion. It was also occasionally applied in poultices to cuts and inflammations.

Some stores feature bayberry candles and soap, but you'll enjoy these

BAYBERRY

even more if you make them yourself. First, you'll need a lot of bayberries. Free these of twigs and leaves and, by washing them a few at a time in a colander, of all dust. Put them in a large kettle filled with water and heat them very slowly so that as the sediment floats to the top, where it should be removed, it will not cook into the wax. Then set everything aside to cool. Left in the cold for several hours, the wax will form a hard cake.

Take this out and remove as much of the adhering dirt as you can. Then put the cake into a smaller kettle filled with fresh water and set it again over low heat. Once the wax has remelted, run everything through a strainer and then through cheesecloth. Do this in the warm kitchen, but then set the mixture in the cold once more. If the rehardening wax does not seem clean enough, go through the whole procedure again. The block of wax you have left can be melted for making tapers or soap.

It takes ten pounds of bayberries to give a pound of wax. This, in turn, will supply two substantial candles. The housewives of yore had plenty of time, but even today the work is satisfying. And what makes better Christmas gifts?

The art of dipping candles is an ancient one. Today you'll be best advised, though, to buy your wicks, perhaps in a hobby shop. You can also purchase molds, for that matter, although there is something particularly eye-catching about the gratifying roughness of candles you dip by hand.

Just melt your wax in a deep container, perhaps a clean tall can you have reserved for the purpose. Start by tying some weight, if only a pebble, to the bottom of the wick, so as to straighten it out as you immerse it in the wax that is just warm enough to remain in the melted state. Once your taper has been started, you can cut off this weight so as to have a flat base.

As soon as each layer of wax has cooled, dip the candle again. Tying the tops of the wicks apart from one another on a short stick, you can be dipping two or three candles at once. When they have built up nearly to the desired size, shave them a bit perhaps with a knife. Then the final dip or two will give them the desired rugged slickness.

Pioneers used hollow lengths of cane and carefully rolled cylinders of birch bark for their molds, and you can do the same thing. Start by suspending the wick from a short stick laid across the top of the upright mold. Then fill the latter with the odoriferous bayberry wax, perhaps pouring this handily from an old teapot.

Fasten the mold so that it will remain undisturbed in an upright position for half a day in the cold. Then, loosening the base with a sharp knife, pull it out by the cross stick. If it does not slide readily, the trouble may be that your wax was not clean enough. All you'll have to do, though, is run hot water over the mold. Then once the candle is loose, hold it upright until it is firm enough to lay down.

Some use bayberry soap the year around. In making this, use enamel, iron, or earthenware utensils. Do not employ aluminum. Avoid fumes and watch out you do not splash lye on your hands. If lye is spilled, rinse the object with weak vinegar. Lye becomes very hot and may break a glass container.

For 9 pounds of soap, use:
    6 pounds bayberry wax
    ¼ cup borax (optional)
    1 can lye (3 ounces)
    2½ pints soft water

For 1 bar of soap, use:
    1 cup bayberry wax
    1 teaspoon borax (optional)
    5 teaspoons lye
    ½ cup soft water

Dissolve the lye in soft water a little at a time. Use rain water, snow water, or melted ice. If no soft water is available, "break" hard water by adding 1 to 2 tablespoons of lye to a gallon. Let stand overnight and then remove the scum. Bring this solution to a lukewarm 85 degrees.

Melt your wax and then cool it to 110 degrees, slightly warmer than body heat. Add the borax to the melted wax and stir. This will improve the sudsing action of the soap.

Add the lye solution to the wax in a steady, thin stream. Stir evenly and slowly. If you stir too fast, the soap will curdle and not combine. Continue mixing in this fashion for 10 to 20 minutes or until the solution is like thin honey. A greasy layer indicates it is too warm. Then put the kettle in cool water and stir from sides and bottom. If it is lumpy, it is too cold. Put it in a pan of hot water. Within a half-hour, the mixture should thicken.

Pour the thickened mixture into a mold. For a mold, use a flat enameled pan or a wood or cardboard box lined with wet cotton cloth. Cover with a heavy rug or blanket for a day and a night, depending on where you live, as freezing will spoil the soap. Cut into bars of desired size with a string. Stack these bars in an airy place and age them for two weeks before you use any.

If this soap separates, or is crumbly or greasy, reclaim it by boiling in a large kettle. Add 7 pints of soft water to the large recipe or 1 cup of soft water to the small recipe. Dissolve the soap slowly. Then increase heat and boil until it thickens. Since it boils over readily, select a large kettle and stir constantly. Then pour into the mold as above.

BUFFALO BERRY

(Shepherdia)

The three varieties of buffalo berry native to the continental United States are the only species of the sort in the world. One or more of them flourishes in nearly every part of the country except the Southeast, including Alaska, making them prime emergency foods.

Black bears eat the fruit, and so do quail and flocks of other birds. Indians used to devour tremendous amounts of the berries, gathering them by the bushel. They used them as we do the currants they resemble, often making a pudding of them and the flour of the prairie turnip, described elsewhere in this book. Vast quantities, dried for winter use, were cooked with buffalo meat; hence the name.

BUFFALO BERRY

Shepherdia canadensis is the type of buffalo berry with which many are most acquainted. Growing from Alaska and British Columbia to Newfoundland, south to the northern states and along the Rockies, this is a shrub some three to five feet tall. It prefers dry, well-drained habitats. The young buds and twigs are rough with reddish brown scales. The oval leaves, growing opposite to one another, are up to about two and one-half inches long and have smooth margins. Green above, beneath they are silvery or rusty with scales and dense hair. Small yellow flowers appear at the same time, growing in the angle between leaf and branch. The berries are small, round, translucent, and either a striking orange or scarlet.

The presence of saponin, found in many plants and used commercially as a foam producer, makes these berries a little too bitter ordinarily to be enjoyed raw in any quantity, although they are good when sweetened by frost and then dried with sugar. Indians, however, consider them great delicacies at any time. Their *modus operandi,* even today, is to mix the fruit with a little sugar, then beat it until it foams into a salmon-colored mass. Both tasty and nutritious, this is enjoyed on desserts as we use whipped cream.

*unspoiled
vitamins
and minerals*

Nature's Own Salad Greens

EVEN THOSE WHO don't like to cook will enjoy making the easy-to-fix tossed and wilted salads described below. Nature's own salad greens provide a blend of the familiar and the exotic. Many of them—like prickly lettuce, wild lettuce, and lettuce saxifrage—can be used just like the common varieties of lettuce found in supermarkets, but they are much more versatile. Prickly lettuce, for instance, can be used to make a tasty casserole. Wild lettuce makes an excellent cream soup and an intriguing baked loaf. Lettuce saxifrage pie is an epicurean delight.

Among other versatile greens often found growing wild are live-forever, which makes a zippy relish as well as an uncommonly good tossed salad, and rock cress, whose pungent flavor can do anything for salads that radishes can do.

Best of all, all these greens are widely distributed and are free for the picking.

LIVE-FOREVER

(Sedum)

Youngsters often know this wild vegetable as frog plant because of the way one of its fleshy green leaves, after being loosened by being held between the warm tongue and the roof of the mouth, can be blown up like a distended frog's throat. Our pioneer ancestors went one step farther and used the insides of the leaves, once they had been blown or cut apart, to apply to warts. The fresh leaves also have a cooling quality and have long been used to soothe bruises, insect stings, burns, and other such irritations.

The well-known live-forever, also called Aaron's rod, is a close cousin of roseroot, whose succulencies are discussed in Part I. As with roseroot, both the plant tops and the roots are deliciously edible, making them both pleasant table companions as well as prime survival foods.

The live-forever, which like roseroot is rich in sometimes life-saving amounts of Vitamin C, grows from Canada's Gaspé Peninsula to Wisconsin and as far south as Maryland. Good from early spring to late fall, it is a familiar of damp woods, moist fields, shaded roadways, and rich, stony banks.

The oblong, thickish leaves of the live-forever ascend stems one or two feet high in crowded spirals. Because of the way they can be inflated by blowing into the loosened slit at the base, they are unmistakable. Broad round clusters of tiny flowers, vaying in color from crimson and garnet to whitish, appear in midsummer.

The stout, rounded or finger-like tuberous roots become stringy and tough when the plant blooms. Again in late fall, however, large masses of new-grown, crisp white tubers can again be located.

If you find them near home, you may enjoy making the following tasty relish from the roots, unless you prefer to wash and eat them raw as is or turn them into a sliced salad component. For the relish, concoct a pickle in the proportions of a cup of cider vinegar, a teaspoon salt, and 1½ teaspoon apiece of cloves, allspice, and cumin. Bring to a boil. Then pour it over scrubbed young live-forever tubers that have been packed in hot, sterilized jars. Seal immediately, protect from drafts until cool, label, and store in a cool, dark place for at least a month before using.

Both the stems and leaves when very young are tender enough to enjoy raw. Later—until the plant flowers, in fact—they may be briefly cooked until tender by any of the methods suggested in this book for other greens. For a particularly appetizing topping for cooked live-forever, melt a stick of butter or margarine in a frypan. Add ½ cup of dry white bread crumbs and ¼ teaspoon oregano. Heat until lightly tanned. Sprinkle this over the hot, freshly cooked vegetable.

The young tubers and greens together in the spring make a provocative salad. Rub a salad bowl with a halved clove of garlic. Then lay a bed of watercress in it. For each portion, spread on ½ cup of washed and sliced

LIVE-FOREVER

live-forever leaves and stems. Sprinkle over this 2 tablespoons of the coarsely chopped tubers.

If you are serving four, sprinkle 5 tablespoons of salad oil over the greens and toss. Mix ¼ teaspoon salt and a scant pinch of dry mustard with 1½ tablespoons of vinegar. Add that, grind pepper over the top, toss again, and apportion. If you are serving live-forever salads often and ever want a taste change, just sprinkle on a little paprika and freshly grated Parmesan cheese.

PRICKLY LETTUCE

(Lactuca)

One of the more succulent members of the wild lettuce family is the distinctive prickly lettuce, one of the ancient foods of Europe, from which it is an immigrant. Some botanists theorize that the lettuce we now buy in stores got its start from this species.

Like such Boy Scout familiars as rosinweed and prairie dock, the prickly lettuce indicates north and south, its sharply toothed and tipped

PRICKLY LETTUCE

leaves twisting edgewise to the sun. Both the lower part of the stem and the center leaf ribs bristle with prickles which, however, quickly lose their sharpness in boiling water. In fact, if you gather prickly lettuce young enough, it is tender enough for the most delicate of salads. Later, the leaf-clasped stalks of this wild lettuce grow up to about five feet tall.

When just a few inches high, it makes salads difficult to surpass. Wash enough of the tender young greens for four (four cups), shake gently dry, and keep in a cool place while you complete the other preparations. For the dressing, blend ½ teaspoon celery salt, ½ teaspoon dry mustard, ¼ teaspoon pepper, and a minced clove of garlic in a bowl. Stirring, add ¼ cup of lemon juice slowly to the mixture. Stir in a teaspoon of finely chopped pickles. Then gradually mix in ¾ cup salad oil.

Fry 8 slices of bacon until crisp, starting with a cold frypan and tilting it so that the grease accumulates to one side. Toss the greens with the dressing and with 2 tablespoons hot bacon fat. Garnish with the crumbled bits of bacon. Serve at once.

Or, still for 4 cups of loosely packed young greens, take 2 tablespoons of butter or margarine, 2 tablespoons flour, ½ cup sour cream, and ½ teaspoon of diced onion. Blend the butter or margarine and the flour over very low heat in a frypan, stirring constantly. Then turn up the heat slightly, add the sour cream and onion, and cook, still stirring, until everything thickens. You now have your choice. Either pour the sauce over the tender raw greens and toss. Or add the greens to the sauce and cook over low heat until they are limp. In either instance, season at once with salt and pepper to taste and serve immediately.

When the prickly lettuce is slightly older, in the late spring and early summer, here is a way to prepare it that is guaranteed to have the family eating with gusto. Stirring, sauté a teaspoon of finely grated onion in 3 tablespoons of butter or margarine until the bits are tender. Then add enough undrained young greens for four, scissored into bite sizes and then washed in cold water. Scatter on ⅛ teaspoon rosemary. Cook, covered, over high heat 3 or 4 minutes or until the lettuce is limp. Season to taste with salt and pepper. Serve hot.

Prickly lettuce also goes well in a casserole. To go with 2 cups of chopped or scissored prickly lettuce, heat in a frypan 3 tablespoons of salad oil and 3 tablespoons of butter or margarine. Add a finely minced small onion, a finely chopped garlic clove, and the leaves that have been washed in cold water but not drained. Cook over low heat for 5 minutes or until the lettuce is tender, salting and peppering it to taste. Then remove from the heat, allow to cool, and stir in 2 beaten egg yolks. Tip into a buttered casserole, dot with butter or margarine, strew with freshly grated Parmesan cheese, and brown in an oven preheated to a moderate 400 degrees.

A vinegar and bacon sauce brings out the singular taste of prickly lettuce in the following dish. To go with 2 cups of cooked greens, sauté a small diced onion and 2 tablespoons of diced green pepper in ¼ cup of bacon drippings. When they are soft, add ¼ cup lemon juice, ½ teaspoon salt, and ⅛ teaspoon pepper. Allow to bubble several minutes. Then add the well-drained lettuce and heat well. Serve steaming, garnished with mealy slices of hard-cooked eggs that have been touched up with paprika and the merest suggestion of oregano.

You can top off the prickly lettuce season by bringing 2 tablespoons each of salad oil and butter or margarine, along with the two halves of a clove of garlic, to a sizzle in the bottom of a saucepan. Add enough washed, undrained greens for four. Stir until they start to go limp. Then cover and cook until thoroughly tender. Take out the garlic. Puree what's left in the blender or press through a sieve.

Return to the saucepan. Season to taste with pepper and salt. Stir in ½ teaspoon lemon juice. Then add a cup of rich milk, bring slowly to a simmer, and serve on hot buttered toast with a sliced hard-cooked egg garnishing each portion.

ROCK CRESS

(Arabis)

The finest big game hunting and freshwater fishing in this hemisphere is now in the Far North. But this is also the land of the great hunger. Storm, ice, fog, or other conditions can delay scheduled plane or boat pickups. Too, fresh greens are often lacking in regular food supplies. There may be a time when you'll be glad to know rock cress.

This grows in Alaska, on the islands of the Bering Sea and the Aleutians, and in the Yukon. Alpine cress (*Arabis alpina*), which is similar, thrives in the eastern Arctic, south to Newfoundland and the Gaspé Peninsula. Both are seen on ledges, cliffs, gravelly shores, cool rocks, and along the banks of roads and streams.

Rock cress has a slender stem, often much branched from the base, up to about a foot high. Narrow, alternate, sometimes toothed leaves, gradually tapering at the bottom but not clasping the stalk, are scattered along the stem. Lobed basal leaves, up to an inch and one-half long, form characteristic rosettes. Long, loose clusters of pretty white flowers, each with four petals, appear in the spring. These develop into slender, long seedpods.

The somewhat radishlike flavor of the rosettes, gathered while tender, will enhance tossed salads as well as cook up into tasty greens. The flowers, too, are edible, but the stem leaves are apt to be bitter.

One of the tastiest northern salads is started by washing 4 cups of tender young rock cress and 2 cups of one of the blander greens. Dry thoroughly in a towel; then tear into bite sizes and mix in a large bowl. Prepare the dressing by shaking in a jar ½ cup of salad oil, 2 tablespoons

ROCK CRESS

wine vinegar, 2 tablespoons honey, a teaspoon salt, and ⅛ teaspoon pepper. Pour over the greens and toss diligently. Serve at once.

Rock cress also makes a better than usual wilted salad. Wash, dry thoroughly in a towel, tear into bite sizes, and drop into a salad bowl enough young rosettes for four. Starting with a cold frypan, sauté 4 slices of bacon over low heat, tilting the pan so that the grease will flow to one side and the bacon will become crisp. Remove the slices and tip the hot fat over the greens. Quickly heat a tablespoon of vinegar in the same pan. Pour this over the greens as well and toss until the leaves are thoroughly coated. Crumble the bacon over the top and serve immediately.

The radishlike taste of rock cress really touches up a soup. Wash 4 cups of some bland young greens, such as one of the wild lettuces, and ½ cup of rock cress rosettes, tearing all into bite sizes. Melt 3 tablespoons of butter or margarine in a large saucepan, add a small chopped onion, and sauté until tender. Add the greens, salt and pepper to taste, and cook over low heat until wilted. Then pour in a quart of poultry stock, made with bouillon cubes if necessary, and bring to a simmer.

Now mix 2 egg yolks with ½ cup of heavy cream. Add that. Stirring, heat only until a few bubbles are plopping lazily to the surface. Correct the seasonings. Place a buttered, crisply toasted slice of some substantial white bread, such as sourdough, in each of the quartet of soup plates. Pour the repast over them.

WILD LETTUCE

(Lactuca)

A delectable and vitamin-teeming relative of domesticated varieties, wild lettuce grows all the way across the continent from British Columbia to Newfoundland, south throughout the United States. About a dozen species of these tall, white-juiced edibles are common in the rich, moist soil of fields, yards, roadsides, and open thickets.

Ring-necked pheasants are among the birds feasting on the seeds. The prairie dog enjoys the foliage, while antelope and deer browse on the entire plants. Saddle and pack horses seem to find these delicately flavored greens particulárly toothsome, too, even when they're too tough and old for the table.

Sometimes growing as high as a basketball player's reach, wild lettuce is hollow-stemmed and leafy. The generally smooth stalks have a whitish cast to them, as do the underneaths of the clasping stem leaves, which are abundant up to the loosely branched flower clusters. The deeply indented leaves growing from the base of the stalk become from several to twelve inches long. The numerous little narrow flowers range in color from bronze to yellow and blue.

If you like the slightly bitter taste of cooked dandelions, you'll enjoy wild lettuce as a potherb. Otherwise, discard the first water in which it is boiled. The leaves and stems are tender enough to cook until the edible is about sixteen inches high.

When just a few inches tall, wild lettuce makes a tasty salad, especially if you help things along by serving it on chilled plates.

For example, pick over, wash, and dry in a towel enough young wild lettuce for four. Tear into convenient pieces. Stirring, slowly pour the juice of a lemon into ½ cup of thick cream. Thoroughly mix in a teaspoon sugar, ¼ teaspoon dry mustard, and ⅛ teaspoon paprika. Pour over the greens, season lightly to taste with salt, and toss. Serve immediately.

WILD LETTUCE

Bacon in particular brings out the taste of young wild lettuce. To go with 4 rather compactly filled cups of leaves that have been torn into bite-size portions in a salad bowl, start with a cold frypan and slowly cook 4 diced slices of bacon until crisp, tilting the fat to one side while the bits brown. Then add ¼ cup cider vinegar, 2 teaspoons sugar, ½ teaspoon salt, and ⅛ teaspoon apiece of pepper, dry mustard, and paprika. Stir until well blended, pour hot over the greens, toss thoroughly, and serve.

Wild lettuce goes well with watercress, considered at length in Part I. Tear enough young wild lettuce for four into bite sizes and mix with ½ cup of chopped water cress. Toss with a dressing made by dissolving ¼ teaspoon of salt in 2 tablespoons tarragon vinegar, adding ⅛ teaspoon pepper and the merest pinch of curry powder, and then whipping in 6 tablespoons of salad oil. Top with tiny pieces of white toast, well covered with garlic spread concocted by softening ½ stick of butter or margarine, then beating in with a fork a chopped clove of garlic and salt and pepper to taste. What spread you don't use on the spot can be kept covered in the refrigerator.

When wild lettuce is a little older, you'll prefer it cooked. Depending on the size, it is often pc ,sible to lift this green directly from the rinse to the saucepan and heat it without added water. If this edible is no longer quite young, add 2 tablespoons of boiling water. In either event, cover and cook over high heat only until tender. Then drain if necessary. The following four recipes are particularly effective with wild lettuce, torn into bite-size pieces and cooked this way. Each is geared to four people.

For the first, season the hot greens to taste with salt and pepper. Mix in ½ cup each of cubed cooked ham and hot croutons, freshly browned in butter or margarine. Serve immediately.

For the second, bring ½ cup of sour cream, along with a tablespoon of butter or margarine, to a bubble in a separate saucepan. Season to taste with salt and pepper. Add the hot greens, cook over low heat until bubbles again begin plopping to the surface, and serve hot.

For the third, drench the hot greens with a cup of preferably heavy cream. Add 3 tablespoons of butter or margarine. Sprinkle on salt and pepper to taste. Simmer for 5 minutes. Then rapidly stir in an egg yolk. Serve at once, garnished with the paprika-brightened slices of 4 hard-cooked eggs.

For the fourth, be sautéing a medium-size onion in a stick of butter or margarine until the bits are tan and tender. Add the hot greens and 2 cups of cooked rice, preferably wild. Mix well and get steaming hot. Season to taste with salt and pepper. Sprinkle with paprika, dust sparingly with nutmeg, and serve hot.

Cream of wild lettuce soup is well worth the making. You'll need 1½ cups of cooked, well-drained greens for this recipe. Chop them and either press them through a sieve or puree them in the blender. Add them, along with a cup of milk and a teaspoon of grated onion, to a sauce made by melting 3 tablespoons of butter or margarine in a saucepan over moderate heat and blending 3 tablespoons of flour with it. Stirring hard, add 3 cups of hot milk and bring to a bubble. Stir in a well-beaten egg yolk, season to taste with salt and pepper, simmer 3 minutes, and serve.

Or turn 1½ cups of cooked, drained, and chopped wild lettuce into a loaf that will be a delight to both eye and palate. Sauté a medium-size, finely chopped onion until golden in ½ stick of butter or margarine over low heat. Mix ¼ cup of flour to a paste with a minimum of cold milk. Blend this smoothly with the remainder of 1½ cups of milk. Stir into the onions and, continuing to stir, bring to a simmer, whereupon everything will thicken. Mix with the greens.

Beat 3 egg yolks with a teaspoon salt, ¼ teaspoon black pepper, and ⅛ teaspoon rosemary. Add to the greens mixture. Then beat the 3 whites until they are stiff and fold them in. Smooth out in a pan measuring about 8 by 4 inches.

Get ¾ of a cup of fresh crumbs, perhaps by cutting the crusts from soft white bread, tearing the remainder into small pieces, and feeding these a bit at a time into your electric blender. Stir the crumbs and 2 tablespoons of grated Parmesan cheese with a tablespoon of melted butter or margarine. Then sprinkle over the top of the loaf.

Bake in a preheated moderate 350-degree oven about an hour or until a knife inserted in the middle comes out clean. Allow to cool and firm for 15 minutes. Then invert on a hot platter, cut into half-inch slices, and serve.

LETTUCE SAXIFRAGE

(Saxifraga) (Micranthes)

The "saxifrage" part of the name comes from the Latin word meaning rock-breaker, a redoubtable and amusing designation for such a fragile little edible. Because it sometimes grows in rock fissures, the supposition arose that it split the stones. The lettuce saxifrage also abounds in moist meadows, along the cool edges of brooks, in marshy places, and on damp slopes from Pennsylvania on through the Appalachians to Tennessee. Edible cousins prosper over much of the country, except for the west central states, from Alaska and California to Georgia.

Also known as deer tongue because of the shape of its leaves and as mountain lettuce because of their edibility, lettuce saxifrage concentrates its growth in a crisp green rosette of leaves. The members of this thick mat are up to about eleven inches long, shaped like an animal's tongue and serrated with keen, short teeth.

When these leaves start to age and lose their tenderness, a flower stalk rises one or two feet from their midst, ending in a loosely branched cluster of small white flowers. These later develop sharply pointed, two-pronged seed capsules. In Alaska, with the *Saxifraga punctata,* this may be delayed until very late in the season in mountain and shoreline gulches where snow persists until midsummer.

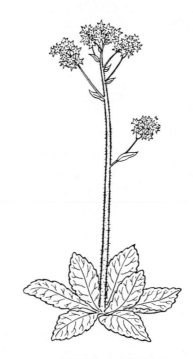

LETTUCE SAXIFRAGE

The young, tender leaves, picked before the plant flowers, will supply considerable amounts of vitamins and flavor to salads. You may like them shredded with the fingers, tossed with 2 tablespoons of olive oil and the juice of ½ lemon, salted to taste, and garnished with sliced hard-cooked egg. Slices of cold lamb or chicken added to such a salad make a convenient and quickly prepared luncheon dish. Too, cold flaked fish is exceedingly nice mixed with it.

Wilted lettuce saxifrage is a favorite in numerous localities. Sauté 4 diced slices of bacon until crisp. Add 3 tablespoons cider vinegar, a tablespoon water, a teaspoon salt, and ⅛ teaspoon apiece of pepper and dry mustard. A little sour cream is also good. When everything is bubbling, tip in 4 cups of coarsely shredded young greens. Cook only until wilted. For a change on occasion, slice hot hard-cooked eggs over the top.

For lettuce saxifrage soup, a whiff of which will start the nostrils of a hungry man trembling, shred 4 cups of the young greens, again enough for four. Sauté a diced, medium-size onion in 2 tablespoons of butter or margarine until the bits are soft but not browned. Then stir in the greens, cover, and steam for 3 minutes. Add 3 cups of beef stock, made with bouillon cubes if necessary, and bring to a bubble for 10 minutes. Correct the seasoning. If you'd like something a bit more substantial, add 1½ cups of cooked rice, a blend of the wild and the domestic being tasty. Serve steaming.

Finally, there is a vitamin-teeming lettuce saxifrage pie, as stimulating to the tongue as to the gastric fluids. Bring a small amount of salted water to a boil. Toss in 4 cups of the young greens, ½ cup of watercress, and ¼ cup of chopped chives. Boil, covered, only until tender. Then drain, chop, and season to taste with salt, pepper, and a liberal amount of paprika.

Beat 3 eggs with a pint of half-and-half. Stir in ¼ cup of flour until you have a smooth thin batter. Mix this well with the vegetables and pour into a casserole. Cook in a moderate 350-degree oven until an appetizing crust covers the top. Start 2 tablespoons of chipped butter or margarine melting over everything, sprinkle on more paprika, and serve.

ORACH

(Atriplex)

In a lot of homes across the continent the acknowledged pick of the edible greens is orach. The tender tips and juicy young leaves of this wild edible are delicious from spring to late fall. Connoisseurs pronounce them equal to, if not better than, the green amaranth, to which the plant bears some resemblance.

Orach provides top eating from British Columbia to Labrador, south to California and Virginia, growing luxuriantly on salt marshes and wet flats along the coasts and on moist alkaline lands in the interior. Shaped somewhat like lance heads, the leaves are grayish to bright green, smooth-edged, and characteristically lighter and mealy-looking underneath. The small, green flowers grow in narrow spikelike clusters. Later there is an abundance of small, starchy seeds, once ground by some of the Indian tribes for meal.

Also known as saltbush and as shad scale, orach is a favorite food of the big Canada goose, which feeds on its seeds, leaves, and stems. Quail are among the upland game birds dining on the seeds. Deer, rabbits, antelopes, mountain sheep, and some of the remaining herds of bison browse on the twigs and foliage.

ORACH

You have to be careful not to add too much salt to orach, but outside of that it can be used in any of the recipes in this book for wild greens. Too, there are these particularly efficacious dishes.

Few green salads are as tasty as those made with young orach, washed, dried, and, if you're not going to use it right away, wrapped in a towel to stay crisp in the refrigerator. For something a little different, mix orach with sliced apples, slivers of peeled lemon, a few broken walnut meats, and a generous sprinkling of grated Cheddar cheese. A dressing that will really bring out the flavor of all this is made by mixing and chilling ½ cup olive oil, 3 tablespoons lemon juice, a tablespoon of finely chopped pickles, ½ teaspoon finely minced chives, ½ teaspoon chopped parsley, ¼ teaspoon paprika, ⅛ teaspoon pepper, and salt to taste.

Orach brings out the savor of fruit, and you may like to blend it in a salad bowl with such availables as thin slices of orange, pear, apples, and slivers of banana touched up with lemon juice. Dress this salad liberally with mayonnaise and paprika just before serving.

For a wilted salad of tender young orach, wash and dry 4 cups of the greens. Place them in a salad bowl that has been well rubbed with a later discarded halved clove of garlic. Brown 4 diced slices of bacon over low heat in a frypan. When it is crisp, turn off the heat and quickly stir in ¼ cup of wine vinegar, a teaspoon of chopped chives, and ⅛ teaspoon pepper. As soon as everything is steaming, pour over the orach, cover, and let stand 5 minutes. Then toss again, using a spoon and fork gently as always so as not to bruise the leaves, and serve.

Young orach cooks up quickly. Just wash it well, then put it into a saucepan without added water and cook it, tightly covered, until barely tender. Serve hot with pepper, a little salt if you want, and a scattering of lemon juice.

Baked orach provides an artful change of pace. Toss 4 cups of the greens in ½ stick of butter or margarine over low heat in a frypan until everything is well mixed. Then put in a casserole and pepper and salt to taste, being careful not to add too much of the latter. Mix ½ cup of dried white bread crumbs with a cup of cream and pour over the top. Sprinkle with grated Parmesan cheese, touch up with paprika and a suggestion of parsley flakes, and bake in a moderate 350-degree oven until very hot.

For a cream soup with a delicate warmth of color, aroma, and taste, you'll need a cup of cooked, chopped orach. Mix this in the blender with 3 cups of milk, or if you want something really luxurious, cream. Add 3 tablespoons butter, 1 tablespoon flour, ¼ teaspoon dry mustard, and ⅛ teaspoon pepper. Blend until everything is smooth. Then tip into a saucepan and bring to a simmer, salting to taste and stirring until the soup is somewhat thick and has a full-bodied savor.

Another particularly tasty soup for four is started by slowly heating a cup of chopped orach and ½ cup of chopped watercress in 2 tablespoons of butter or margarine for 5 minutes. Then add 4 cups of some broth, made with bouillon cubes if necessary. Cover and simmer 10 minutes.

Remove from the heat, stir in ½ cup of heavy cream that has been beaten with an egg yolk, check for salt, strew with pepper and with a little paprika for contrast, and ladle out.

Fritters, anyone? For four satisfied diners cook 4 cups of orach until tender, tightly covered, in the water that clings to them after rinsing. Then strain, chop, and place in a bowl. Stir in the yolks of 2 eggs, ½ cup freshly grated Parmesan cheese, a tablespoon of butter or margarine, and ¼ teaspoon nutmeg. When the mixture has cooled to room temperature, beat the 2 egg whites and fold them in. Drop the batter by the tablespoon into very shallow hot fat and fry until golden all over. Drain on absorbent paper, and you're in business.

Nature's Own Potherbs

IT ISN'T NECESSARY to become used to wild potherbs; they are like old friends. They resemble the vegetables sold in stores but often surpass them in flavor and have many more uses. Green amaranth, for instance, can be used just like spinach, but it has a more delicate flavor than that common green. Silverweed and salsify both resemble parsnips in flavor, but both can be used in many ways in which parsnips are not. Both milkweed and knotweed can be cooked just like asparagus, but they have a taste all their own. One variety of knotweed can even be prepared just like rhubarb.

Whether these potherbs are merely served plain with butter or are creamed or used in soups or casseroles, they furnish some of the most delectable eating known to man.

COWSLIP

(Caltha)

The glossy yellow flowers of the cowslip, also known as marsh marigold and by over two dozen other common names, are among the first to gleam in the spring along stream banks and in marshy coolnesses from Alaska to Newfoundland and as far south as Tennessee and South Carolina. This wild edible is also eagerly awaited in Europe.

One reason this member of the crowfoot family gained its name of cowslip is that you often see it growing in wet barnyards and meadows and in the trampled soggy ground where cattle drink. Few wild blossoms are more familiar or beautiful, and New Englanders find few wild greens that boil us so delicately so soon after the long, white winters.

The bright golden blossoms, which grow up to an inch and a half broad and which somewhat resemble large buttercups, have from five to nine petal-like divisions which do not last long, falling off and being replaced by clusters of seed-crammed pods. These flowers grow, singly and in groups, on slippery stems that lift hollowly among the leaves.

Cowslips, growing up to one and two feet tall, have crisp, shiny, heart-shaped lower leaves, some three to seven inches broad. These grow on long, fleshy stems. On the other hand, the upper leaves appear almost directly from the smooth stalks themselves. The leaf edges, sometimes wavy, frequently are divided into rounded segments.

There are two things to watch out for if you are going to enjoy the succulent cowslip. First, this plant must be served as a potherb, as the raw leaves contain the poison helleborin, which is destroyed by cooking. It is, therefore, a good idea to gather cowslips by themselves to avoid the mistake of mixing them with salad greens. Secondly, ordinary care must be taken not to include any of the easily differentiated poisonous hellebore or water hemlocks that sometimes grow in the same places.

The two poisonous plants are entirely different in appearance from the distinctive cowslip. The water hemlock plant superficially resembles the domestic carrot plant but has coarser leaves and a taller, thicker stem. The white hellebore, which can be mistaken for a loose-leaved cabbage, is a leafy plant which somewhat resembles skunk cabbage, one reason why that not altogether agreeable edible has been omitted from these pages.

The dark green leaves and thick, fleshy stems of the cowslip are at their tastiest before the plant flowers. The way many know them best is boiled for an hour in 2 changes of salted water, then lifted out in liberal forkfuls and topped with quickly spreading pads of butter.

For a change, you can cream them, too. Tear the cowslips into small pieces and boil for an hour in 2 changes of salted water. Then drain. In

COWSLIP

the meantime, be melting 3 tablespoons of butter or margarine, either in a saucepan over low heat or in the top of a double boiler. Stir in 3 tablespoons of flour and cook a minute. Then gradually add ½ cup of cream. Salt and pepper to taste, and stir until thickened. Add the cooked greens, mix well, and serve.

Parmesan cheese also goes well with cowslips on occasion. Just use the above recipe, adding 3 tablespoons of grated cheese after the flour and other ingredients have started to thicken. Then stir until the Parmesan has melted and the sauce is creamy.

The leaves and stems aren't the only deliciously edible portions of this bright little harbinger of spring. You can make pickles from the buds, soaking them first for several hours in salted water, draining, and then simmering them in spiced vinegar, whereupon they take on the flavor of capers.

MILKWEED

(Asclepias)

Although milkweed grows from coast to coast and was long used by the Indians, it is the common milkweed, *Asclepias syriaca*, with which many are most familiar. This native perennial, thriving from the Maritimes to Saskatchewan and south to Kansas and the Carolinas, has stout stems reaching from two to five feet high.

This milkweed is abundant in meadows, old fields, marshes, and along roadsides, where in the fall its seeds with their familiar parachutes waft away by the thousands into the wind. These, plus a milky juice—latex, the subject of numerous experiments seeking a native rubber—are the plant's two predominant characteristics. However, these edibles should never be identified by this milky sap alone.

The leaves of this branchless edible grow in opposite pairs. Their short stems, like the stalks, are stout and sturdy. From four to nine inches long, and about half as wide, these oblong to ovate leaves taper at both top and bottom. They have wide central ribs.

The clusters of numerous tiny flowers have a memorable fragrance. They vary in color from greenish lilac to almost white. Each of the components of the delicate blossoms, which are deadly traps to many of the insects that seek their nectar, is divided into five parts. They eventually produce large green pods, some three to five inches long. The warty coverings of these finally split, exposing silk-tufted seeds.

Young milkweed sprouts, when up to some eight inches tall, are excellent asparagus substitutes, especially when cooked with a small piece of salt pork—if "substitute" is the right word, their being so regally satisfying in their own right. Then the young leaves provide cooking greens. The flower buds are a delicacy. Running the sprouts a close second, and even surpassing them in some estimations, are the firm, young pods. If they are at all elastic in your fingers, however, the silken wings of the seeds have developed too far to make for good eating.

There is one thing to keep in mind, however. All parts of the plant are bitter with the pervasive latex. However, this is readily soluble in water. Put your milkweed—whether sprouts, young leaves, flower buds, or seedpods—all ready for cooking, in a saucepan. Cover it with boiling water, bring again to a boil over high heat, and pour off. Do

MILKWEED

this at least once again, maybe more times, depending on your palate. To some, a slight bitterish tinge is invigorating. In any event, finally re-cover with boiling water, add a bit of salt, and simmer until tender. This may require a bit longer than expected, as milkweed takes more cooking than most other greens. Serve with margarine or butter melting on top.

I've also used the similar *Asclepias speciosa* with its purplish flowers on the western side of the continent, from British Columbia to California.

The tough fibers of the mature stalks of this milkweed were employed by the Indians for making string and rope and for coarse weaving. The milky juice was applied to warts and to ringworm infections, as well as to ordinary sores and cuts. The exquisitely packed ripe seeds were gathered just before soaring and skittering over the landscape, their hairy protuberances burned off, and the remainder ground into a salve for sores. These seeds were also boiled in a minimum of water and the concentrated liquid applied to draw the poison out of rattlesnake bites.

Besides serving as a cough medicine, a hot beverage made by steeping the roots was taken to bring out the rash in measles. Externally, it was supposed to help rheumatism. The root, mashed with water, was applied as a poultice to reduce swelling.

Once the shoots are more than eight inches tall and too old to eat, the bottom leaves can no longer be used but the young top leaves are still tender and tasty before the green flowers. These are fine mixed with young dandelion leaves, although they are good by themselves, too. Then there are the buds themselves, prepared and cooked the same way. Finally, the young pods are fine served on the side with roast or steak, or you may like what they can do for a stew.

Getting back to the blossoms, the Indians are supposed to have used them for sweetening on summer mornings, shaking the dew-laden nectar onto their foods before this dampness evaporated in the heat of the day. This has never worked for me, however, perhaps because I've become too lazy too soon.

KNOTWEED

(Polygonum)

Some thirty or so species of knotweed occur in practically every part of the United States. Grouse, mourning doves, pheasants, quail, prairie chickens, woodcocks, and partridges devour the rather large, dark seeds. Antelope and deer eat the plants.

Man has long dined on the knotweed, using various members of the family as vegetable, fruit, and even as nut. The fleshy and starchy rootstocks of the *Polygonum bistorta* in British Columbia and the Yukon are cooked and eaten as a substitute for nuts because of their almondlike taste, and in the Arctic south to New England and Colorado, the raw roots of the *Polygonum bistorta* are emjoyed for the same nutlike characteristic.

It is the Japanese knotweed, *Polygonum cuspidatum*, with which many are most familiar. This is well known, although not always by name, from North Carolina to Missouri, north to southern Canada, growing in large, coarse stands from about three to eight feet high. The enlarged joints of

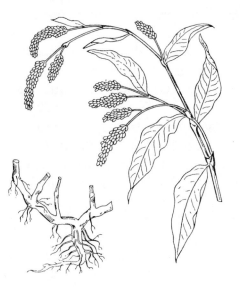

KNOTWEED

the stalks are encased with thin, papery sheaths. When these hollow stalks die, they form bamboolike thickets which clack and rattle in the wind and which serve to identify the young, edible sprouts when, somewhat resembling asparagus in shape although not in taste, these shoot up lustily in the spring.

The stemmed green leaves of this knotweed are roundly egg-shaped, being broad at their bases but rather abruptly pointed at their tips. The whitish green flowers, each with its five outer lobes, grow profusely in branching clusters that appear in the angles between leaves and stalk.

Knotweed shoots, before the leaves start to unfurl, are delicately delicious when some twelve to fifteen inches high. They cook up much more rapidly than asparagus. Three or four minutes in boiling salted water will do the job. Their toothsome acidity is then brought out with melted butter or margarine. Its shoots also taste good cold with mayonnaise. Both ways they go well with hot buttered toast.

To lift this wild edible to a heavenly level, cook and drain enough for four. Lay in a well-greased casserole, strew to taste with pepper and salt, and mix gently with ½ cup cream. Roof with ⅔ cup of fresh white bread crumbs mixed with 2 tablespoons of melted butter or margarine. For a variation on occasion, sprinkle with ¼ cup grated Parmesan cheese. In either event, bake in a preheated hot 400-degree oven until the top is golden brown. Try this sometime with cold ham, hard-cooked eggs, and sliced tomatoes.

One of the knotweeds in Alaska, *Polygonum alaskanum*, is called wild rhubarb because the young stems in early spring are used the same way as domesticated rhubarb. This will work, too, with Japanese knotweed. First, carefully peel the outer skin from the thinly fleshed stalks. Then cut into segments. Four cups of these, plus a cup of sugar and ⅛ teaspoon nutmeg, will give you enough tart sauce for four. If you'll let this stand a few minutes, it'll quickly simmer to softness in its own juice. Many like it hot with a little cream. It's tangy ice cold, too.

SILVERWEED

(Potentilla)

The bright golden blossoms of silverweed are common in damp places, haunting seacoast and stream banks, tarrying about stagnant ponds, and even shoving up amid salt meadow grasses. The white underneaths of the leaves are responsible for one of the common names of this edible. The roots, tasting like particularly good parsnips with overtones of sweet potato, have sometimes nourished people for months when other provisions were lacking.

Called argentine in French-speaking Canada, this food which grows in Europe and Asia as well as on this continent is also known as wild sweet potato, good tansy, wild tansy, cramp weed, and moor grass. It is luxuriant on the beaches and adjacent meadows of Alaska, where the natives and sourdoughs collect the fleshy roots in early spring as well as late fall, and extends over the roof of North America to Newfoundland. From there its range extends across the northern states, south along the Rocky Mountains to California and New Mexico.

Silverweed's relationship to the rose family is evinced by its lone, long-stemmed, five-petaled, inch-wide, bright yellow blossoms, which have the appearance of solitary roses. These eventually produce fruit that make one think of dry strawberries. The leaves, all produced from the roots, are long and featherlike, being composed of many, stemless, oblong, toothed leaflets that are shining green above and silvery below.

SILVERWEED

The roots, which on this continent were Indian favorites, are the parts used, although ruffed grouse, woodcock, rabbit, and mountain sheep feast on the foliage. Good both raw and cooked, these roots are thick and fleshy.

The easiest way to prepare them is by roasting or boiling. Candied, they are really special. For four, scrub about a pound of the roots. Simmer in a small amount of salted water until tender. Drain and slice. You'll need a stick of butter or margarine, ½ cup orange juice, ¼ cup honey, ½ teaspoon grated orange rind, and ½ teaspoon salt. Place the silverweed, layer by layer, in a greased baking dish, flavoring each tier with dots of butter or margarine and some of the orange juice, honey, rind, and salt. Cover and bake in a moderate 350-degree oven for half an hour, carefully basting occasionally.

Silverweed patties are excellent, too, and can be quickly prepared in any amount. Just cook the scrubbed and sliced roots until tender in a minimum of salted water. Then mash and season with pepper, salt, and a liberal amount of butter or margarine. Shape in little cakes perhaps 2½ inches broad. Dip in bread crumbs and sauté in butter or margarine until temptingly tanned on both sides.

These roots are also good with salt pork. Scrub and slice about a pound of the former, enough for four. Simmer, covered, in a small amount of salted water until tender. Then dice ½ pound of salt pork. Spread alternate layers of vegetables and meat in a greased casserole. Blend a tablespoon sugar, ½ teaspoon salt, and ⅛ teaspoon pepper, and sprinkle a little over each tier. Then pour ⅔ cup of beef broth over everything. Bake in a preheated moderate 350-degree oven for a half-hour and serve hot.

It is reasonable that so popular an edible as silverweed should have assumed a certain position in the medicine chest. The pioneers found silverweed tea efficacious in allaying diarrhea. This beverage was made by steeping a teaspoon of leaves in a cup of boiling water. It was drunk cold, one or two cupfuls a day, a few sips at a time.

GREEN AMARANTH

(Amaranthus)

Plants manufacture their own vitamins, and the nutritious green amaranth is rich in minerals as well. In addition, it is one of the most delicious of the greens, wild or otherwise. The tender tops, stalks, and leaves of this wild spinach, which has none of the strong taste of market varieties, are delightfully esculent from early spring to frost-blighting fall.

Growing as a weed over much of the continent including the tropics, the green amaranth is familiar to most individuals, although not necessarily as an edible. The stout, rough stalks, usually unbranched, sometimes reach the height of a man, but small, tender plants can usually be found growing in the same patch. These stems are slightly hairy.

The dull green leaves are long-pointed ovals with wavy edges. Their stems, also edible, are nearly as long as they are themselves. The roots, the reason for the occasional name of redroot and wild beet, are attractively red. Another name is pigweed, applied because the green amaranth prefers rich soil such as that found around pigpens and barns.

GREEN AMARANTH

The flowers are greenish and, being such, are usually not recognized as blossoms. They grow in long, loosely branched clusters. Exuding the faint, evocative scent of spring, they have a pleasant taste raw. The resulting shiny black seeds were threshed by the Indians, roasted, and then used for cakes and porridge. Some outdoorsmen like to scatter a handful atop a bannock before consigning this frying pan bread to the heat.

The extremely delicate flavor of green amaranth is something many prefer to that of almost any other green. This fragility of taste lends itself to a wide range of cooking procedures. You can also influence the final results by including some less bland vegetable, such as watercress.

But at least try some just started in a minimum of boiled salted water and cooked, covered, as briefly and as rapidly as possible. Young green amaranth can be lifted directly from rinse to saucepan, salted spraingly, and cooked without additional fluid. Serve with just margarine or butter melting yellowly over the top.

Young green amaranth is also notable raw. Wash, dry, and tear into bite-sized pieces enough tender greens for four. Toast 4 slices of white bread, rub both sides with a halved clove of garlic, cut into small cubes, and sauté with golden in butter or margarine. Season the greens to taste with salt and pepper, add the croutons, a cup of French dressing, 4 tablespoons crumbled Roquefort cheese, toss thoroughly, and serve.

Or for another highly pleasing dinner salad, prepare the dressing sometime during the afternoon by mixing in the bottom of your salad bowl a minced clove of garlic, ½ cup of salad oil, 2 tablespoons wine vinegar, 2 teaspoons chopped watercress, ¼ teaspoon black pepper, and salt to taste. Leave at room temperature, stirring occasionally. Just before the meal, toss with enough washed, towel-dried, and shredded greens for four.

Wilted green amaranth is also excellent. Tear 4 loosely packed cups of washed and well-dried young greens into bite-sized segments. Put into a bowl that has been freshly rubbed with a halved clove of garlic. Sauté 4 chopped slices of bacon over low heat until crisp, starting with a cold frypan and tilting it so that the grease will run to one side. Add 6 tablespoons salad oil, 2 tablespoons tarragon vinegar, ¼ teaspoon celery salt, and ⅛ teaspoon of preferably freshly ground black pepper. Bring to a simmer, pour over the amaranth, cover with a plate, and allow to steam 5 minutes. Then toss and serve on warm dishes.

Here's another version that adds even more flavor to these bland greens. Wash, dry, and shred 4 cups of loosely packed amaranth. Heap in a salad bowl and sprinkle with ¼ teaspoon salt. Mix in a teaspoon of chopped watercress and ½ teaspoon grated onion. Chop 4 slices of bacon and sauté this until the bits are crisp and golden. Add ½ cup wine vinegar and a teaspoon of sugar to the bacon grease and bring to a bubble for 3 minutes.

You now have your choice. You may turn the hot sauce over the raw greens and blend well. Or you may tip the greens into the frypan and cook over low heat until they are limp. In either event, serve immediately, garnished with the bacon bits and 2 sliced, hard-cooked eggs.

There's a pristine delicacy to creamed green amaranth. Simmer enough whole greens for four in a very small amount of salted water. While they are seething, tightly covered, prepare your sauce by melting 2 tablespoons of butter or margarine in a pan over heat so low that the grease doesn't color. Then smoothly stir in an equal volume of flour. Be bringing a cup of milk to a simmer. Stirring to prevent lumping, add this. Bring to a bubble, whereupon it will thicken. Keep bubbling for 5 minutes, seasoning to taste with salt and pepper and with ⅛ teaspoon nutmeg. As soon as the greens are tender, drain them, chop them, and blend them with the steaming sauce. Serve immediately.

Green amaranth cream soup will enhance the finest dinner. For enough for four, you'll need 2 cups of pureed green amaranth, made by cooking the wild vegetable until soft and then reducing it to a pulp by putting it through a sieve or the blender. Warm this with a quart of milk.

In the bottom of a saucepan, melt 3 tablespoons of butter or margarine. Blend 2 teaspoons of cornstarch with this, not letting either brown. Gradually stir in the puree and milk. Season to taste with salt and pepper. Heat at no more than a simmer until the soup thickens slightly. Then stir in 2 eggs that have been beaten with ½ cup of cream, warm a minute more, and ladle out.

Feel like a little well-spent effort? To go with 2 cups of cooked green amaranth, drained thoroughly and then either put through a colander or such or pureed in the blender, sauté 1½ tablespoons of finely minced onion in ½ stick of butter or margarine in a large frypan until well tanned. Smoothly blend in 4 tablespoons of flour. Then, stirring until everything thickens, slowly add a cup of light cream.

Turning the heat to low, beat 4 egg yolks until frothy. Stir in a bit of the hot mixture from the frypan. Then turn the yolks into the pan, mix in a cup of white bread crumbs, and, stirring, cook 2 minutes. Add the greens and heat. Season to taste with about a teaspoon of salt and ¼ teaspoon of pepper.

Take off the heat. Beat the 4 egg whites until they are stiff and fold them into the mixture. Pour into a well-greased ring mold. Set this in a pan of boiling water. Bake in a preheated moderate 325-degree oven for about a half-hour or until a knife inserted in the mousse comes out dry. Then turn upside down on a hot platter, fill the center with creamed young carrots, and serve at once.

Then there are green amaranth molds that some always enjoy at least once each spring. To go with 1½ cups of cooked amaranth, well drained and chopped fine, add a cup of milk and heat to a bubble only. Beat until frothy 4 eggs, a teaspoon salt, ½ teaspoon lemon juice, and ⅛ teaspoon pepper. Mix in a bit of the greens. Then stir into the greens and milk. Bring again to a bubble.

Turn the simmering mixture into 4 well-greased cups or molds. Set these in a pan, pour boiling water around them, and bake in a preheated moderate 350-degree oven for about a half-hour or until a knife inserted into one of the centers comes out dry. Turn onto hot plates and eat immediately.

You can have a fine one-dish meal with green amaranth, too. Get things going by placing 8 eggs, one by one with a spoon, in enough boiling water to cover them by an inch. Let the temperature immediately drop to a simmer and keep it that way for 10 minutes. Then remove the eggs from the heat and plunge them into cold water. If the shells are cracked slightly before the eggs cook, peeling will be easier. Slice the eggs carefully.

In the meantime, be simmering enough green amaranth in a minimum of salted water to fill 2 cups when drained. Cook, covered, only until a test piece, still slightly crisp, proves soft enough to eat.

You'll need to prepare your sauce, too. Melt 6 tablespoons of butter or margarine in a pan over moderate heat, not letting it brown. Stir in 6 tablespoons of flour until it is well blended. Still stirring, pour in 2 cups of milk that has been brought to a bubble in another pan. Season to taste with salt and pepper and with ⅛ teaspoon of mace. As soon as this sauce comes to a simmer, it will thicken. Then stir in 1½ cups of grated Cheddar cheese bit by bit, lower the heat, and continue stirring until the cheese has smoothly melted.

Spread a portion of the greens over the bottom of a greased casserole. Top this with a roofing of chopped eggs. Keep on doing this until the green amaranth and the eggs are all gone, ending with the vegetable. Pour the cheese sauce over everything, sprinkle with paprika, and bake in a moderate 350-degree oven for half an hour. This will serve four.

SALSIFY

(Tragopogon)

The three species of salsify that thrive from coast to coast in this country and in southern Canada are also known as goatsbeard and as oyster plant. The last name takes note of salsify's similarity in taste, to some palates, to that of the shellfish. To others, however, the roots have more the pleasant flavor of parsnips. The only secret is to get those roots while they are tender. The tops are used, too, both for salads and for cooked greens.

In many localities salsify is common along roadsides and in fields. Often growing two and three feet high, salsify is a tall perennial with a primary root that extends vertically downward. This becomes too pithy for use once the tall, leafy flowering stem develops the second year, producing either yellow or purple blooms not unlike large dandelion blossoms.

Also like dandelions, the leaves exude a milky juice when scraped or broken. They resemble wide blades of grass. Salsify is so good that the roots are grown commercially both on this continent and in Europe, the only difference between them and the wild variety being that the latter are usually smaller.

Salsify roots can be a treat. Scrub them. Then scrape them. If you are preparing them beforehand, keep them in cold water along with a tablespoon of vinegar to prevent their discoloring. When ready to use, cut into half-inch slices. Bring to a simmer in lightly salted water, in a covered saucepan, and cook until a table fork will easily penetrate the center of a test slab. Drain, salt and pepper to taste, and serve with melting butter or margarine.

Salsify cooked this way is also tasty with white sauce. A good one for this purpose can be made by melting 2 tablespoons of butter or margarine in a saucepan over moderate heat. Sauté 2 slices of onion briefly in this without letting either the grease or the vegetable brown. Then blend in 2 tablespoons of flour. Still stirring, slowly add a cup of milk and simmer for 5 minutes. Season to taste with salt and pepper. Then strain and serve. Incidentally, cold boiled salsify can be reheated in such a sauce.

Cold boiled salsify can also be very satisfactorily sautéed in a liberal amount of butter, margarine, or salad oil. Turn the pieces until they are well browned on both sides. Then season them with salt and pepper. If

239

you prefer, first roll them well in seasoned flour instead of salting and peppering them later.

Sometime when you're having another couple over for dinner and really want to show them what can be accomplished with a wild vegetable, dice 2 cups of scrubbed and scraped salsify. Drop the bits, along with a cup of light cream, into the top of a double boiler over boiling water. Season with salt and, in this case particularly, preferably with freshly ground black pepper. This salsify, stirred about every 15 minutes, will take about 2 hours to become tender. Keep hot until ready to serve.

SALSIFY

French-fried salsify goes well with steak. Scrub and scrape enough roots for four. Then cut each lengthwise as you would potatoes. Simmer in salted water until nearly tender. Drain and chill.

In the meantime, beat 2 eggs with ½ cup of light cream. Season a cup of flour with salt and pepper. Dredge the salsify in the flour. Dip in the liquid. Then roll in white bread crumbs, pressing on all that you can. Melt 2 sticks of butter or margarine in a shallow frypan. As soon as it starts to color, put in the salsify so that each piece is separate. Fry, turning, until golden. Serve sizzling.

Salsify is also good sugared. Again scrub, scrape, and slice lengthwise enough of the roots for four. Simmer in salted water until nearly tender. In the meantime, mix a tablespoon of sugar with ¼ teaspoon of salt and ⅛ teaspoons each of cinnamon, pepper, nutmeg, and mace. Melt a stick of butter or margarine. Have ¼ cup of flour ready. Roll each piece in the sugar mixture. Then dip into the fat. Dredge with flour. Sprinkle with sugar. Fry in 2 sticks of butter or margarine, turning until golden.

The leaves are well worth eating when you catch them young. Wash a quart of greens, dry them thoroughly with a towel, tear into bite-size segments, and pile in a salad bowl that has been rubbed with a halved clove of garlic.

Fry 4 diced slices of bacon, starting as always with a cold frypan and tilting the accumulating grease to one side. When the bits are brown, remove them. Add to the frypan ½ teaspoon salt, and ⅛ teaspoon pepper. Simmer over low heat for 3 minutes. Then pour over the greens and toss thoroughly. Garnish with the bacon, 2 sliced hard-cooked eggs, and a tablespoon of chopped watercress. Serve immediately.

PRAIRIE TURNIP

(Psoralea)

When John Colter, a mountain man once with the Lewis and Clark expedition, escaped from the Indians and came back safely with his incredible story of what now is Yellowstone National Park, he lived for a week largely on prairie turnips. This famous vegetable of the plains and the West, a mainstay of such Indians as the Sioux, is also known as the prairie apple, Indian breadroot, wild potato, *pomme blanche, pomme de prairie,* and wild turnip. Early plainsmen, frontiersmen, settlers, trappers, traders, and explorers soon came to relish its starchy, sweetish, and somewhat turnip-like taste.

The prairie turnip is a member of the pea family. It is a perennial whose large root, or sometimes group of roots, resembling sweet potato roots, lies entirely beneath the ground. The generally branched stalks, characterized by soft, whitish bristles, are erect and from about six to eighteen inches tall. Five inversely ovate leaflets, narrowest at their bases, comprise each leaf. These leaflets are about one-half to an inch wide and twice as long. The plant blooms with dense spikes of small, bluish, pealike flowers which eventually become tiny pods.

The tops of the prairie turnips mature early, breaking off in the unfettered winds and bounding over the plains like tumbleweed, which incidentally is also edible when gathered very young and simmered until tender. The roots, thus, are left unmarked. To find them, the Indians had to harvest them in the early summer. They were then peeled and hung up in long strings to dry for winter use.

PRAIRIE TURNIP

Prairie turnips, edible peeled and raw, were even better liked by the early settlers when boiled or roasted in small lone campfires. They can also be enjoyed in cakes. If you'd like to try some of these, wash, peel, and slice your wild tubers. You'll need about a pound to serve four. Simmer them, covered in a small amount of salted water until a fork will penetrate the largest of the pieces easily. Then drain and mash.

For every cup of mashed prairie turnips, mix in a tablespoon of butter or margarine. Whip together a teaspoon of flour, ½ teaspoon salt, ⅛ teaspoon pepper, and an egg yolk. Mix this with the prairie turnips. Mold into small, flat cakes, press into dry white bread crumbs, and sauté in a liberal amount of butter or margarine, turning them so as to brown them evenly.

Sometime when you want to serve four with a soup with a tantalizing flavor, simmer ½ pound of peeled and sliced prairie turnips in a minimum of salted water with a large sliced carrot and a large diced onion until everything is soft. Then drain and either strain or reduce to a pulp in a blender.

Put this pulp in a pan with a quart of milk, a tablespoon of butter or margarine, and salt and pepper to taste. Bring to a simmer, strew with a tablespoon of chopped watercress, and serve with thin, hot, buttered toast. If you'd really like to add a bit of tang and zip to the taste, allow ½ stick of butter or margarine to soften at room temperature and then mix 2 or 3 drops of tabasco with it. Spread the hot toast lightly with this.

WILD ONION

(Allium)

Wild onions, including the leeks, the chives, and the garlics, grow wild all over North America except in the far northern regions. Indians used them extensively, not only for the provocative taste they impart to blander foods, but also as a main part of the meal. Settlers and frontiersmen soon followed suit.

When Père Marquette and his band journeyed from Green Bay, Wisconsin in 1674 to near our present Chicago—whose name is taken from the Indian word "shikato," meaning place where wild onions are strong-smelling—their main food was wild leeks, probably *Allium tricoccum*, whose flat leaves, some one to three inches broad, nod in the breezes from the Maritime Provinces to Iowa and Minnesota, south to the Carolinas.

For the most part, though, the wild onions have slender, quill-like leaves, similar to those of domestic varieties. They grow from bulbs. Flowers appear on otherwise naked shafts, arising like the ribs of an umbrella. The one characteristic on which to depend is the characteristic odor.

Although you probably won't like all the breed—especially not the strong-tasting field garlic, *Allium vineale*, which is an immigrant from

Europe and which is beloved by cows in the East to the detriment of milk, cream, and butter—wild onions are all good to eat. The best way to find out your likes and dislikes is by trying them. Often you can use the entire plant.

However, have nothing whatsoever to do with any plants, wild or otherwise, that resemble the onion but do not have its familiar odor! Some bulbs whose appearance is superficially like that of onions are

WILD ONION

among the most concentrated of poisons. Your nose will be your own best protection.

By the way, it has been found that the odors that sometimes linger on the breath after one has eaten onions, chives, leeks, and garlic are entirely the result of solid particles remaining in the mouth. Brushing the teeth and tongue and rinsing the mouth after eating will do away with any fear of offending.

Wild onions simmered until tender in a small amount of lightly salted water, then drained and topped with butter or margarine, or, for a change, mayonnaise, are fine fare. Save the liquid for soup or for other cooking.

If you want to go to a little more trouble, glazed wild onions are succulent. Simmer, covered, until they are nearly tender enough wild onions for four in a cup of either broth or water in which a chicken bouillon cube has been dissolved. Then drain off all but 3 tablespoons of the liquid. Add ½ stick of butter or margarine and 2 tablespoons of sugar. Simmer, uncovered now, for 20 minutes, basting and stirring gently every 5 minutes.

The Indians ate grouse, duck, quail, plover, and other wild eggs whenever possible, often cooking them with wild onions. Eggs and this wild vegetable still really go together. If you like fried eggs and have the time to impress some friends, try this recipe.

Blend thoroughly 2 tablespoons salad oil, 2 teaspoons lemon juice, ¼ teaspoon salt, and a slight darkening of pepper. Cook a tablespoon of grated wild onion in this over low heat for 2 or 3 minutes. Then add a tablespoon of hot water and bring up the heat a bit. As soon as the liquid steams, slip 8 shelled eggs carefully from a dish into the frypan, cover, lower the heat again, and cook briefly until the whites are set. The results are so far from the tough, leathery objects so often served as "fried eggs" that you have to eat them to believe them.

When you don't want to go to that much trouble, why not scramble your eggs and wild onion. There's a trick to this, too, that you may care to adopt as your own. First, let the eggs come to room temperature. Then break 8 eggs into a bowl, add a tablespoon of cool water for each egg, and mix with a fork until well blended but not frothy. Add a teaspoon of chopped wild onion.

Melt 2 tablespoons of butter or margarine in a frypan just hot enough to sizzle a drop of water. Tip in the egg mixture and reduce the heat to low. When the eggs have started to harden, begin stirring them constantly with a fork. Remove them while they are still creamy and soft. Season to taste with pepper and salt. Serve at once on hot plates.

Then there's wild onion pie. Starting with a cold frypan, slowly cook 4 diced slices of bacon until the bits begin to color. Then melt ½ stick of butter or margarine around them. Sauté 3 cups of thinly sliced wild onions in this until they are golden. Then set off the heat. After they have cooled, mix them with 4 eggs that have been beaten with ¼ cup of evaporated milk. Pour into an uncooked, 9-inch pastry shell, the recipe for wild grape pie being an apt one. Bake in a preheated moderate 350-degree oven about 45 minutes or until the crust is flaky and the contents set and temptingly tan. Eat while still steaming.

As the Indian nations knew well, wild onions will enhance the flavor of almost any game or wild vegetable. An odorous sauce that will really touch up the somewhat bland flavor of pheasant breasts, when the hunter of the house comes home with limits and you are assigning the rest of the bird to the soup kettle, is started by gently sautéing ½ cup of chopped wild onions in 3 tablespoons of butter or margarine until the still uncolored bits are just tender.

Then blend in 1½ teaspoons flour, stirring all the time. Add 2 cups of sour cream and a tablespoon of lemon juice. Salt and pepper to taste. Bring to a bubble and, giving it an occasional stir, cook over low heat for 10 minutes. Strew with a tablespoon of chopped parsley, sprinkle with paprika, and cascade over the bronzed white meat.

For hot weather you can make a delicate chilled soup with wild onions. Using a deep saucepan, sauté until no more than a very light tan a cup of thinly sliced wild onions in ¼ stick of butter or margarine. Then add 4 equally thinly sliced, medium-size potatoes and a cup of water. Simmer until everything is very tender. Drain, saving the liquid, and put the vegetables through a strainer or the blender.

Slowly cook 2 tablespoons of flour and 2 tablespoons of butter or margarine over very low heat, stirring until golden. Then pour in the fluid from the vegetables and 3 cups of rich milk. Bring to a simmer, add the vegetables, season to taste with salt and pepper, and allow to bubble for 5 minutes. Remove from the heat. Allow to cool and then chill in the refrigerator. Serve garnished with a tablespoon of chopped watercress and if possible with one of chopped wild chives.

Then there is a robust soup to make on cool fall days when you have plenty of odds and ends of venison with which to brew a sturdy, forthright stock. Moose is a favorite, but beef will do. You'll need 5 cups of stock for a wild onion soup to serve four.

Sauté 2 cups of sliced wild onions in a stick of butter or margarine, stirring until they are well browned. Then transfer them to a saucepan containing the stock, seasoned to taste with salt and pepper, ⅛ teaspoon mace, and a bay leaf. Simmer very gently for 15 minutes, removing the bay leaf after 5 minutes.

Then set 4 slices of toasted sourdough or other substantial white bread in a large casserole. Pour the soup over it and sprinkle with ½ cup of freshly grated Parmesan cheese. Place the casserole either in a preheated hot 425-degree oven or under the broiler. Heat until the cheese is melted and golden.

For a superb one-dish meal for four that can be stirred together in minutes, first sauté ½ cup of chopped wild onions until limp in 3 tablespoons of butter or margarine. Before the onions brown, add the contents of a large can of tomatoes, ⅛ teaspoon each of tarragon and basil, and a minced clove of garlic. Cook until bubbling throughout. Then add 9 eggs and stir continuously and slowly to scramble. Serve while everything is seething.

Or simmer your wild onions for four in a small amount of salted water until, still whole, they are just tender. Then arrange them in a greased casserole. In the meantime, be preparing a sauce by melting 3 tablespoons of butter or margarine in a saucepan over moderate heat, then smoothly stirring in 3 tablespoons of flour. Still stirring, pour in a cup of hot milk. All this will thicken when it comes to a bubble. Season to taste with pepper and salt. Now pour this over the onions, sprinkle liberally with white bread crumbs, and place in a moderate 350-degree oven for a half-hour or until browned.

POKEWEED

(Phytolacca)

The first wild greens of the spring in many a happy household, pokeweed flourishes in the eastern half of the country except along the Canadian border, west to Texas and south to the tropics. The Indians found it delicious, and some of the first European adventurers on these shores were in such agreement that they took the seeds back to France and southern Europe, where the vegetable became popular. Today pokeweed finds its way into many of our stores as a springtime delicacy. Some devotees like it so well that they even grow it in their cellars.

Also known as pokeberry, poke, scoke, pigeonberry, garget, coakum, and inkberry, this wild vegetable has a huge perennial root often as large as a man's forearm. Fibrous and covered with a thin tannish bark, this can be easily broken to size and planted in garden soil in a deep, flat box. Best are the medium-size roots, some three or four inches in diameter, broken or cut into six-inch lengths, dug and replanted indoors after the first heavy freeze of fall. Kept in a dark, warm cellar and regularly watered, these will regularly send up shoots for months. For a family of three, you'll want about a dozen such roots.

The fat young sprouts, especially when they are some six to eight inches high, are the only part of pokeweed that is good to eat. The bitter roots—cathartic, emetic, and somewhat narcotic—are poisonous. So are the mature stalks when they take on a purplish cast. You may have seen birds get tipsy on the berries.

You'll want to be able to recognize the full-grown plants, however, as in the spring it is near their dried remains that the tender young shoots will arrow upward. These annuals grow into round stalks, about an inch in diameter, which reach and branch upwards from four to nine feet. The leaves, which are shaped like rounded lances, have stems on one end and points on the other. Scattered, smooth on both sides, and wavy-margined, they are up to about ten inches long.

Both flowers and fruit grow in long clusters on short stems. The numerous, small flowers are a greenish white. The round, ripe berries are a deep purple and are an important source of food for the mourning dove. Their reddish purple juice, as boys sometimes used to confirm in the fall when school classes were first resuming, will serve as an ink for steel pen points.

Gather your small, tender pokeweed shoots when they are no more than about eight inches tall. Remove skin and leaves, saving the latter for greens. Simmer the whole stems in a small amount of lightly salted water for 10 minutes or until tender. Serve on hot buttered toast, steaming with sauce.

One sauce whose flavor really brings out the springlike deliciousness of young pokeweed is started by finely chopping 2 slices of a medium-size onion, then tanning the bits in 2 tablespoons of butter or margarine. Then blend in 3 tablespoons flour. Slowly add a cup of milk, stirring vigorously. Mix in a teaspoon of chopped watercress. Salt and pepper to taste, sprinkle with ⅛ teaspoon nutmeg, and simmer gently for 5 minutes, stirring occasionally. Add ¼ cup of heavy cream, bring again to a bubble, and serve.

A tantalizing cheese sauce to touch up the flavor of such pokeweed on toast can be made by slowly melting 2 tablespoons of butter or margarine in a saucepan over moderate heat, not allowing it to brown. Then smoothly stir in an equal volume of flour. Stirring vigorously, gradually add 1¼ cups of milk and bring to a bubble. Season with ¼ teaspoon salt and ⅛ teaspoon pepper. Still stirring, simmer for 5 minutes to take away the raw taste of the flour. Now remove from the heat for several minutes. Add a bit at a time, stirring energetically until each portion has melted before adding more, ¾ cup of good grated

POKEWEED

American cheese. Return to low heat but do not allow to boil. Spoon over each serving, dust with paprika and with parsley flakes, and see what everyone's idea is for vegetables the next day.

Pokeweed is also good with eggs. For this dish, skin the shoots but leave on the little unfurled leaves at the top. Wash well. Then boil whole for 8 minutes in salted water until nearly tender. Drain, saving ¼ cup of the fluid. Mix this liquid with 3 beaten eggs, 3 tablespoons salad oil, a halved clove of garlic, and salt and pepper to taste. Add to the pokeweed and, stirring occasionally, cook about 2 minutes or until the latter is ready for the table. Remove the garlic and serve.

For a rich, aromatic soup, simmer 2 cups of pokeweed shoots until soft and then put either through a sieve or the blender. Bring 2 cups of milk to a bubble along with a halved clove of garlic. Then discard the garlic and add the pureed vegetable. Mix 3 tablespoons flour smoothly with a small amount of cold water. Stir that, along with 3 tablespoons of butter or margarine, into the soup. Season to taste with salt and pepper. Bring again to a bubble, add a tablespoon of chopped watercress and a cup of heavy cream, sprinkle with paprika, and serve steaming.

Those times when bachelors are doing the cooking they sometimes go in a lot for one-dish meals, and this wild vegetable is one of those lending itself well to such production. Simmer until tender in a minimum amount of salted water enough young pokeweed for four. In the meantime, be preparing a white sauce by melting ½ stick of butter or margarine in a saucepan, smoothly stirring in ¼ cup flour, and then, still stirring, slowly add 2 cups milk. Season to taste with salt and pepper. Stir in 2 tablespoons of finely diced green pepper. Bring to a simmer.

Also be simmering 4 eggs, completely covered with water, for 8 to 10 minutes depending on their size. Then remove them from the heat and plunge them into cold water. Crack the shells slightly before the eggs cool, so that peeling will be easier. Slice.

Spread a base of pokeweed over the bottom of a well-greased casserole. Cover with white sauce, then with sliced egg. Repeat until all the ingredients are used. Top with ½ cup of buttered white bread crumbs. Bake in a moderate 325-degree oven for half an hour. Serve hot. Just a whiff of this will have your customers waiting eagerly.

little treats
that top off
the meal

Snacks, Confections, and Condiments

BESIDES SUPPLYING VEGETABLES for the main course, wild plants also furnish some of the best condiments known anywhere and confections and beverages which top off any meal superbly or can be enjoyed between meals. Take horseradish, for instance. Everyone knows that horseradish enlivens the flavor of meat dishes, but those who haven't tried it freshly grated just don't know how good it can be. Another masterful condiment from nature's larder is sweet sea pickles made from giant kelp.

As desserts or between-meals nibbles, candied wild ginger and candied sweet flag excel. Syrup made with wild ginger is an exciting topping for ice cream.

For snacks that are good any time, chips made from chufa are hard to beat. Chufa also furnishes the makings of a delicious wild coffee. Like chufa, sunflowers are also used to make coffee; and their seeds make excellent snacks.

As anyone who begins to seriously investigate edible wild plants will soon discover, nature's amazing bill of fare includes everything from soup to nuts.

CHUFA

(Cyperus)

Chufa was so valued as a nutriment during early centuries that as long as 4,000 years ago the Egyptians were including it among the choice foods placed in their tombs. Wildlife was enjoying it long before that. Both the edible tubers of this plant, also known as earth almond and as nut grass, and the seeds are sought by waterfowl, upland game birds, and other wildlife. Often abundant in mud flats that glisten with water in the late fall and early winter, the nutritious tubers are readily accessible to duck. Where chufa occurs as a robust weed in other places, especially in sandy soil and loam, upland game birds and rodents are seen vigorously digging for the tubers.

Abounding from Mexico to Alaska, and from one coast to the other, this edible sedge also grows in Europe, Asia, and Africa, being cultivated in some localities for its tubers. Sweet, nutty, and milky with juice, these are clustered about the base of the plant, particularly when it grows in sandy or loose soil where a few tugs will give a hungry man his dinner. In hard dirt, the nuts are widely scattered as well as being difficult to excavate.

Except for several smaller leaves at the top of the stalk supporting the flower clusters, all the light green, grasslike leaves of the chufa grow from the roots. These latter are comprised of long runners, terminating in little nutlike tubers. The numerous flowers grow in little, flat, yellowish spikes.

Chufa furnishes one of the wild coffees. Just separate the little tubers from their roots, wash them, and spread them out to dry. Then roast them in an oven with the door ajar until they are rich brown throughout, grind them as in the blender, and brew and serve like the store-bought beverage. So prepared, chufa tastes more like a cereal "coffee" than like the regular brew. But it is wholesome, pleasant, and it contains none of the sleep-retarding ingredients of the commercial grinds.

All you have to do is wash and eat chufas, but if you are going to have a wild-foods dinner for guests, why not go one step further and have some really different chips to serve with your dip during the cocktail hour? The chufas first have to be very well dried, as in a slow oven, then ground to powder as in the ubiquitous blender. This powder can be mixed with regular wheat flour for all sorts of appetizing vitamin-and-mineral-rich cakes, breads, and cookies.

For these chips, which resemble fat little pillows, sift together a cup of

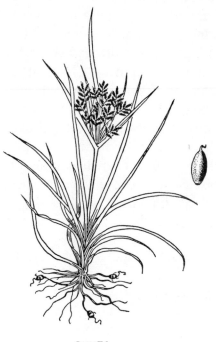

CHUFA

powdered chufa, a cup of all-purpose flour, 3 teaspoons baking powder, and a teaspoon of salt. Then cut in 2 tablespoons of shortening with a pastry blender or a pair of knives. Not wasting any time, work in ¾ cup of cold water bit by bit to make your dough. Roll this out as thinly as you can. Cut into 2-inch squares and fry these one by one in hot fat. They'll puff as they bronze. If you'll turn them, the other side will expand, too. Drain the some 30 resulting chips on paper toweling. They are particularly tasty, by the way, in an avocado and tomato dip touched up with grated wild onion.

The Spanish make a refreshing cold drink from the chufa, enjoyed both as is and as a base for stronger concoctions. A popular alcoholic drink is made by partially freezing this beverage in the refrigerator, then adding an equal volume of light rum to make a sort of wild frozen Daiquiri. The Spanish recipe calls for soaking ½ pound of the well-washed tubers for 2 days. Then drain them and either mash them or put them through the blender along with 4 cups of water and ⅓ cup sugar. Strain the white, milky results, and you're in business.

Europeans in the Mediterranean area, northward as far as Great Britain, used to make a conserve of chufa that is still very much worth the trouble. Again, begin by soaking the scrubbed tubers for 2 days in cold water. You'll need a quart of the drained vegetables for this recipe.

Make a syrup by boiling together a cup of sugar, a cup of corn syrup, and 1⅔ cups of water for 10 minutes. Add the drained chufas. Simmer, stirring occasionally, until the tubers are tender and the syrup thickened. Then take off the stove. Cover and let stand overnight. The next day, reheat to boiling. Pack the chufas in hot, sterile pint jars. Bring the liquid once more to a boil and pour it over the chufas, filling the jars to within ½ inch of their tops. Seal at once, cover if necessary to protect from drafts, allow to cool, label, and store.

SUNFLOWER

(Helianthus)

Almost two-thirds of the sunflowers that brighten the world, some sixty species, thrive in this country. Although they grow in every state, sunflowers spring up in greater abundance in the West, especially on the prairies. Indians used them everywhere, but it was here they were most useful to the tribes, often taking the place of maize.

However, sunflowers had, and have, many more uses. The Indians found they could boil the crushed seeds, then skim an extremely nutritious oil from the surface. This was used at mealtimes and in cooking. It was also one of this continent's earliest hair oils.

In medicine, the seeds were regarded as diuretic and the entire plant as antimalarial. The roots were boiled and the warm liquid used as a liniment. They were also supposed to be efficacious in snakebite remedies. A strong extract from wild sunflower roots was one of the original baths used to allay the severe inflammations that plague most who come in contact with poison oak and poison ivy.

Indians obtained black and purple dyes from the seeds, and a brilliant yellow dye from the plants, with which to beautify clothes, baskets, and ornaments. As if that weren't enough, the stalks can be utilized in an emergency like those of the tall, widely cultivated hemp to give delicate, silky threads.

SUNFLOWER

The American wilderness is well stocked with teas, but wild coffees are scarcer. Sunflowers give one of the latter. The Senecas were among the Indians roasting sunflower seeds, after the kernels had been extracted, and pouring hot water over them to produce a coffeelike beverage.

The stately forms of wild sunflowers, reaching up to some six feet tall but seldom rivaling the size of domesticated species, are common sights in open fields and meadows and along roads. A few tolerate woodland shade. One sunflower, *Helianthus annuus*, is the state flower of Kansas, growing as far west as California and western Mexico.

Sunflowers, which are annuals, are all relatively tall. Their stems, for the most part, are rough and stout. Their alternate, stemmed leaves, shaggy on both sides, are coarse and toothed. The blossoms are made up of many ray and disk flowers. Their total diameters in the wild plants range from about three to six inches, with disks from one to two inches broad. The disk flowers vary in color from brown and purple to yellow. The showy rays, often brilliantly turning fields into almost solid expanses of gold, usually run in number from about ten to twenty-five. Although the season of blooming is supposed to be later, they are sometimes seen blossoming gaily in early spring.

The agreeably oily seeds of the wild sunflowers are important to such game birds as snipe, quail, grouse, partridge, dove and pheasant. Antelope, deer, and moose dine on the plants.

Sunflower seeds are nutritious and, particularly when roasted in an oven or beside a campfire, delicious. Because the tedious job of shelling does not fit in with the high-speed tempo of American living, we enjoy them far less in the United States than, for example, do millions in eastern Europe. However, there continues to be a steady demand for the little bags of toasted, salted nuts at candy counters across the nation.

The fact remains that in an emergency the wild seeds could make all the difference. This would be true whether or not you just ate them raw or, as Lewis and Clark found the Indians doing along the Missouri River, pounded the kernels to a fine meal to drink with water, to make into bread, to stir into soups as thickening, or to mix with marrow.

This last is especially tasty, besides being of important interest from a survival standpoint. The mineral-rich marrow found in the bones of animals that were in good physical condition at their demise is not surpassed by any other natural food in caloric strength. What is, at the same time, the most delectable of tidbits is too often wasted by the common practice of roasting such bones until they are on the point of crumbling or of boiling them for hours. A more conservative procedure is to crack them near the onset, with two stones if nothing handier is available, or to poke out the soft vascular tissue with the flattened end of a stick. The less the marrow is then cooked, the better it will remain as far as nutrition is concerned.

To shell sunflower seeds in quantity, first break them up, as with a rolling pin, hammer, or food chopper. Then scatter the results in a large container filled with water. Stir vigorously so as to bring all the kernels in contact with the fluid and to break the surface tension. The kernels will sink to the bottom. The shells will remain floating, for use as a wild coffee if you want. The nuts can then be briefly dried and roasted, as in an open oven pan, and used in any recipe calling for nuts. Or the entire mass of kernels can be ground or pounded into a fine meal.

One of the Indian ways of making sunflower cakes is still a good one. For this recipe, you'll need 2 cups of hulled sunflower seeds and 2 cups of water. Put the two together in a saucepan, add 1½ teaspoons salt, cover, and simmer for an hour, stirring occasionally. Then, unless you started with a meal, puree the mixture in your blender. Allow to cool.

Mix in about 4 tablespoons of cornmeal, a scattering at a time, until you have a dough firm enough to shape. Mold this into round, flat cakes about 2 inches wide. Get ⅔ cup of shortening or cooking oil warming in a frypan. When it is hot enough to make a drop of water dance, put the cakes carefully in with a spatula. Turning, bronze them well on both sides. Then drain on absorbent paper. Most prefer these hot, but they're still tasty cold.

WILD GINGER

(Asarum)

Some of the Indian tribes regularly used wild ginger roots for flavoring. This plant, one of the better-known wild flowers, grows in fertile woods from the Maritime Provinces to Manitoba, south to North Carolina and Kansas. A related species follows the coast ranges from British Columbia down into California.

Although the leaves are aromatic, emitting a pleasant fragrance when bruised or crushed, the roots are the part used and are milder than the unrelated ginger from the Orient. The plant is also known as Indian ginger, Canada snakeroot, and Vermont snakeroot—the latter two names resulting from the proclivity of the branching, easily gathered rootstalks to creep along the surface of the ground.

The beautiful long-stalked leaves of the wild ginger rise upon the rims of many a shaded stream, almost as if they enjoyed the gossiping of the brook as it gurgles past. These leaves, often heart-shaped and some three to seven inches broad, have sharp points and broad bases. Deep green above, lighter below, these are generally velvety with short hairs.

In the early spring a warm hue appears among the still undeveloped leaves. Presently a strange, dull bud—one to every pair of leaves—protrudes its long tip from their midst. The flowers eventually bloom in May, often on short stems so close to the ground that the purplish red blossoms with their three long prongs are sometimes nearly invisible on the forest floor. These eventually develop seeds, nurturing them until they ripen.

WILD GINGER

There are two ways to use the roots of wild ginger, often gathered in early spring, after they have been well scrubbed. The first of these, common among the pioneers, is merely to dry them, grind them into a powder, and use them like the commercial spice they then resemble. Once regarded as efficacious in treating whooping cough, this is still commonly used in parts of eastern Canada as a remedy for flatulency. If you'd like to try it, just add ½ teaspoonful of the powdered or granulated root to a cup of boiling water. Drink this 2 tablespoons at a time as often as necessary.

Candied wild ginger comes close to being some woodsmen's favorite sweet. Wash the roots well and then cut them into short pieces. Simmer these until tender, barely covered with liquid made by dissolving 2 cups of sugar in each cup of water. Then drain, cooking the fluid longer if it still does not seem to be quite thick enough.

You can keep the wild ginger in the syrup, but many prefer to bottle both separately, first letting the pieces dry on waxed paper or foil for several days and then rolling them in granulated white sugar. This way you can use the syrup as a sauce for desserts, such as ice cream or sliced bananas, or you can mix a tablespoon with a cup of hot water and enjoy a steaming beverage that is both delicious and medicinal, especially after a heavy meal. The candied tidbits make wonderful nibbles. For a taste thrill, try some one day with a bit of cream cheese.

SWEET FLAG

(Acorus)

Candied sweet flag has somewhat the same aromatic pungency as the now difficult-to-obtain candied ginger. To make your own, cut the tender bases of the stalks into very thin slices. Parboil in several changes of water to moderate the strong taste.

Then simmer, stirring frequently, barely covered with a syrup composed proportionately of 2 cups of sugar to every cup of water until most of the sugar has been absorbed. Drain, dry apart from one another on waxed paper or foil for several days, roll in granulated sugar, and pack what you don't devour on the spot in tightly closing jars.

The fleshy rootstalks were often used for this purpose in the days of wood fires, but they usually need to be kept on the back of a warm stove for several days to become sufficiently tender.

Sweet flag, a cousin of our friend the jack-in-the-pulpit, which also belongs to the arum family, grows in a wide band throughout southern Canada and the contiguous states, as well as in Europe and Asia. You see broad stands of it in marshes, swamps, damp grasslands, and along stagnant waters, where it is also known as calamus, myrtle flag, sweet rush, and sweet grass. The latter two names were inspired not only by the flavor of the stalk's interior but by the pleasantly aromatic fragrance of the bruised foliage. This was a major reason why our pioneer ancestors often chose these leaves to spread cleanly on the floors of their cabins.

This aroma is one characteristic that distinguishes the edible from the blue flag, the state flower of Tennessee. Also, the sweet flag has glossy, yellowish green leaves, whereas those of the blue flag are both dull and bluish green. There is also the spicy pungency of the sweet flag's rootstock, a little of which is sometimes eaten raw as a remedy for indigestion.

Or you can make a tea from the roots, which can be dried and grated for the purpose. Stored in a tightly closed jar, these roots will

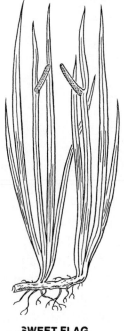

₃WEET FLAG

keep for months. The recommended dosage is a teaspoonful to a cup of boiling water, drunk cold one or two cupfuls a day, several sips at a time. You may prefer this sweetened. In pioneer days it was held to be a remedy for sour or upset stomach, as well as a general stimulant to digestion.

The sharp, thin, swordlike leaves of the sweet flag grow up to about four feet tall. They sheathe one another tightly at the base, often beneath the surface of the ground or mud. Stout, horizontal roots with their unmistakable gingery taste spread from them in closely inter-twined mats.

The flower stalk grows almost as tall as the leaves. About halfway up it the spikelike spadix, several inches long and reminiscent of the "jack" of the jack-in-the-pulpit, grows off on an angle. This becomes closely covered with tiny yellowish green flowers.

Raw sweet flag offers prime emergency food in the spring, when the partially grown flower stalks are edible and when the interiors of the young stalks, crammed with half-formed leaves, are sweet and tasty enough to be taken home for salads.

HORSERADISH

(Armoracia)

There is little comparison between the freshly grated horseradish you can prepare yourself, using the wild roots and lemon juice instead of the commonly employed wine vinegar, and that from a store. Mouth-tickling horseradish, popular the world over, has been used as a food seasoning for centuries.

The perennial horseradish, regrowing in the same places for dozens of years and spreading where there is sufficient moisture, came to the New World from England. Originally planted about the cabins and other buildings of northeastern United States and southern Canada, it has thrived and dispersed until it now grows wild throughout much of the same general area. The nose-stinging, eye-watering white roots, so good when used in moderation with less tasty foods, are edible the year around.

The small white flowers of the horseradish, like those of all other members of the mustard family, have just four petals. They grow in short-stemmed, loosely branched clusters. Although seeds are seldom produced, there are the occasional round pods, each of which is divided into two cells with perhaps four to six seeds in each.

Numerous large leaves grow from the root on strong, long stalks. These leaves, often six inches wide and nearly twice as long, have wavy, scalloped edges. The much smaller, stemless leaves that grow directly from a smooth, round, erect, central spike, often several feet long, are oblong and serrated.

The leaves when tender in the spring make greens that are tastier than most when dropped into a small amount of boiling salted water, cooked uncovered only until tender, and then served immediately with a crowning pat of butter or margarine.

But it is for its heartily peppery roots that horseradish has been famous for thousands of years. These fleshy roots, sometimes as long as

HORSERADISH

a foot and as thick as one or two inches, are tapering, conical at the top, and many times abruptly branched near the end. They are white both within and without. When bruised or scraped, they give off a strongly pungent odor. When a particle is transferred to the tongue, it is immediately hot and biting.

The simplest way to prepare this masterful condiment for the table is by scraping some of the scrubbed root into a small dish, then stirring in fresh lemon juice to taste. Or you can use wine vinegar, instead.

Then there are innumerable refinements, the easiest of which is to add a small amount of sugar to the original mixture, again by taste. In any event, for the most pleasing results make only small amounts of the sauce at a time, an easy thing to do as horseradish roots can be freshly gathered the year around.

Keep the sauce covered when not in use, preferably in a tightly closed jar or bottle. You may want to keep this in the refrigerator. For best results, however, it should be allowed to return to room temperature before being used. Otherwise, part of its taste-tingling piquancy will be trapped by the cold, and more will have to be used to achieve the same result.

Grated horseradish and sour cream make a combination that really brings out the flavor of game meats such as roast moose and bear, not to forget good honest beef. Two parts of sour cream by volume to 1 part of horseradish blend excellently.

You can use regular cream, too. Mix 2 teaspoons of finely grated horseradish with ¼ teaspoon salt and 2 tablespoons water. Then whip ½ cup of heavy cream. Stir the first mixture into the cream. Allow to stand half an hour before using.

Here's a way to make horseradish sauce more pleasantly assertive. Begin by whipping the same ½ cup of heavy cream. When it starts to thicken, gradually tip in a tablespoon of lemon juice. Once everything thickens, add ½ teaspoon paprika, ¼ teaspoon dry mustard, and ¼ teaspoon salt. Then fold in 2 tablespoons of freshly grated horseradish. Before putting on the table, allow to stand a half-hour until the flavors can affirm themselves.

Freshly grated horseradish will also do much for sandwiches and for small crisp crackers—tidbits that will arouse the appetite even more if decorated with slices of pimento-stuffed olives. For this spread, cream butter or margarine with an equal volume of horseradish. Then gradually add a little lemon juice, salt, paprika, and, if you want, sugar to taste. If you ever tire of this, substitute cream cheese for the butter or margarine. Or use mayonnaise for the base.

Besides enjoying horseradish roots and leaves, pioneers used to apply the freshly scraped roots externally as they would mustard plasters. Horseradish was also used as an internal medicine, a teaspoon of the scraped root to a cup of boiling water. This was allowed to cool. One or two cupfuls were then drunk throughout the day, several sips at a time, as a stimulant to the stomach.

GIANT KELP

(Nereocystis)

If you live or vacation where giant kelp grows, this abundant marine alga, which often thrives in beds acres wide, makes unusual and excellent pickles.

Giant kelp has round, hollow stalks up to about seventy-five feet long, gradually widening from less than one-half inch at the base to perhaps four inches at the top and ending in a floating round bulb

GIANT KELP

which may be up to eight inches in diameter. Two rows of narrow, leathery, leaflike blades, ten to thirty feet long, stem from the bulbs. These blades float on the ocean surface, and on the Pacific Coast from Mexico to Alaska you can often watch sea lions, whales, and sometimes sea otters swimming among them.

The long, hollow stalks, used by the Indians of southeastern Alaska as fishing lines for deep-sea angling, may be collected during June,

July, and August, when they are at their prime. Although it is preferable to use only the ones rooted to the bottom, fresh stalks are also common along the beaches, especially after storms.

The kelp is washed, peeled, and used the same as green cucumbers or tomatoes for relish and pickles. It may also be used like watermelon rind for preserving.

For some memorable sweet sea pickles, you'll need 4 pounds giant kelp, 3½ cups sugar, 2 cups white vinegar, 1 cup salt, ½ teaspoon alum, ½ teaspoon oil of cloves, ½ teaspoon oil of cinnamon, and water.

Cut the stalks into 12-inch lengths and split the bulbs. Using a vegetable parer, remove the dark surface layer and discard. Keep the pieces covered in a brine solution, 1 cup of salt to 2 gallons of water, for 2 hours. After the giant kelp is taken out of the brine, wash it thoroughly with cold water.

Then cut it into 1-inch cubes. Soak these in a solution of ½ teaspoon of alum to 2 quarts of cold water for 15 minutes. Drain, wash in cold water, and redrain. Drop the cubes into an enamel kettle and cover them with boiling water. Simmer only until a few test cubes can be easily pierced with a fork. Then drain again.

Combine the sugar, vinegar, and oils. Simmer this for 2 minutes and then pour over the cooked kelp. Let stand overnight in the enamel kettle or in a crock. In the morning, drain and save the syrup. Reheat the kelp to the boiling point with just enough water to prevent sticking, pour off the water, recover with the syrup, and allow to set another 24 hours. On the third morning, heat both kelp and syrup to the boiling point, and seal immediately in 3 hot, sterilized pint jars.

Whole spices, tied in small bags, may be used instead, but the cubes will not then remain so nearly transparently clear. A conservative amount of green food coloring may be put in to make the pickles brighter. If you don't mind sacrificing a certain amount of crispness, omit the salt and alum solutions, merely soaking the kelp in cold water, rinsing, and then cooking until tender.

Other Natural Delicacies

MANY EDIBLE WILD plants, such as seaweeds and lichens, are frequently overlooked as sources of nourishment because they are so inconspicuous or ordinary-looking. Others, like the dandelion (see Part I) or wild grape, are passed by because they are so conspicuous or widely distributed that they are taken for granted simply as being common plants, with no thought of their nutritional value. This is truly regrettable because many of these plants so widely ignored have unique nutritional qualities.

Seaweeds, for example, are extremely rich in minerals, including vitally important iodine. One of the seaweeds, Irish moss, has long been known as a food especially suitable for convalescents.

Lichens, especially valuable because they grow in the Far North, where other edible plants are often scarce, are not only a prime emergency food but can be used to supplement the nutrients found in other foods—especially flour, soups, and stews. Other nutritious additives for flour can be obtained from the chia and jack-in-the-pulpit.

All in all, the study of edible wild plants will well repay a lifetime of effort. The more a person knows about them, the less likely he will be to overlook valuable sources of nourishment which can save his life during an emergency and provide delicious eating anytime.

IRISH MOSS

(Chondrus)

Scientists are finding a rich and nearly inexhaustible store of foods in the oceans that cover almost three-fourths of the globe's surface. Not the least of these is Irish moss, familiar on the eastern shores of this continent as well as in Europe, where it has been eaten for centuries.

Replete in such valuable elements as sodium, potassium, magnesium, copper, calcium, phosphorus, chlorine, and sulphur, this starchy seaweed is also an excellent source of iodine. Furthermore, it is so digestible that it is recommended for convalescents. As if all that weren't enough, it is good the year around.

Also known as sea moss, pearl moss, and carrageen moss, this marine alga was widely gathered and kept for years by our forefathers who settled along the Atlantic Coast. Clinging to submerged rocks, it is gathered during low tides. Irish moss that has been cast up along the shore by tides can also be harvested, often already bleached by the sun. Commercial processors bleach their product in the sunlight to a creamy white. However, the natural, dark Irish moss has even more vitamins.

Irish moss is naturally greenish, purplish, reddish, brown, and blackish. Attached to submerged rocks by small disks, it consists of flat, cartilaginous, forked stems or fronds up to about a foot long. Although it has a rather pleasant mucilaginous, saline taste, it is too tough to eat raw. Drying it makes it almost bonelike.

But just a small amount of cooking after it has been well washed in fresh water will tenderize it, and it can be eaten in a number of ways. It is just the extract that is commonly used. However, a handful cut up and cooked with a soup or stew makes a tasty and thickening additive. Soup made from Irish moss and fresh water alone, or the jelly that it forms upon cooling, is a palatable and nourishing emergency food.

Irish moss, as well as being nutritious, is also soothing to the digestive tract, and it used to be considered useful in allaying diarrhea. The dose was a teaspoon of the dried plant in a cup of boiling water, drunk cold one or two cupfuls a day, several sips at a time.

Irish moss lemonade used to be recommended for anyone who was suffering from a cold or otherwise indisposed. To make a quart of this, start by soaking ½ cup of the moss until soft in enough cold water to cover.

IRISH MOSS

Then drain, add the moss and a quart of boiling water to the top of a double boiler, and simmer about half an hour until the moss is dissolved. Strain, add the juice of 2 fresh lemons, sweeten to taste, and share with your patient.

Blancmange can be a treat for both invalid and gourmet. Properly, you'll need the bleached variety for this. Wash the moss well to remove any sand and pick out any discolored pieces. Add the remainder to a quart of milk in the top of a double boiler and cook half an hour. Then strain. Flavor to taste with salt, sugar, and one of the extracts such as vanilla. Pour into molds that have been immersed in cold water. Set aside, perhaps in the refrigerator, to become firm. Many like this with cream and sliced, sugared oranges. Another tasty variation is a chocolate sauce with overtones of peppermint extract.

If you like meat jelly, there's an easy way to have it with Irish moss. Just wash ½ cup of the moss in fresh water. Add it to a quart of broth and let stand half an hour. Then bring it to a simmer, preferably in the top of a double boiler Stirring, cook it for 10 minutes. Then strain and, if you want, pour into molds.

Irish moss salad is different as well as delicious. Start by washing some of the picked-over seaweed in hot water, then placing it in a soup plate, and covering it with the heated juice of 3 lemons. After several hours the moss will have dissolved, hardening everything into a yellow jelly. Place this in the refrigerator to chill and become even firmer. If you start all this in the early afternoon, it will be ready by dinnertime.

Then arrange a few cool, crisp lettuce leaves on each of four chilled salad plates. Cut the moss mixture into sparkling golden cubes and center them on the lettuce. Cut into small cubes 2 cups of the tastiest apples you can come by. Mix these with 1¼ cups of finely diced celery and 3 tablespoons mayonnaise. Distribute this among the individual salads and top each with a few walnuts. This is so good it's almost voluptuous.

LAVER

(Porphyra)

Anyone near the Atlantic or Pacific shores of this continent seldom need worry about going without food in an emergency. Laver is one of the reasons.

Far from being just an emergency sustenance, though, this abundant seaweed furnishes a regular food crop in the Orient, and some has long been exported to this country. But exactly the same delicacy can be harvested here. And in a tight spot, it might even save your life.

Laver is the thin frond spied at low tide growing from rock ledges, boulders, and pier supports. You can see it wavering beneath the surface in still water, and heavy seas tear considerable quantities of it loose and toss it up on the shore. Very wavy edges characterize these long, narrow, sometimes leaflike seaweeds that grow up to about a foot long and from one to two inches wide. A second characteristic is the satiny gloss of these fronds with their filmy red, green, purple, and purplish brown elasticity.

Although laver is perfectly edible raw, it is better dried. In Alaska, for example, the natives gather it during the low tides of May and early June. It is separated from any foreign matter, then partially air- and

LAVER

sun-dried by being spread outdoors on fair days on a large cloth laid on the ground or on a table. It is chopped or ground in a food chopper, then again put out on sunny days, being repeatedly turned over and over until, blackening, it is thoroughly dried. Stored in closed containers in a dry, cool place, this dried laver can be kept indefinitely.

Dried laver is widely used in fish stews and soups, a cup to every 2 cups of liquid, after first being soaked for about an hour until tender. Too, it is commonly enjoyed raw, its crisp, salty taste being reminiscent of popcorn.

If you live close to the seacoast, a laver soup you can easily enjoy is started by simmering 2 cups of laver in a quart of water, stirring occasionally, until the water plant is tender. You can use fresh laver, or, for tastier results, dried laver that has been soaked an hour covered with fresh water, then drained.

In the meantime, slice a bunch of leeks very thinly almost to the root ends. Wash thoroughly, making sure all the grit is removed. Melt 2 tablespoons of butter or margarine in a preferably heavy frypan. Sauté the leeks in this until they are soft and just starting to tan. Add the boiling water with the laver, as well as a peeled and chopped tomato. Pepper to taste. Then boil rapidly for 10 minutes. Served with thin, hot toast, this is something most individuals want to repeat. Who says the best things in life aren't free?

DULSE

(Rhodymenia)

Dulse is so prolific along our Atlantic and Pacific coasts that it grows from other seaweeds as well as from submerged rocks and ledges. Rich in vital minerals including iodine, the ingredient necessary for the proper functioning of the thyroid gland, this popular chewable is more popular in Europe than on this continent, although in places like New Brunswick you find it for sale in small grocery stores.

These sea plants have extremely brief stems that rapidly widen into thin, elastic fronds. Varying in color from purplish to redish, these smooth flat expanses are frequently lobed and cleft. The whole seaweed grows from a few inches to about a foot in length.

The Indians in southeast Alaska still gather this seaweed in quantity, usually during the low tides of May and early June. They then dry it in the sun and air as they do laver, eventually storing it for adding during the winter to soups and stews. It is also used fresh. Chewed directly from the sea, it is tough and rubbery. The trick is to hang it or spread it out until it is partially dry. Or if you don't want to wait that long, just singe the fresh dulse on a hot stove, griddle, or campfire rock.

A premium you sometimes come by when harvesting dulse in Alaska during the midsummer herring runs is herring roe. All you have to do is drain this roe, season it with pepper and salt, and sauté it in butter or margarine in moderate heat until brown on both sides. About 12 minutes will do the job. Then add lemon juice to butter or margarine that's been heated to a delicate brown and pour this over the hot roe. Enjoy at once.

This dulse-enmeshed herring roe is also scrambled with eggs in Alaska. For about ½ pound of roe, add a tablespoon of vinegar and

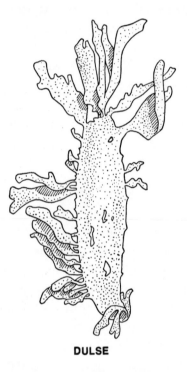

DULSE

another of salt to 2 cups of boiling water. Put in the roe and simmer it for 15 minutes before draining it and removing the membrane. Then mash. Combine with 6 eggs, 6 tablespoons cream, ½ teaspoon salt, and ⅛ teaspoon pepper. Scramble in 2 tablespoons butter or margarine in a frypan over low heat. Garnish with chopped dried dulse and serve hot.

As for the dulse itself, it can be used to add character to such dishes as otherwise rather tasteless tuna loaf. Mix 2 cups of flakes or grated cooked tuna with ½ cup of the chopped soft fronds of dried dulse. Add

½ cup of soft bread crumbs, ½ stick butter or margarine, 2 well-beaten eggs, a tablespoon apiece of chopped onion and watercress, and pepper and Worcestershire to taste. Turn into a buttered baking dish and bake in a preheated 375-degree oven until firm. This is excellent hot, swimming in a sauce made by heating a cup of white sauce with ¼ cup each of mayonnaise and chopped stuffed olives.

ROCK TRIPE

(Umbilicaria)

Probably the most widely known of the wild foods of the Far North is the lichen called rock tripe, whose growth reaches into the southern states. Rock tripe resembles a leathery dark lettuce leaf, up to some three inches across, attached at its center to a rocky surface. Unless the day is wet, rock tripe is apt to be rather dry. It can be eaten raw, especially in small amounts, but you'll probably prefer it much of the time boiled to thicken soups and stews.

ROCK TRIPE

Rock tripe is one of the lichens that manufacture soil by disintegrating rock, so it is apt to be rather gritty. Wash it as well as possible, preferably soaking it in water for several hours to rid it of its purgative, bitter character. The flavor will then be improved if you roast it in a pan, before the campfire or in a partially open oven, until it is dry and crisp.

Then simmer it slowly for an hour or so, or until tender, whereupon it will impart a gumbolike thickness to the stew or soup. Depending on the main ingredients, this may be short on taste, but it will be surpassingly long on nourishment.

This lichen was widely used as an emergency food in early trapping and Arctic-exploring days. Franklin, Richardson, and other northern adventurers lived on rock tripe for months with hardly any change of diet.

ICELAND MOSS

(Cetraria)

Icelanders say that by virtue of Iceland moss a munificent Heaven has provided them bread from the very rocks. In Iceland, northern Europe, and across the treeless top of Alaska and Canada, it has kept actual thousands from starving. In this country it grows across the northern states, down into New Jersey, Pennsylvania, and the high country of North Carolina.

Iceland moss, one of the edible lichens, consists of a fungus and an alga growing in close partnership. It is eaten by moose, deer, elk, and grouse to a certain extent. In the Arctic realms, however, it is one of the main foods of such widely ranging browsers as the reindeer and caribou. These primitive plants, incidentally, are pioneers when it comes to soil manufacture. The bitter organic acids that are characteristic of them assist in decomposing the very rocks on which many of them grow.

Iceland moss is a low, mosslike plant with a structure of branching stems in place of leaves. Forming tufts and tangled masses on the ground, it grows some two to four inches tall. Forking and branching freely, it is variously colored brown and grayish white to reddish.

From the odorless mats formed by this lichen arise numerous stalks, the majority of them being thin, flattened, and less than one-tenth of an inch wide. The upper surfaces of these are generally smooth, the under expanses being paler, with wrinkles or channels toward the base. These stalks roll in at the edges, forming funnel-like tubes which terminate in flattened lobes with finely toothed edges. The spores, or fruits, when present grow mainly along the edges of the lobes.

Iceland moss has a marked rubbery texture during the summer. In winter the cold and the winds dehydrate the plants to brittleness. Upon soaking, they regain their rubbery characteristic.

Like most others, this lichen must be soaked before it is edible by humans. Otherwise, the unpleasantly bitter acids are apt to cause severe intestinal irritation. These acids can be removed easily enough, however, by soaking the Iceland moss in two changes of water, prefera-

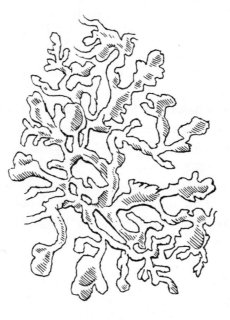

ICELAND MOSS

bly with a teaspoon of baking soda added each time, then draining, drying, and finally crushing and pounding it to a powder. The result is so digestible that it is sold in some drugstores as a nutritive for invalids and convalescents.

When simmered with water or milk, this powder forms a jellylike gruel, becoming firm upon cooling. The powder is added, too, to soups and stews. You can also use it, either as is or mixed half and half with wheat flour, to make cakes and bread.

Frying pan bread made with soaked and powdered Iceland moss is nutritious and substantial. Mix dry 2 cups of the powder, 2 teaspoons of baking powder, and ½ teaspoon of salt, taking all the time you need to do this thoroughly. Have your frypan warm and greased. Working quickly from now on, stir in enough cold water to make a firm dough. Shape this, with as little handling as possible, into a cake about an inch thick.

Lay the bannock in the warm frypan. Place it over low heat until a bottom crust forms, rotating the pan a little so that the loaf will shift and not become stuck. Once the dough has hardened enough to hold together, you can turn the bannock over. This, if you've practiced a bit and have the confidence to flip strongly enough, can be easily accomplished with a slight swing of the arm and snap of the wrist. Or you can use a spatula or plate, supporting the loaf long enough to invert the frypan over it and then turning everything together. When a crust has formed all around, you may if you wish turn the bannock over a few more times while it is baking to an appetizing brown.

When is your Iceland moss bannock done? After you've been cooking them awhile, you will be able to tap one and gauge this by the hollowness of the sound. Meanwhile, test by shoving in a straw or toothpick. If any dough adheres, the loaf needs more heat. Cooking can be accomplished in about 15 minutes. The loaf should then be broken apart, never cut, and devoured piping hot, although cold bannock is good, too.

CHIA

(Salvia)

When Cortez and his conquistadores advanced through the dry, open Southwest, they saw the Indians of that region using the tiny little brown, gray, and white seeds of the chia for food. A teaspoonful of these was regarded as sufficient to sustain an Indian for a day on a forced march. Too, when added to a cup of water and soaked for several minutes, the same teaspoon of chia seeds makes a nearly tasteless but extremely refreshing drink, especially valuable on the desert not only for its thirst-assuaging qualities but because it offsets to a certain degree the harshness of alkaline springs. Today chia is much more widely used in the back country of Mexico than in the United States.

You can go into some of the swankiest restaurants in interior Mexico and get a chia drink, either non-alcoholic or stronger. The basis for this is simply chia seeds soaked in cold water and used unstrained. A quarter-pound of chia to 1½ quarts of water provides the

CHIA

usual proportion. The method is to mix these in a large jar or jug and allow them to stand for at least 5 minutes, long enough for the seeds to swell and to become opaquely surrounded with a gelatinous coating. Then add lemon or lime juice and sugar to taste. This is usually chilled before serving.

This sage, a member of the mint family and one of the best known of all the Indian foods, thrives over much of California and northern

277

Mexico. An annual that commences its growth when the winter rains start to sheet the plains and hills, it is nearly dead and rich with seeds by July. These, often beautifully mottled, are like the tiniest of slippery little flattened eggs.

The flowers themselves, blooming from March to May, grow in interrupted spikes of from one to four little, round, bright blue masses similar to others in the mint family. The projections of their outer parts are prickly. Below each of these heads arises a number of leafy bracts, often a bright wine color in contrast to the blueness of the blossoms.

The coarse, rough, deeply indented, dark green leaves occur mostly at the base of the small stiff plants, which are generally from six to eighteen inches high. Several pairs, however, decorate the stems, not enough to give the wind much purchase on these seed-heavy edibles.

The easiest way to gather chia is to take a large paper bag in one hand and a stick in the other, then to knock the seeds into the bag by striking the dessicated flower heads. Using large flat baskets, Indians used to do the same thing. Too, some of them cut and bundled the plants into the encampment. There they were laid on hard ground and the seeds threshed with rods. The women then winnowed out the seeds. In either event, they were cleaned and dried.

Some were ground into meal. This was turned into gruel or into hard, dark, highly nutritious cakes. The meal today is usually mixed in equal proportions with wheat flour or cornmeal, whereupon it adds a pleasantly nutty flavor to dishes prepared in the normal manner from those staples. But all you have to do to get all the vitamins, minerals, and other nutriments is to eat a pinch of the seeds dry, dilute them to a drink in which each will become separately suspended in its own whitish mucilaginous coat, or mix them with water to form an easily digestible sort of gruel.

Chia is still highly regarded medically in some circles. Because of their glutinous characteristics, the seeds are sometimes used as demulcents and emollients instead of linseed. Too, several seeds placed under the eyelids at night will help clear the eyes of minor inflammation. A paste made by soaking a few seeds in a little water is used for soothing inflamed membranes and as a poultice for gunshot wounds. The drink made by stirring a teaspoonful of the seeds into a glass of cold water, then letting it stand for several minutes, is soothing to inflamed digestive organs. And you can enjoy it, too.

JACK-IN-THE-PULPIT

(Arisaema)

Many Indians relied on the dried and powdered roots of the familiar jack-in-the-pulpit for flour. Today, however, this edible has its principal value as an emergency food, especially for people stranded in one place for a long time. Widely known and easily recognizable, it can then be a lifesaver.

Indian turnip, wake-robin, and dragonroot are among the local names for this North and South American member of the great *Arum* family, used for food by people the world over. Both the leaves and the bright red fruit are eaten by the ring-necked pheasant and the wild turkey.

In the moist, sequestered woodlands of April and May, the jack-in-the-pulpit preaches his silent sermon to a congregation of wild violets and other spring neighbors. Unmistakable, the brown, green, and purplish "pulpit" is a striped two- to four-inch spathe terminating with a hood over the top. The "preacher" is a clublike spadix, two or three inches long, with small greenish yellow flowers, occasionally varying greatly in hues and in brightness, near its base.

The plant, growing in rich woods from the Maritime Provinces to Florida, west to Minnesota and Louisiana, becomes from one to three feet high. The two leaves, growing on long stems, are each composed of three egg-shaped, sometimes lobed, pointed leaflets. Green clusters of berries become handsome scarlet masses that brighten the dark woods in late August.

All parts of the plant, especially the round roots, will burn the mouth like liquid fire if eaten raw. Many youngsters used to have a standard ceremony for initiating newcomers to town, and perhaps still do. This consisted of offering the tenderfoot the tiniest morsel of what they claimed was the finest delicacy their woods had to offer. At first contact, this innocent-looking tidbit was palatable enough. But then the taste became as bitingly hot as a teaspoon of red pepper. This burning sensation, which was followed by inflammation and tenderness, seemed to permeate every part of tongue, mouth, and throat and to linger for hours, although cold milk did appear to allay it some.

The wonder is that aborigines the world over have learned to rid *Arum* roots of this corrosive acridness and thus capitalize upon their

279

nutritious, delicate, white starchiness. Boiling won't do it! Drying will. The fastest way to do this is by roasting. The simplest method is just to cut the fresh roots into very thin slices, then set these aside in a dry place for upwards of three months. They then provide pleasant snacks, either as is or with a potato chip dip. Or you can crumble the crisp slices into flour and use it in regular recipes, preferably half and half with wheat flour.

JACK-IN-THE-PULPIT

Jack-in-the-pulpits and hazelnuts, often growing in the same habitats, go together in the following cookies which always seem to call for seconds and thirds whenever guests get their first samples of them. Beat 2 egg yolks until thick. Add, bit by bit, a cup of brown sugar and beat that in well. Then mix in a cup of chopped hazelnuts and a scant ⅛ teaspoon salt.

Beat the 2 egg whites until they form peaks and fold them in. Sift together 3 tablespoons jack-in-the-pulpit flour and 3 tablespoons all-purpose flour. Stir that in. Distribute by the teaspoonful on cooky sheets or heavy foil, press gently flat with a spatula, transfer to a preheated 350-degree oven, and bake about 7 minutes or until firm. After they have cooled, keep the 4 dozen or so cookies in a closed container for as long as they last, which isn't likely to be long.

Once the fire had been taken out of them, jack-in-the-pulpit roots were also held to be medicinally valuable. One prescription for spasms of asthma consisted of a handful of the dried and chipped roots, aged for three days in a quart of whisky. Even then, the dosage was conservative. It was a single tablespoonful twice a day.

GRAPE

(Vitis)

The various species of broad-leaved, tendril-clinging, high-climbing or trailing wild grapes, one of the survival foods of the Lewis and Clark expedition and long an Indian mainstay throughout much of the continent, include the large fox grape, the aromatic muscadine, the pleasant pigeon grape, and the notable scuppernong. All are too familiar to require description.

At least half the world's wild grapes are native to this country, some two dozen or so species being widely distributed over the United States. Favoring moist, fertile ground, they frequently twine towards sunlight along stream banks, beaches, fences, stone walls, and near the edges of woods. Birds find the dense foliage excellent sanctuary and even use the bark for some of their nests.

Fruit, leaves, and young shoots are all edible. Among the game making use of them are deer, black bear, opossum, rabbit, squirrel, dove, wood duck, ruffed grouse, ring-necked pheasant, bobwhite, prairie chicken, and wild turkey. Even when clusters of fruit dry like raisins on the vines, they are sought by birds and animals during all seasons.

There are two satisfactory ways of securing wild grape juice for use in the home. For the first, wash, pick over, and stem your grapes. Have hot, sterilized quart jars waiting, arranged on toweling out of drafts, and have water boiling. Tip 2 cupfuls of wild grapes into each jar. Add a cup of sugar to each, planning to sweeten it more later if necessary.

Fill with boiling water. Seal immediately, allow to cool, label, and then store in a dark, cool place for about 10 weeks before straining and using.

For the second, again wash, pick over, and stem your wild fruit. Mash the grapes in a kettle, not crushing the seeds. Cover with a minimum of water and bring to a simmer only. Heat that way for a half-hour, with only an occasional bubble plopping to the top. Press through a sieve and then strain through a jelly bag. Season to taste with white sugar. Bring once more to a simmer, not a boil, for 15 minutes.

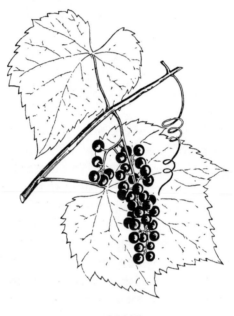

GRAPE

Pour into hot, sterilized jars set on a towel, seal, cool as always away from drafts that might break the glass, label, and store in a dark, cool, dry place.

For a sherbet with a satisfying bouquet, mix and chill in ice trays—with the refrigerator control set for fast freezing—2 cups of wild grape juice, 3 cups milk, ¼ cup crushed pineapple, a tablespoon lemon juice, and sugar to taste. This is even better when you use half-and-half instead of the whole milk. Freeze until nearly firm. Then turn into a chilled bowl and beat, with either a rotary hand or electric beater, until smoothly blended. Turn back into the trays and freeze, stirring once or twice, until almost firm.

Wild grape jelly is luscious, but it takes some doing. The majority of the grapes should be on the underripe side. Wash, drain, and stem these. Relegate them to a kettle, mash them without crushing the seeds, and simmer until the fruit comes apart. Press through a sieve and then, not exerting any pressure, allow to drip through a jelly bag.

When the time comes to make the jelly, prepare only a quart of this juice at a time for perfect jelly. Here's another secret, too. Ordinary grape jelly has a tendency to crystallize upon standing. An easy way to prevent this? When preparing the juice, just cook a cup of diced tart apples with each 4 cups of wild grapes.

Allow 4 cups of sugar to every 4 cups of juice. Bring rapidly to a boil. Continue boiling until 2 drops form on the edge of a metal spoon, then flow together to make a sheet. The jelling point will near at 220 to 222 degrees if you're using the thermometer. Skim off the foam. Then pour the sweetened juice into hot, sterilized glasses, filling these to within ¼ inch of the top.

Either vacuum seal, if you are using that kind of a container, or seal with paraffin, melting this in small bits over hot water and pouring a tin layer atop the jelly, carefully turning and tipping the glass so that the seal is perfect. Allow to cool. Then pour on a second thin layer of paraffin, cool, cover with a lid or with foil, label, and store in a cool, dark sanctuary.

Some may recall their grandmothers making wild grape conserve. They may even remember being allowed to help her, until their interest waned, for the pleasure of squeezing the individual wild grapes—which perhaps grew luxuriously on the edge of the apple orchard—until the insides plopped out of their skins.

The pulp goes into one pan, the skins along with a cup of water for every 4 pounds of washed and stemmed grapes in another. Both are simmered over low heat for 15 minutes, until the skins cook down and the seeds become dislodged from the pulp. Then press the pulp through a sieve to remove the seeds. You'll have a smoother conserve if you now take time to chop the skins, along with the cup of seedless raisins that go in next. Also chop a navel orange, plus a segment of skin about the size of a silver dollar.

Combine all this in a single pan, stir in 4 cups of sugar and ½ teaspoon of salt, and simmer over moderate heat for half an hour, stirring frequently and spooning off any foam. When everything has thickened, you can give it a little added substance by stirring in a cup of finely chopped nutmeats. Many in the East use hazelnuts but if you're away from where they thrive, try substituting a cup of slivered almonds. Pour the thick mixture into small, hot, sterilized jars, seal immediately, and treat as usual. You owe it to yourself to try this with venison or savory beef.

Pie, anyone? Squeeze the skins from 4 cups of ripe wild grapes. Simmer the pulp until it comes apart and press it through a sieve to remove the seeds. Chop the skins into fine bits. Now blend the strained pulp and the chopped skins with 1½ cups sugar, 2 tablespoons flour, a well-beaten egg, a tablespoon of lemon juice, and ¼ teaspoon salt.

Turn into an uncooked 9-inch pie shell, dot with 2 tablespoons of chipped butter or margarine, tightly fit on a top crust, and cut a pine tree of slits in the center. Bake in a preheated hot 450-degree oven for 10 minutes. Then lower the heat to a moderate 350 degrees and bake 20 minutes longer or until the crust is attractively bronzed.

Unless you have your own favorite pastry recipe, here is a good one for wild grape pie. Cut ⅔ of a cup of shortening into 2 cups of sifted all-purpose flour and a teaspoon salt until you have particles the size of peas. Stir in about ⅓ cup of cold water, a bit at a time, enough to make a wad of dough. Divide this into 2 parts and lightly roll out about ⅛-inch thick.

If you, too, enjoy dining occasionally at Middle East restaurants, you are already acquainted with the delicate acid savor grape leaves lend to food. To use them for cooking, these should be gathered in the spring when they have achieved their growth but are still tender.

A convenient way to keep several dozen for future use is to divide such freshly gathered leaves into piles of 2 dozen each. Fold each of these stacks once and tie it together with a string. Bring a large pot of water to a boil and add salt until no more will dissolve—about ¾ cup of salt to 3 quarts of water. Then dip each bundle into the boiling brine for 5 seconds.

Press the stacks tightly into sterilized jars, tip in a bit of the saturated salt solution to condense and keep the leaves from becoming too brittle. Store in a dark, cool, dry place. These can be used—as long as they last—until the following spring, by which time you'll have a new crop of raw material. Before employing any of them, incidentally, always wash the leaves well in cold fresh water.

Stuffed grape leaves, far simpler to prepare than they may sound, are as exciting as they are exotic. Mix 1½ pounds ground lean beef, venison, lamb, or veal with ¾ cup of raw rice, 2 raw eggs, a small grated onion, ¼ cup minced celery, ⅛ teaspoon apiece of marjoram and thyme, and salt and pepper to taste. Place about a tablespoon of this mixture on each grape leaf, well washed if they have been salted down, and wrap each neatly around it.

Sauté 4 diced slices of bacon in the bottom of a large kettle until they start to tan. Pour in 3 cups of canned tomatoes and bring to a simmer. Now carefully spoon the stuffed grape leaves into the hot mixture, top with another 3 cups of canned tomatoes, cover, and cook over moderate heat for an hour with only an occasional bubble ballooning to the top. Serve hot.

Such game birds as grouse take on added zest when cooked with grape leaves. Rub each cleaned and plucked small fowl inside and out with lemon juice, salt, and a sprinkling of powdered ginger and black pepper. Lard generously with thin strips of salt pork.

Place atop a nest of grape leaves in a shallow baking dish. Cover with additional leaves. Roast 30 to 40 minutes in a slow 300-degree oven until a sharp fork can be easily inserted and withdrawn. Remove the top leaves and the lardons. Then turn the heat up to a hot 500 degrees just long enough to give the birds an appetizing bronze. Sprinkle with white bread crumbs, browned in an abundance of butter or margarine, and clear a way to the table.